Contents

Blackstone's
Police Q&A

Crime
2014

Twelfth edition

Huw Smart and John Watson

OXFORD
UNIVERSITY PRESS

OXFORD
UNIVERSITY PRESS

Great Clarendon Street, Oxford, OX2 6DP,
United Kingdom

Oxford University Press is a department of the University of Oxford.
It furthers the University's objective of excellence in research, scholarship,
and education by publishing worldwide. Oxford is a registered trade mark of
Oxford University Press in the UK and in certain other countries

© Huw Smart and John Watson, 2013

The moral rights of the authors have been asserted

First published in 2013

Impression: 1

Crown copyright material is reproduced under Class Licence
Number C01P0000148 with the permission of OPSI
and the Queen's Printer for Scotland

Published in the United States of America by Oxford University Press
198 Madison Avenue, New York, NY 10016, United States of America

British Library Cataloguing in Publication Data

Data available

ISBN 978–0–19–968206–5

Printed and bound in Great Britain by
CPI Group (UK) Ltd, Croydon, CRO 4YY

Introduction

Before you get into the detail of this book, there are two myths about multiple-choice questions (MCQs) that we need to get out of the way right at the start:

1. that they are easy to answer;
2. that they are easy to write.

Take one look at a professionally designed and properly developed exam paper such as those used by the Police Promotion Examinations Board or the National Board of Medical Examiners in the US and the first myth collapses straight away. Contrary to what some people believe, MCQs are not an easy solution for examiners and not a 'multiple-guess' soft option for examinees.

That is not to say that *all* MCQs are taxing, or even testing—in the psychometric sense. If MCQs are to have any real value at all, they need to be carefully designed and follow some agreed basic rules.

And this leads us to myth number 2.

It is widely assumed by many people and educational organisations that anyone with the knowledge of a subject can write MCQs. You need only look at how few MCQ writing courses are offered by training providers in the UK to see just how far this myth is believed. Similarly, you need only to have a go at a few badly designed MCQs to realise that it is a myth none the less. Writing bad MCQs is easy; writing good ones is no easier than answering them!

As with many things, the design of MCQs benefits considerably from time, training and experience. Many MCQ writers fall easily and often unwittingly into the trap of making their questions too hard, too easy or too obscure, or completely different from the type of question that you will eventually encounter in your own particular exam. Others seem to use the MCQ as a way to catch people out or to show how smart they, the authors, are (or think they are).

There are several purposes for which MCQs are very useful. The first is in producing a reliable, valid and fair test of knowledge and understanding across a wide range of subject matter. Another is an aid to study, preparation and revision for such examinations and tests. The differences in objective mean that there are slight differences in the rules that the MCQ writers follow. Whereas the design of fully validated MCQs to be used in high stakes examinations which will effectively determine who passes and who fails has very strict guidelines as to construction, content and style, less stringent rules apply to MCQs that are being used for teaching and revision. For that reason, there may be types of MCQ that are appropriate in the latter setting which would not be used in the former. However, in developing the MCQs for this book, the authors have tried to follow the fundamental rules of MCQ design but they would not claim to have replicated the level of psychometric rigour that is—and has to be—adopted by the type of examining bodies referred to previously.

These MCQs are designed to reinforce your knowledge and understanding, to highlight any gaps or weaknesses in that knowledge and understanding; and to help focus your revision of the relevant topics.

I hope that we have achieved that aim.

Good luck!

Blackstone's Police Q&As—Special Features

References to Blackstone's Police Manuals

Every answer is followed by a paragraph reference to Blackstone's Police Manuals. This means that once you have attempted a question and looked at an answer, the Manual can immediately be referred to for help and clarification.

Unique numbers for each question

Each question and answer has the same unique number. This should ensure that there is no confusion as to which question is linked to which answer. For example, Question 2.1 is linked to Answer 2.1.

Checklists

The checklists are designed to help you keep track of your progress when answering the multiple-choice questions. If you fill in the checklist after attempting a question, you will be able to check how many you got right on the first attempt and will know immediately which questions need to be revisited a second time. Please visit www. blackstonespolicemanuals.com and click through to the Blackstone's Police Q&As 2014 page. You will then find electronic versions of the checklists to download and print out. Email any queries or comments on the book to: police.uk@oup.com.

Acknowledgements

This book has been written as an accompaniment to Blackstone's Police Manuals, and will test the knowledge you have accrued through reading that series. It is of the essence that full study of the relevant chapters in each Police Manual is completed prior to attempting the Questions and Answers. As qualified police trainers we recognise that students tend to answer questions incorrectly either because they don't read the question properly, or because one of the 'distracters' has done its work. The distracter is one of the three incorrect answers in a multiple-choice question (MCQ), and is designed to distract you from the correct answer and in this way discriminate between candidates: the better-prepared candidate not being 'distracted'.

So particular attention should be paid to the *Answers* sections, and students should ask themselves 'Why did I get that question wrong?' and, just as importantly, 'Why did I get that question right?'. Combining the information gained in the *Answers* section together with re-reading the chapter in the Police Manuals should lead to greater understanding of the subject matter.

The authors wish to thank all the staff at Oxford University Press who have helped put this publication together. We would particularly like to dedicate these books to Alistair McQueen who sadly passed away in 2008. It was his vision and support that got this project off the ground. Without his help neither Huw nor John would have been able to make these Q&As the success they are. We would also like to show appreciation to Fraser Sampson, consultant editor of Blackstone's Police Manuals, whose influence on these Q&As is appreciated.

Huw would like to thank Caroline for her constant love, support and understanding over the past year and her ability to withstand the pressures of being the partner to a workaholic! Special thanks to Lawrence and Maddie—two perfect young adults. Last but not least, love and special affection to Haf and Nia, two beautiful young girls.

John would like to thank Sue, David, Catherine and Andrew for their continued support, and the occasional use of the computer.

1 | State of Mind

STUDY PREPARATION

This chapter looks at the 'recipe ingredients' that make the offence cake, in other words what has to be present for the offence to be made out.

One of the most important ingredients is *mens rea*, a person's awareness of the fact that his or her conduct is criminal, and is the mental element. Your knowledge of this is tested together with other important states of mind like intent, negligence and recklessness, and even 'strict liability' which requires no fault element.

The chapter goes on to test how some states of mind can be 'transferred'.

When answering questions in this chapter you should remember that although they are based on substantive offences committed, they are testing the general principle of criminal law.

QUESTIONS

Question 1.1

DEAKINS finds out his wife is having an affair and he is considering killing her. He is wondering whether he could poison her whilst she is still asleep. He puts poison in her bedtime drink, intending to cause her serious injury, however she has a violent allergic reaction to it and dies.

Considering only the *mens rea* for murder has DEAKINS committed that offence?

A Yes, even though he was only *considering* murder.
B Yes, as he intended to cause serious injury.
C No, as he was only ever considering murder, no clear intention to kill.
D No, as he only intended serious injury he could never be guilty of murder.

Question 1.2

SZARBO has been arrested for being in possession of Class A drugs which he has secreted in his mouth. The arresting officer attempts to put his fingers in SZARBO's mouth to try and seize the evidence, but SZARBO keeps his mouth firmly shut. The officer then applies a lawful pressure point technique and SZARBO opens his mouth and immediately tries to spit the drugs out to get rid of them. At this point the officer places his fingers in SZARBO's mouth which shuts on them at that exact moment causing injury to the officer's fingers.

Considering the concept of 'recklessness' has SZARBO committed an assault on the police officer?

A Yes, as there should have been an obvious risk of contact with the officer's hand and the defendant took that risk.

B Yes, as it would have been obvious to a 'reasonable person' that there was an obvious risk of contact with the officer's hand and the defendant took that risk.

C No, the assault was committed accidentally; there was no intention to injure the officer.

D No, the defendant was not reckless as to whether he injured the officer; he was attempting to destroy the evidence.

Question 1.3

Criminal offences generally can be classified in terms of the level of *mens rea* required, i.e. the 'mental' element of an offence. However a few offences can be committed through 'negligence' which in itself may not be a state of mind.

In relation to 'negligence' in a criminal sense, which of the following is correct?

A There has to be a blame element and the defendant's compliance with the standards of ordinary people.

B There has to be a blame element and the defendant's compliance with the standards of reasonableness of ordinary people.

C There doesn't have to be a blame element, it concerns only the defendant's compliance with the standards of ordinary people.

D There doesn't have to be a blame element, it concerns only the defendant's compliance with the standards of reasonableness of ordinary people.

Question 1.4

STUCKEY was in a crowded pub and was larking about with his friends. He decided that as a laugh he would try to pretend to slap his friend by going as close to his face as he could. However, due to his drunken state he overbalances and hits someone in the face who was standing next to his intended prank victim.

Considering the legal concept of recklessness which of the following is correct in relation to assaulting the bystander?

A Recklessness of the act and the outcome would have to be proven.

B Recklessness only about the act would be enough for there to be an assault.

C Recklessness is irrelevant here as this was an 'accidental' encounter.

D Recklessness here would be affected by the fact that STUCKEY was drunk.

Question 1.5

Recklessness is a concept in law; the concept itself goes beyond a statutory expression and is important in proving criminal offences and is often enough to fulfil the requirement of *mens rea*.

In relation to recklessness as defined in law which of the following is correct?

A The defendant foresaw that harm (though not the extent of that harm) may be caused but nevertheless went on to take that risk.

B The defendant foresaw that harm (including the extent of that harm) may be caused but nevertheless went on to take that risk.

C The defendant anticipated that harm (though not the extent of that harm) may be caused but nevertheless went on to take that risk.

D The defendant anticipated that harm (including the extent of that harm) may be caused but nevertheless went on to take that risk.

Question 1.6

Some criminal offences are said to be offences of 'strict liability'. Consider an offence where it is illegal to take a person aged 16 years or under on a rollercoaster (note this is a fictitious offence!).

Assuming this offence is one of 'strict liability' which of the following is correct in relation to this 'strict liability'?

A You only have to show the child was taken on the rollercoaster.

B You only have to show the person taken on to the rollercoaster was aged 16 years or under.

C You have to show the child was taken on the rollercoaster and that they were aged 16 years or under.

D You have to show that the accused knew or should have been aware that the person taken on to the rollercoaster was aged 16 years or under.

Question 1.7

MUSTAQ lives with his partner, who is six months' pregnant. They have frequent rows and in the past MUSTAQ has been violent towards her. During a blazing row MUSTAQ takes a knife, stabbing his partner in the upper arm and slashing her face. She is hospitalised and requires extensive treatment, but does not die from her injuries. However the shock of the incident causes her to go into early labour, and the child is born, but dies about an hour after birth. When interviewed MUSTAQ admits he intended to cause grievous bodily harm to his partner, but did not intend to kill her, although he states 'she had it coming'. He also states he had no intentions at all to harm the baby and deeply regrets the death of the child.

Considering only the doctrine of transferred malice, which of the following is correct in relation to the death of the child?

A MUSTAQ is guilty of murder as his intention was to cause grievous bodily harm to his partner, and this malice can be transferred to the child.

B MUSTAQ is guilty of murder as he was reckless as to whether he would kill his partner or not, even though that was not his intention and this malice can be transferred to the child.

C MUSTAQ would not be guilty of murder as the malice cannot be transferred, but he may well be guilty of manslaughter of the child.

D MUSTAQ would not be guilty of murder or manslaughter, as the malice cannot be transferred in relation to either offence.

Question 1.8

AZIZ has a grudge against SMITH (his neighbour) and intends seeking revenge against him. He intends to frighten SMITH and pours paraffin through his letter box and sets fire to it; he believes paraffin to be less flammable than petrol and is aware that the house is occupied at the time he does this. The blaze he starts spreads and a child in the house dies from smoke inhalation caused by the fire.

Consider 'foresight' as it applies to the legal concept of 'intent'. Which of the following is correct in relation to whether AZIZ has murdered the child?

A The jury should be directed that they are not entitled to infer the necessary intention, unless they feel sure that death or serious bodily harm was a virtual certainty as a result of the defendant's actions.

B The jury should be directed that they are not entitled to infer the necessary intention, unless they feel sure that death or serious bodily harm was a virtual certainty as a result of the defendant's actions, and that the defendant appreciated that such was the case.

C The jury should be directed that they are not entitled to infer the necessary intention, unless they feel sure that death or serious bodily harm was almost certain as a result of the defendant's actions.

D The jury should be directed that they are not entitled to infer the necessary intention, unless they feel sure that death or serious bodily harm was almost certain as a result of the defendant's actions, and that the defendant appreciated that such was the case.

Question 1.9

GREENWOOD buys a dog and, due completely to lack of knowledge and utter stupidity, does not feed it at all. He lets in run in nearby fields believing it will kill another animal and feed itself. The dog dies and the RSPCA are considering an offence of animal cruelty.

In relation to the term 'wilful', what must the prosecution show in respect of GREENWOOD's state of mind, in order to prove this offence?

A That GREENWOOD must have intended the dog to be ill as a result of not feeding her, or providing medical aid.

B That GREENWOOD must have intended to be cruel to the dog but not necessarily by not feeding it.

C That GREENWOOD had considered the consequences of not feeding the dog.

D That GREENWOOD was aware of the risk but took it anyway due to not caring whether the dog's health was at risk or not.

ANSWERS

Answer 1.1

Answer **B** — Offences, generally speaking require a state of mind; a *mens rea*. Offences requiring a particular *mens rea* are often referred to in legal textbooks as crimes of specific intent or ulterior intent. 'Intention' is a word that is usually used in relation to consequences. A person clearly intends a consequence if he wants that consequence to follow from his action. Murder is such a crime, requiring proof of an intention to kill or seriously injure.

The question asks you to consider only *mens rea* and gives you the intention of causing serious injury. Although other factors may come into the legal equation at a later stage, in these circumstances there is *mens rea* for murder and therefore the offence is complete even though there is no intention to murder; answers A, C and D are therefore incorrect.

Crime, para. 1.1.2

Answer 1.2

Answer **D** — Consider the statutory expressions that exist in English law; the more common expressions are:

- intent;
- recklessness;
- wilfully;
- dishonestly.

Looking at the differences between intent and recklessness, then, an advantage of recklessness over intention is that the former is easier to prove by the attendant circumstances; a disadvantage is the different elements attributed to the word 'reckless' by different courts considering different offences.

An example of this dilemma occurs in *D* v *DPP* [2005] EWHC 967. A police officer attended a domestic incident involving a dispute as to the defendant's access to his newborn daughter. The defendant was outside the property. He was arrested to prevent a breach of the peace. When he had calmed down he was allowed to see his daughter. He then ran away pursued by the officer to his home address. During a subsequent struggle the defendant bit the officer on the left hand. The defendant was arrested for assaulting a police constable. He was charged with an offence contrary to

s. 89 of the Police Act 1996. The justices found that the defendant was guilty of assaulting the officer by biting him, on the basis that the defendant's actions were reckless. The defendant appealed, arguing that a bite could not be reckless; either it was deliberate or it was accidental.

The Divisional Court held, dismissing the appeal, the test of recklessness in an assault of this kind involved foresight of the risk that the complainant would be subjected to unlawful force and the taking of that risk, that state of mind being coincident with the act of biting, so even accidental injury could be 'reckless' and therefore an assault; answer C is therefore incorrect.

While the case (D) endorses the view that there can be a reckless 'battery' the facts of it are not so convincing as, say, an occasion where the defendant causes injury by thrashing his arms around to avoid being handcuffed or by attempting to throw away some property during an arrest. In this scenario the defendant's motive in opening his mouth was to dispose of the drugs, not come into contact with the officer's fingers (indeed the officer appears to be more 'reckless' in his actions). Due to the defendant's state of mind there can be no 'reckless' assault; answers A and B are therefore incorrect.

Crime, para. 1.1.4

Answer 1.3

Answer **B** — Negligence is generally concerned with the defendant's compliance with the standards of reasonableness of ordinary people, not just the standards of ordinary people; answers A and C are therefore incorrect.

Like strict liability, the concept of negligence focuses on the consequences of the defendant's conduct rather than demanding proof of a particular state of mind at the time.

Unlike strict liability, negligence still ascribes some notion of 'fault' or 'blame' to the defendant who must be shown to have acted in a way that runs contrary to the expectations of the reasonable person; answers C and D are therefore incorrect.

Crime, para. 1.1.10

Answer 1.4

Answer **B** — The concept of recklessness goes beyond a statutory expression and has probably become more important in proving criminal offences than the concept of 'intent' as proof of recklessness is often enough to fulfil the requirement of *mens rea*.

An advantage of recklessness over intention is that the former is easier to prove by the attendant circumstances; a disadvantage is the different elements attributed to the word 'reckless' by different courts considering different offences.

In assault cases recklessness can suffice in proving the mental element (*R* v *Venna* [1976] QB 421); answer C is therefore incorrect. But recklessness as to what? The defendant may have been reckless as to the assault itself and/or to the harm that was actually caused by the assault. The courts have held that assault occasioning actual bodily harm only requires proof of recklessness as to the assault and there is no need to show that the defendant was reckless as to the extent of the harm caused by his/her assault (see *R* v *Savage* [1992] 1 AC 699); answer A is therefore incorrect.

Intoxication is not relevant to where someone is assaulted 'recklessly'; answer D is therefore incorrect.

Crime, para. 1.1.4

Answer 1.5

Answer **A** — The concept of recklessness itself goes beyond a statutory expression and has probably become more important in proving criminal offences than the concept of 'intent' above as proof of recklessness is often enough to fulfil the requirement of *mens rea*.

Following decades of complex differences between objective and subjective recklessness (the former applying only to a very limited number of offences), the law was eventually clarified so that the standard approach to dealing with the term 'recklessness' will be that 'subjective recklessness' is the order of the day.

In *R* v *G & R* [2003] UKHL 50, the House of Lords decided that the former *Caldwell* (*Metropolitan Police Commissioner* v *Caldwell*) [1982] AC 341) decision should be departed from and that recklessness in criminal damage matters should be viewed subjectively.

What the prosecution will need to show is that the defendant either intended to do harm to the victim or that he/she foresaw that harm (though not the extent of that harm) may be caused but nevertheless went on to take that risk (*R* v *Savage* [1992] 1 AC 699).

The risk is foreseen and not anticipated; answers C and D are therefore incorrect and the extent of the harm need not be foreseen; answer B is therefore incorrect.

Crime, para. 1.1.4

Answer 1.6

Answer **C** — The term 'strict liability' is sometimes loosely explained as meaning 'liability without fault' but this is misleading insofar as it suggests that no mental or fault element whatsoever is required. Strict liability offences are normally those where no fault element is required in relation to one (perhaps crucial) element of the *actus reus* but where *mens rea* is required in relation to other aspects.

In relation to our fictitious offence there is absolutely no mental element required; taking a person on a rollercoaster is an absolute offence which would be committed where:

• a person is aged 16 or under, and
• is taken on a rollercoaster.

Both elements would need to be shown however; answers A and B are therefore incorrect.

The wording of the statute leaves no room for manoeuvre for the accused, there would be no defence of 'I honestly thought he was 17'; answer D is therefore incorrect.

If the caveat of 'without the person's parents or legal guardian's permission' were added to the rollercoaster offence it would add a mental element to it, however it would still be an offence of 'strict liability' in relation to the facts outlined above.

Crime, para. 1.1.11

Answer 1.7

Answer **C** — The state of mind required for one offence can, on occasions, be 'transferred' from the original target or victim to another. Known generally as the doctrine of 'transferred malice' because it originates from a case involving malicious wounding the doctrine only operates if the crime remains the same. For example, in the original case (*R v Latimer* (1886) 17 QBD 359) the defendant lashed out with his belt at one person but missed, striking a third party instead. As it was proved that the defendant had the required *mens rea* when he swung the belt, the court held that the same *mens rea* could support a charge of wounding against any other victim injured by the same act. The House of Lords has acknowledged that this doctrine is somewhat arbitrary and is an exception to the general principles of law (*Attorney General's Reference (No. 3 of 1994)* [1998] AC 245).

If the nature of the offence changes, then the doctrine will not operate. Therefore if a defendant is shown to have thrown a rock at a crowd of people intending to injure one of them, the *mens rea* required for that offence cannot be 'transferred' to an offence of criminal damage if the rock misses them and breaks a window instead, although this is not exclusive to offences of an entirely different nature.

The defendant intended only to injure his partner, and although had she died this would have been enough to support a charge of murder, she did not die. Attempted murder requires intention to kill, which is absent here. As there is no intention of the defendant in relation to murder, this intention cannot be transferred; answers A and B are therefore incorrect.

There was, however, intention to harm, which can be transferred and therefore support a charge of manslaughter; answer D is therefore incorrect.

Crime, para. 1.1.12

Answer 1.8

Answer **B** — Section 8 of the Criminal Justice Act 1967 states:

A court or jury, in determining whether a person has committed an offence,—
(a) shall not be bound in law to infer that he intended or foresaw a result of his actions by reason only of its being a natural and probable consequence of those actions; but
(b) shall decide whether he did intend or foresee that result by reference to all the evidence, drawing such inferences from the evidence as appear proper in the circumstances.

Both the Court of Appeal and the House of Lords have clearly indicated that, normally, there will be no necessity to refer expressly to the accused's foresight. In the words of Lord Lane CJ in *R* v *Nedrick* [1986] 1 WLR 1025:

Where the charge is murder and in the rare cases where the simple direction is not enough, the jury should be directed that they are not entitled to infer the necessary intention, unless they feel sure that death or serious bodily harm was a virtual certainty (barring some unforeseen intervention) as a result of the defendant's actions and that the defendant appreciated that such was the case.

Note it is 'virtual' and not 'almost' certainty; answers C and D are therefore incorrect. The defendant must also be aware of that risk; answer A is therefore incorrect.

Crime, para. 1.1.3

Answer 1.9

Answer **D** — 'Wilfully' is mentioned in offences such as child cruelty (s. 1 of the Children and Young Persons Act 1933) and obstructing a police officer (s. 89(2) of the Police Act 1996).

Like the term 'maliciously', the term 'wilfully' should not be understood in a literal sense as meaning 'deliberate' or 'voluntary'. It is taken to mean intentionally or recklessly (subjective) (*Attorney General's Reference (No 3 of 2003)* [2005] QB 73).

The requirements of subjective recklessness can be found in the case of *R v Cunningham* [1957] 2 QB 396 and are satisfied in situations where the defendant foresees the consequences of their action as being probable or even possible.

Answers A and B both say there must be intention but as this term includes recklessness as well they are incorrect. It is not enough just to consider the consequences, they have to foresee the consequences as being probable or possible; answer C is therefore incorrect.

Crime, paras 1.1.4, 1.1.6

2 | Criminal Conduct

STUDY PREPARATION

This chapter goes on from the first chapter to look at how all the ingredients are physically put together to make the offence cake.

Where *mens rea* is the mental element, *actus reus* is the conduct or positive act by the accused. This chapter examines how the principle of 'an act does not make a person guilty unless (their) mind is also guilty' by examining the interface that *mens rea* has with *actus reus*.

Once this is established there are other factors to consider like voluntary acts, omissions, causal links and intervening acts.

You are also tested on how one offender can link with an accessory, and how 'acts' and 'states of mind' are affected in joint offending. Also 'the responsibility of the superior for the acts of their subordinate' is examined; how organisations can commit offences, as well as being responsible for the acts of their staff.

QUESTIONS

Question 2.1

JOHNSON was trying to import drugs into the UK from Pakistan; she had arranged a series of flights to try to avoid detection. JOHNSON was now in Paris about to book her suitcases onto a flight to London; however, she changed her mind and left the suitcases in a toilet in Paris, and she travelled on to London without any luggage. The suitcases were found and searched in Paris but the drugs were not found, the authorities then arranged for their onward journey to London.

In relation to importation of drugs, and in particular the criminal conduct of JOHNSON which of the following is correct?

A JOHNSON's loss of *mens rea* will not prevent her being guilty of an importation offence.

B JOHNSON's loss of *mens rea* will not prevent her being guilty of an importation offence; however, this will be mitigated by the fact she tried not to import the drugs by leaving them behind.

C JOHNSON's loss of *mens rea* will not prevent her being guilty of an importation offence; however, she won't be guilty as she didn't actually import the drugs.

D JOHNSON's loss of *mens rea* will prevent her being guilty of an importation offence as she didn't have the *mens rea* when the drugs were imported.

Question 2.2

ALBARETTI worked for a major retail company on the night shift. The company, to save money, had unisex facilities including changing and toilet facilities. The night shift manager walks in on ALBARETTI whilst she is changing and is standing in her underwear. The manager walks over to her and takes his penis out inviting ALBA-RETTI to put it in her mouth, he then grabs her bra strap. The manager is charged with an offence under the Sexual Offences Act 2003.

What, if any, is the company's corporate liability in relation to the activity of its manager?

A They would be liable as he is effectively their representative on night shift.

B They would be liable as they introduced unisex facilities, thus increasing the risk of this type of activity.

C They would not be liable at all for the actions of their employee in these circumstances.

D They could be liable as accessories for aiding and abetting the activity should relevant evidence exist.

Question 2.3

MARRINER gives a lift to his friend FILCH and notices that FILCH has a shotgun in his bag. MARRINER asks what the shotgun is for and FILCH tells him to mind his own business; MARRINER suspects that FILCH may use the gun to shoot someone. About 15 hours later FILCH shoots a male who dies of his injuries at the address where MAR-RINER dropped him off.

In relation to causation, which of the following is true in relation to MARRINER's liability as an accessory?

A MARRINER is guilty as he suspected FILCH may commit a crime and did nothing about it.

B MARRINER is guilty as there is no intervening act between him dropping FILCH off and the shooting.

C MARRINER is not guilty as there is a time delay between him dropping FILCH off and the murder.

D MARRINER is not guilty as there is no evidence he knew about the murder therefore there is no chain of causation to him.

Question 2.4

PRETORIOUS and his girlfriend agreed to take care of his sister who had been diagnosed with anorexia. The sister was initially able to look after herself; gradually, however, her condition deteriorated, until she became bedridden. She needed medical help, but none was summoned and she eventually died in squalor, covered in bed sores and filth. PRETORIOUS and his girlfriend were jointly charged with manslaughter due to their failure to act to prevent the sister's death.

Which of the following is correct?

A Only PRETORIOUS will be guilty as it was his sister and there is a clear duty of care.

B Both will be guilty, they both assumed a duty of responsibility, and had failed to carry out that duty.

C Neither will be guilty as at the time they assumed responsibility the sister was able to look after herself.

D Neither will be guilty as the disease she was suffering from was self-induced.

Question 2.5

MULLER intends to commit a burglary at a local electrical goods shop. He confides in BERGSTROM, who tells his wife who works in that shop. BERGSTROM's wife tells her husband that as far as she knows the security guard is always asleep at night, but she does not tell him that the rear door alarm is currently broken. BERGSTROM tells MULLER to commit the offence at 4 am, which he does by entering through the back door.

What is the BERGSTROM'S liability, if any, for the burglary?

A Both husband and wife are guilty as counsellors of the offence.

B Both husband and wife are guilty as procurers of the offence.

C Only Mr BERGSTROM is guilty as counsellor of the offence.

D Only Mr BERGSTROM is guilty as procurer of the offence.

Question 2.6

TIMKINS wishes to take revenge on someone who owes him a lot of money but won't pay it back. He goes to STRUTHERS who he knows supplies imitation firearms and asks for a handgun; STRUTHERS supplies what he believes to be an inactive weapon that has had the firing mechanism removed. TIMKINS approaches the male who owes him money, his intention is to put the gun to his head and pull the trigger believing it won't go off; however STRUTHERS has given him a 'live' gun by mistake and TIMKINS fatally wounds the man who owed him money.

Is STRUTHERS an accessory to an offence that resulted in the death of that male?

A No, he did not intend helping TIMKINS commit the murder.

B No, as he only intended supplying an imitation firearm.

C Yes, he is reckless when he supplies a 'live' weapon, even by accident.

D Yes, he is an accessory, as he knowingly supplied the weapon, whatever the circumstances of the death.

Question 2.7

PAGETT commits an armed robbery and is pursued by armed police officers. PAGETT grabs a woman at a bus stop and uses her as a human shield and starts shooting at the police officers; they return fire and kill the woman. PAGETT is unhurt but as he has used all his ammunition he surrenders to the officers. He is charged with manslaughter of the woman he used as a human shield.

Considering the term 'intervening act' which of the following is correct?

A PAGETT cannot be guilty of manslaughter as the officers' actions in returning fire were 'voluntary' therefore an intervening act.

B PAGETT cannot be guilty of manslaughter as the officers' actions in returning fire were 'deliberate' therefore an intervening act.

C PAGETT will be guilty of manslaughter as the woman's death was a natural and foreseeable result of his behaviour.

D PAGETT will be guilty of manslaughter but only if the officers' actions in returning fire were reasonable.

Question 2.8

DONOVAN is part of a gang that always carry weapons. Some of the gang are together one night when they are attacked by a rival gang. During the fight one of the rival gang is stabbed and dies; DONOVAN did not have a knife himself that night and did not inflict the fatal wound, nor does he know who did; although he knows that his gang friends regularly carry knives and often used them in fights.

Is DONOVAN guilty of murder through joint enterprise?

A Yes, as he is aware that his friends often carry knives.

B Yes, as he is aware that his friends often carry knives and may use them.

C No, as DONOVAN himself did not have a knife that night.

D No, as there was not an agreement prior to the incident that a knife might be used.

Question 2.9

KHAIRA is in a gang who wish to push their rivals out of their area. KHAIRA and his associates then all arm themselves with baseball bats, iron bars and various other weapons. The gang become involved in a large-scale fight and one of the rival gang receives three stab wounds, one of which is fatal. KHAIRA is charged with murder by joint enterprise and states he neither knew that anyone had a knife nor that he knew anyone intended to kill; he claims his only joint enterprise was to cause serious harm. In fact KHAIRA did not have a knife on him and the male who caused the fatal injury was never arrested.

Is KHAIRA guilty of murder through joint enterprise?

A Yes, he had the necessary intent and foresaw that serious injury could be caused.

B Yes, he had the necessary intent and was reckless as to whether serious injury could be caused.

C No, he did not see any knife and was not aware that anyone was carrying a knife.

D No, he did not have an intention to kill nor have that intention as the joint enterprise.

Question 2.10

CONDRON was walking through the park one day when he saw two males involved in a bare knuckle fight. As a boxing fan he recognises that these are two trained boxers and he thinks it is a good fight. Indeed he encourages one male more than the other. The male he was encouraging then punches the other breaking his jaw; at this point the police arrive and arrests are made.

Which of the following is correct in relation to CONDRON's liability as an accessory to the assault (the broken jaw)?

A He will be liable as he encourages the male who commits the assault.

B He will be liable as he did nothing to prevent the assault taking place.

C He will not be liable as mere words of encouragement are not enough to be an accessory.

D He would not be guilty unless the fighters state his actions encouraged them to fight.

Question 2.11

RODRICK is driving his car at night when he knocks over a pedestrian walking on the pavement. The pedestrian is not dead, but lies bleeding and severely injured in the road, on the carriageway itself. RODRICK gets out of his car, sees the pedestrian and then, in panic, drives away. CARTER is also driving down the road, but is distracted as he is using his mobile phone. CARTER fails to see the pedestrian lying in the road and drives over his head killing him instantly.

Considering only a 'causal link', which of the following is correct in relation to causing death by dangerous driving?

A RODRICK could *only* be guilty if it was proved the pedestrian would ultimately have died from the injuries he received in the first collision.

B RODRICK could be guilty as, without his collision with the pedestrian, the pedestrian would not have been lying in the road.

C RODRICK would not be guilty even if the injuries he caused would have killed the pedestrian, as there was an intervening act when CARTER hit the pedestrian.

D RODRICK would not be guilty, but only because of the inattentiveness of CARTER who may have seen the pedestrian had he not been on his phone.

Question 2.12

GOLD stabs KHAN in the leg, almost severing the femoral artery. KHAN is rushed to hospital and his life can be saved by blood transfusion. KHAN refuses as he is paranoid that the blood he will be given will contain the HIV virus. This is an unreasonable belief due to the screening process transfusion blood has to go through. In fact KHAN does not die of blood loss as the hospital staff work a small miracle without giving him a blood transfusion; however he contracts multiple antibiotic-resistant staphylo-coccus aureus (MRSA) and dies as a result of that disease.

How culpable is GOLD for the death of KHAN?

A He is fully culpable as the stab wound was the first injury KHAN received.

B He is partly culpable, as the stab wound was not the primary cause of death.

C He is not culpable at all, as KHAN's blood loss did not cause his death.

D He is not culpable at all as there were two new intervening acts between his actions and the death of KHAN.

Question 2.13

GUNNERSON is homeless and enters a shop during opening hours and hides in the storeroom as it has been below freezing all week at night. During the night, the heating is off in the storeroom. Being a former electrician GUNNERSON rigs the heating system, however in doing so he leaves several live wires bare. In the morning he leaves the storeroom in the condition he made it. Later that day an assistant electrocutes herself on a wire that GUNNERSON had made bare.

Is GUNNERSON liable by omission for the assistant's injuries?

A Yes, as he was under an obligation to avert the danger he had caused.

B Yes, as he took it upon himself to assume responsibility for the electrical system in the storeroom.

C No, he is not under any statutory obligation to intervene before the assistant was injured.

D No, there was no proximity between him and the assistant at the time she was injured.

ANSWERS

Answer 2.1

Answer **A** — The general rule is that, to be guilty of a criminal offence requiring *mens rea*, an accused must possess that *mens rea* when performing the act or omission in question, and it must relate to that particular act or omission. If, for example, a man accidentally kills his wife in a car crash on Monday, the fact that he was planning to cut her throat on Tuesday does not make him guilty of her murder, even if he was thinking about the planned murder at the time of the accident, and even if he is subsequently delighted to find that his wife has died.

The general rule as to contemporaneity must nevertheless be qualified in certain respects. First, an accused's *mens rea* need not last beyond the moment at which he causes the *actus reus* to occur. He will not be excused merely because he abandons the crime before that *actus reus* is complete; answer C is therefore incorrect. After inflicting a fatal injury on V with murderous intent, D may repent of his actions and may even do his utmost to save V's life; but if V dies he will be guilty of murder (*R v Jakeman* (1983) 76 Cr App R 223); answer B is therefore incorrect.

In *Jakeman*, the defendant booked suitcases containing drugs onto a series of flights terminating in London. She abandoned them in Paris, allegedly because she no longer intended to import them, but the cases were sent on to London where the drugs were discovered. The Court of Appeal held that the loss of *mens rea* came too late to prevent her being guilty of an importation offence; answer D is therefore incorrect.

Crime, para. 1.2.2.2

Answer 2.2

Answer **D** — This question addresses the issues of corporate liability. Companies have been successfully prosecuted for offences involving strict liability (*Alphacell Ltd v Woodward* [1972] AC 824) as well as offences which require *mens rea* (*Tesco Supermarkets Ltd v Nattrass* [1972] AC 153).

Liability is not limited to summary offences and companies can be liable for the actions of some of their employees as accessories under certain circumstances (*R v Robert Millar (Contractors) Ltd* [1970] 2 QB 54), making answer C incorrect.

Clearly there are some offences that would be conceptually impossible for a legal corporation to commit (e.g. some sexual offences) but, given that companies can be guilty as accessories they may well be capable of aiding and abetting such offences even though they could not commit the offence as a principal; answers A and B are therefore incorrect.

Crime, para. 1.2.7

Answer 2.3

Answer **D** — Although legal causation must be 'operative and substantial', it need not necessarily be a direct cause of the proscribed result. In *R* v *McKechnie* [1992] Crim LR 194, a man inflicted serious head injuries on another man. These were not in themselves fatal, but they prevented doctors from operating on the injured man's duodenal ulcer, and he died when the ulcer burst. In some cases a significant delay can occur between the acts which put in train the criminal consequences. An example is where a defendant transported an accomplice to a place near to the victim's house some 13 hours before the accomplice shot and killed the victim. Despite the delay and despite the fact the accomplice had not fully made up his mind about the proposed shooting at the time he was dropped off by the defendant, there was no intervening event that diverted or hindered the planned murder (*R* v *Bryce* [2004] EWCA Crim 1231); answer C is therefore incorrect.

However, there must be a chain of causation between the act of the defendant and the ultimate crime. In this scenario MARRINER gives a lift to someone and suspects, as they are carrying a gun, some malfeasance. Although there is ultimately a shooting there is no chain of causation between the lift and that action, even though there had been no intervening act; answers A and B are therefore incorrect.

Crime, para. 1.2.4

Answer 2.4

Answer **B** — Criminal conduct is most often associated with *actions*: damaging or stealing property, injuring or deceiving others, but occasionally liability is brought about by a failure to act.

Most of the occasions where failure or omission will attract liability are where a *duty to act* has been created. Such a duty can arise from a number of circumstances, the main ones being:

D The creation of a **D**angerous situation by the defendant. See, for example, *R* v *Miller* [1983] 2 AC 161 where the defendant, having accidentally started a fire in a house, moved to another room taking no action to counteract the danger he had created.

U Under statute, contract or a person's public 'office'. Examples would be where a police officer failed to intervene to prevent an assault (*R* v *Dytham* [1979] QB 722) or where a crossing keeper omitted to close the gates at a level crossing and a person was subsequently killed by a train (*R* v *Pittwood* (1902) 19 TLR 37).

T Where the defendant has taken it upon himself/herself to carry out a duty and then fails to do so. Such a duty was taken up by the defendant in *R* v *Stone* [1977] QB 354 when she accepted a duty to care for her partner's mentally ill sister who subsequently died.

Y In circumstances where the defendant is in a parental relationship with a child or a Young person, i.e. an obligation exists for the parent to look after the health and welfare of the child.

In this scenario both PRETORIOUS and his girlfriend had taken his sister into their home, they had assumed a duty of care for her and had been grossly negligent in the performance of that duty. The fact that she was PRETORIOUS's sister was merely incidental to this; answer A is therefore incorrect. The actual reason why the person needed care is irrelevant, it is the duty imposed that is important, and the condition of the person when they first assume that duty is also of no relevance; answers C and D are therefore incorrect.

Crime, para. 1.2.3

Answer 2.5

Answer **C** — A principal offender must meet all the requirements of the particular offence, and for procurement there must be a causal link between his conduct and the offence. Counselling requires no causal link (*R* v *Calhaem* [1985] QB 808); all that is required is the principal offender's awareness of the counsellor's advice or encouragement—and this is true even if the principal would have committed the offence anyway (*Attorney General* v *Able* [1984] QB 795).

Generally, the state of mind (*mens rea*) which is needed to convict an accessory is: 'proof of intention to aid as well as of knowledge of the circumstances' (*National Coal Board* v *Gamble* [1959] 1 QB 11). The minimum state of mind required of an accessory to an offence is set out in *Johnson* v *Youden* [1950] 1 KB 544. In that case the court held that, before anyone can be convicted of aiding and abetting an offence, he or she must at least know the essential matters that constitute that offence. There must also be a further mental element, namely an intention to aid the principal, so in what way is there evidence against Mrs BERGSTROM? None, in fact there is evidence to the contrary in that she did not indicate that the back door alarm was faulty. So only Mr BERGSTROM is an accessory and at that a counsellor; answers A, B and D are therefore incorrect.

Crime, paras 1.2.6, 1.2.6.1

Answer 2.6

Answer **A** — Generally, the state of mind (*mens rea*) which is needed to convict an accessory is: 'proof of intention to aid as well as of knowledge of the circumstances' (*National Coal Board* v *Gamble* [1959] 1 QB 11 at p. 20). The minimum state of mind required of an accessory to an offence is set out in *Johnson* v *Youden* [1950] 1 KB 544. In that case the court held that, before anyone can be convicted of aiding and abetting an offence, he/she must at least know the essential matters that constitute that offence.

There must also be a further mental element, namely an intention to aid the principal. Whether there was such an intention to aid the principal is a question of fact to be decided in the particular circumstances of each case.

Although he knowingly supplied a weapon, he does not fit the criteria of:

- intention to aid
- knowledge of the circumstances

as they relate to the death; therefore he cannot have aided and abetted it as he did not envisage a death occurring; answers B, C and D are therefore incorrect.

Crime, para. 1.2.6.1

Answer 2.7

Answer **C** — A defendant will not be regarded as having caused the consequence for which he stands accused if there was a new intervening act sufficient to break the chain of causation between his original action and the consequence in question, in this case the death of the woman. The causal link can be broken by a new intervening act provided that the 'new' act is 'free, deliberate and informed' (*R* v *Latif* [1996] 1 WLR 104). Were the officers' actions 'free, deliberate and informed'? For that to be the case the officers would have had to have shot the woman deliberately and not whilst trying to take reasonable measures for self-preservation and in the performance of their legal duty to apprehend PAGETT; answers A and B are therefore incorrect.

Even if the police officers were at fault, their conduct was not free, deliberate and informed. PAGETT created a situation in which the woman's life was inevitably endangered, and what happened was a natural and foreseeable consequence of that behaviour; answer D is therefore incorrect.

Crime, para. 1.2.5

Answer 2.8

Answer **B** — The main features that will determine DONOVAN's liability as an accessory in a joint enterprise will be:

- The nature and extent of the agreed offence.
- Whether the accessory knew the principal had a knife.
- Whether a different knife was used.
- Whether the knife was used differently than agreed.

The House of Lords have held that where one party (D) to a joint enterprise to commit an offence foresees as a real possibility that another party (E) may, in the course of it do an act, with the requisite *mens rea*, constituting another offence (and E does so), D is liable for that offence. This is the case even if D has not expressly or tacitly agreed to that offence, and even though he expressly forbids it.

DONOVAN is aware that knives are being carried *and* that they may be used; answer A is therefore incorrect. That makes him an accessory even though there was no agreement and he did not agree to a knife being used; answers C and D are therefore incorrect.

Crime, para. 1.2.6.2

Answer 2.9

Answer **A** — In *R v Powell* [1999] 1 AC 1, two defendants accompanied a third defendant to a drug dealer's house to buy drugs. When the drug dealer came to the door he was shot. It was unclear who had fired the fatal shot but the prosecution argued that, if the third defendant had done so, then the first two defendants were guilty of murder because they knew that the third defendant was armed with a gun. The first two defendants were convicted of murder. They appealed but the House of Lords dismissed the appeal holding that where one party (D) to a joint enterprise to commit an offence foresees as a real possibility that another party (E) may, in the course of it do an act, with the requisite *mens rea*, constituting another offence (and E does so), D is liable for that offence. This is the case even if D has not expressly or tacitly agreed to that offence, and even though he expressly forbids it. This approach was reaffirmed in *R* v *Rahman* [2008] UKHL 45 where the House of Lords considered an appeal by a group of men who chased and attacked their victim with weapons including base-ball bats, iron bars and knives. The victim died from two stab wounds to his back. There was no evidence that the appellants inflicted the fatal injuries; the participant who did probably escaped arrest but this did not prevent the defendants being convicted for their part in the joint enterprise; answers C and D are therefore incorrect.

Their Lordships held that an accessory was liable in respect of an unlawful killing on the basis of his foresight of what the principal might do, not of the intention with which the principal's act might be performed. If a defendant realises (without agree-ing to such conduct being used) that another defendant may kill or intentionally inflict serious injury, but nevertheless continues to participate in that venture, that will amount to a sufficient mental element for them to be guilty of murder if the other defendant goes on to kill. Recklessness plays no factor; answer B is therefore incorrect.

Crime, para. 1.2.6.2

Answer 2.10

Answer **D** — There are two ways of attracting criminal liability for an offence: either as a principal or an accessory.

A principal offender is one whose conduct has met all the requirements of the particular offence. An accessory is someone who helped in or brought about the com-mission of the offence. If an accessory 'aids, abets, counsels or procures' the commis-sion of an offence, he/she will be treated by a court in the same way as a principal offender for an indictable offence (Accessories and Abettors Act 1861, s. 8) or for a summary offence (Magistrates' Courts Act 1980, s. 44). The expression 'aid, abet, counsel and procure' is generally used in its entirety when charging a defendant, without separating out the particular element that applies. Generally speaking, the expressions mean as follows:

- aiding = giving help, support or assistance
- abetting = inciting, instigating or encouraging.

Each of these would usually involve the presence of the secondary party at the scene (unless, for example, part of some prearranged plan):

- counselling = advising or instructing
- procuring = bringing about.

These activities would generally be expected to take place before the commission of the offence.

Presence at the scene of a crime can be capable of constituting encouragement if the accused is present in pursuance of a prior agreement with the principal, but if the accused is only accidentally present then he must know that his presence is actually encouraging the principals, and they must be so encouraged to carry on; answers A and C are therefore incorrect. However, neither mere presence at the scene of a crime nor a failure to prevent an offence will generally give rise to liability (*R* v *Coney* (1882) 8 QBD 534); answer B is therefore incorrect.

Crime, para. 1.2.6

Answer 2.11

Answer **B** — Once the *actus reus* of an offence has been proved, a causal link must then be shown between it and the relevant consequences. That is, it must be proven that the consequences would not have happened 'but for' the defendant's act or omission. The *actus reus* for this offence is that a collision caused the death of a person. So a causal link is required.

As far as CARTER is concerned there is a causal link, the pedestrian would not be dead but for his driving over his head!

With RODRICK it is more complicated. Is there a causal link? Whilst evidence that the pedestrian would have died from his injuries had he not been hit for a second time would be good, and would almost certainly show a causal link, it would probably be very difficult to establish. In fact it is not needed as a *prima facie* causal link. This approach ignores the issue of RODRICK's foresight. Roads are, by their nature, used by vehicles and it is clearly foreseeable that a person left lying on the road is at risk of being further injured by an inattentive driver; answer A is therefore incorrect.

Hence, as RODRICK left the pedestrian on the road with knowledge of that risk and the foreseen event occurred, he remains the more proximate cause of the death. In other words 'but for' RODRICK hitting the pedestrian, and 'but for' RODRICK leaving him in a very vulnerable position on the road, he would not have died. This is the case even had CARTER been paying full attention to the road and still not seen the pedestrian; answer D is therefore incorrect.

Although effectively there has been an intervening act, it was not enough to break the chain of causation that links RODRICK to the death. Had someone approached the pedestrian on the road and fatally stabbed him, then the chain would clearly be broken.

Although the pedestrian died of injuries caused by CARTER, as far as causation is concerned RODRICK is culpable in that death (whether he would be charged or not is questionable however); answer C is therefore incorrect.

Crime, para. 1.2.4

Answer 2.12

Answer **A** — A defendant will not be regarded as having caused the consequence for which it is sought to make him liable if there was a *novus actus interveniens* (or new intervening act) sufficient to break the chain of causation between his original action and the consequence in question.

However, the chain of causation can be broken only where the effect of the intervening act is so overwhelming that any initial injuries are relegated to the status of mere historical background. So what caused KHAN's death? The answer is the stab wound because 'but for' it KHAN would not have been in hospital to contract MRSA. The fact he did not die of blood loss caused by the wound is irrelevant; answer C is therefore incorrect. No matter how many intervening acts there have been, the chain of causation in this case is unbroken; answer D is therefore incorrect.

GOLD is fully culpable, not partly culpable if you apply the 'but for' test; answer B is therefore incorrect.

Crime, paras 1.2.4, 1.2.5

Answer 2.13

Answer **A** — Most criminal offences require the defendant to carry out some positive act before liability can be imposed. There can ordinarily be no liability for failure (or omission) to act, unless the law specifically imposes such a duty upon a particular person. The general rule is illustrated by this example from *Stephen's Digest of the Criminal Law* (3rd edn, 1887):

A sees B drowning and is able to save him by holding out his hand. A abstains from doing so in order that B may be drowned, and B is drowned. A has committed no offence.

Although A may have failed to save B, he did no positive act to cause B's death.

GUNNERSON certainly committed an act that led to the injuries, but how liable is he? Most of the occasions where failure or omission will attract liability are where a *duty to act* has been created. Such a duty can arise from a number of circumstances the main ones being:

D The creation of a **D**angerous situation by the defendant. See, for example, *R v Miller* [1983] 2 AC 161 where the defendant, having accidentally started a fire in a house, moved to another room taking no action to counteract the danger he had created.

U **U**nder statute, contract or a person's public 'office'. Examples would be where a police officer failed to intervene to prevent an assault (*R v Dytham* [1979] QB 722) or where a crossing keeper omitted to close the gates at a level crossing and a person was subsequently killed by a train (*R v Pittwood* (1902) 19 TLR 37).

T Where the defendant has **T**aken it upon himself or herself to carry out a duty and then fails to do so. Such a duty was taken up by the defendant in *R v Stone* [1977] QB 354 when she accepted a duty to care for her partner's mentally ill sister who subsequently died.

Y In circumstances where the defendant is in a parental relationship with a child or a **Y**oung person.

One of those occasions is the duty to avert a danger of one's own making. If a person creates a dangerous situation through his own fault, he may be under a duty to take reasonable steps to avert that danger, and may therefore incur criminal liability for failing to do so.

GUNNERSON had not 'assumed' responsibility for the electrical system, which still remains the shop's responsibility; answer B is therefore incorrect. Although he has no statutory duty as can be seen the almost moral duty he holds does not release him from his liability; answer C is therefore incorrect. Proximity to the victim may be compelling in a duty to protect someone from danger, but it is not a pre-requisite; answer D is therefore incorrect.

Crime, para. 1.2.3

3 | Incomplete Offences and Police Investigations

STUDY PREPARATION

Having looked at the key building blocks of *mens rea* and *actus reus*, you now need to go on to consider specific criminal offences and their constituent parts. Before doing so, however, you need to get a few problematic situations out of the way.

The first of these deals with those occasions where the defendant, despite his or her best or worst endeavours, fails to do what he or she set out to do.

These are 'incomplete' offences. The second area deals with defences to criminal charges—these are addressed in the next chapter.

When dealing with incomplete offences there are two key things to remember: first, that the physical impossibility of actually achieving what the defendant set out to do will not absolve him or her from criminal liability (and why should it?); and secondly, that some offences—such as summary offences and some incomplete offences themselves—cannot be attempted.

Finally, in this chapter we deal with the related area of police operations, where the evidential and substantive issues often overlap with those of the incomplete offences involved.

QUESTIONS

Question 3.1

McCAW is a hypnotherapist who wishes to touch the breasts of his female clients. His profession's guidelines, however, mean he cannot be alone with any female who has been hypnotised, so he approaches his assistant and asks him to assist in his plans by not entering the room when he has a lone female client. The assistant is horrified and tells McCAW that he will not assist in any way and in fact contacts the police who arrest McCAW.

Has McCAW committed an offence contrary to s. 44(1) of the Serious Crime Act 2007?

A McCAW has committed the offence as he has encouraged someone to assist in the commission of an offence.

B McCAW has committed the offence as he has encouraged someone to assist in the commission of an offence and he intended to encourage the commission of an offence.

C McCAW has not committed the offence as the assistant was not encouraged or interested in assisting McCAW.

D McCAW has not committed the offence as he was not asking his assistant to actually assist with the offence, merely to ignore standard practices.

Question 3.2

GREAVES and MALK market a device that can be used to falsify readings of gas and electricity meters and they install it in houses of customers. The device itself does not allow the customers to have free gas or electricity; it simply allows them to have more than the meter reads. Neither GREAVES nor MALK install a device in their houses.

Would this constitute an offence of conspiracy to defraud (contrary to common law)?

A Yes, provided there is intent to defraud a victim.

B Yes, provided an offence is committed intent is irrelevant.

C No, as neither GREAVES nor MALK install a device in their houses.

D No, as there is no attempt to obtain entirely free gas or electricity.

Question 3.3

GRAVES and THORNTON are same sex common law partners and are very friendly with GORTON who is very short of money. To help overcome this they plan to carry out a 'burglary' at GORTON's house and make a false claim to the insurance company.

Who, if anyone, is guilty of conspiracy contrary to the Criminal Law Act 1977, s. 1?

A No one as spouses, common law and civil partners cannot conspire.

B No one as you cannot conspire with the intended victim.

C GRAVES and THORNTON only as GORTON is the intended victim.

D All three of them.

Question 3.4

KHAN is standing in a local election but realises he probably won't have enough votes. His campaign assistants are HUSSAIN and SHORT; together they decide to try to assist KHAN by asking people if they intend using their postal or proxy vote. If they do not they offer to collect the postal ballot paperwork for 'official records'. In fact they use the collected votes to vote for KHAN, who still did not win the election.

Which of the following is correct in relation to the offence of conspiracy to defraud contrary to Common Law?

A This offence is not committed as no one has lost a 'proprietary right'; they voluntarily handed over their votes.

B This offence is not committed as KHAN did not win the election.

C Only KHAN as he was the beneficiary of the conspiracy.

D All three are guilty of this offence.

Question 3.5

Constable HAYWARD is standing in the forthcoming election for police federation representative. Having spoken to many of his colleagues Constable HAYWARD is confident of election as most have indicated they will vote for him. However, to avoid disappointment he makes an agreement with Constable MAPPS to ensure success. They agree to collect voting slips from a number of officers stating that there is a printing error and that another will be sent to them by the federation office. The officers take these forms and complete them in favour of Constable HAYWARD, falsely signing the forms themselves. The result of the election was overwhelming and Constable HAYWARD was elected achieving 90 per cent of the vote. In fact Constable HAYWARD would have won the vote without submitting any of the voting slips that he submitted himself.

In these circumstances have the two officers committed an offence under common law of conspiracy to defraud?

A Yes, the officers have signed the forms dishonestly and in doing so have committed this offence.

B   Yes, the officers have deprived their colleagues of their right to vote for who they want and in doing so have committed this offence.
C   No, there is no statutory offence of 'vote rigging' and as the end result of their action is not an offence they have not committed this offence.
D   No, their actions did not affect the outcome of the vote, and as no one was deprived of their right to be elected they have not committed this offence.

Question 3.6

GENKA climbs onto the back of a trailer on a lorry and intends doing something illegal on there, although he is unsure what he will do. Unfortunately he is spotted by a security guard and arrested on the back of the trailer before he can commit any offence at all.

In relation to s. 9 of the Criminal Attempts Act 1981, interference with vehicles, which of the following is correct?
A   GENKA commits this offence as there is no need to prove what offence he intended to commit.
B   GENKA commits this offence as he was caught on the trailer with the relevant intention to commit an offence.
C   GENKA does not commit this offence as there is no evidence of specific intent at the moment he was arrested.
D   GENKA does not commit this offence as merely climbing on the back of the trailer is not 'interference' under the Act.

Question 3.7

PRETTY wishes to kill his wife who will not grant him a divorce, and looks for a contract killer. The police, however, are aware of his plan and send an undercover officer to meet him. PRETTY and the officer agree that for £2,000 the officer, posing as a contract killer, will shoot and kill PRETTY's wife. Naturally the officer has no intention of committing the murder.

In relation to conspiracy, which of the following is true?
A   As an agreement has been reached to carry out an offence, this is a statutory conspiracy.
B   As an agreement has been reached to carry out an offence, this is a common law conspiracy.
C   As the officer will not carry out the murder, the offence of conspiracy is not made out.

D Although the officer will not carry out the murder, PRETTY is still guilty of conspiracy.

Question 3.8

STRUTHERS is aware that his friend HEWISH is planning to carry out a burglary on a bank and wants to help if he can. STRUTHERS' wife works at the bank and tells STRUTHERS that tonight the alarm will be off from 4 am until 5 am for essential maintenance; she is aware of the plan but doesn't believe that anybody would be stupid enough to try to break into a bank. STRUTHERS tells HEWISH about the alarm and he breaks into the bank, although he is arrested on the way out having been captured on CCTV.

Who, if anybody, has committed an offence of encouraging or assisting an offence contrary to s. 45 of the Serious Crime Act 2007?

A STRUTHERS only.

B Both STRUTHERS and his wife.

C The wife only.

D Neither STRUTHERS or his wife.

Question 3.9

ALEXANDER is found by police officers trespassing in the lavatory block of a school, armed with a large knife and lengths of rope and tape. It appears that he had intended to kidnap a child although he remains silent during police interviews.

At what point, if any, does ALEXANDER commit the offence of attempted kidnap?

A At no point does he commit this offence.

B When he takes possession of the rope and tape,

C When he enters the school boundary.

D When he enters the school lavatory.

Question 3.10

LARK is an undercover officer working on a drugs operation. The police are carrying out an operation on XHOSH, a known drug dealer. LARK is authorised (proper authorities for this operation have been obtained) to purchase drugs from XHOSH. He approaches XHOSH who offers to sell him a wrap of amphetamine. LARK hands over the money and takes the drugs. During the transaction LARK asks XHOSH if he can supply a firearm for a robbery he is planning. XHOSH agrees to this and plans a later meeting.

In relation to LARK's request, which of the following is true?

A This is not entrapment as XHOSH is volunteering to get the firearm.

B This is not entrapment as the undercover operation has been authorised.

C This may be entrapment as LARK is no longer a passive observer.

D This is entrapment as LARK was not authorised by the operation to buy firearms.

Question 3.11

Police officers are carrying out an undercover operation involving drug supply. BEATTIE mistakes one of the undercover officers for a drug supplier and approaches him and asks if he can supply heroin to him. The officer agrees to such supply in order to preserve his cover. Other officers arrest BEATTIE for encouraging or assisting in the commission of an offence. He denies this and argues that the officer could not have been encouraged to commit an offence as the police have defences to drug possession; he also argues that it was impossible for the officer to supply heroin.

Given this is an undercover police operation, which of the following is correct?

A This could be seen as entrapment as the officer agrees to supply the drugs.

B The fact BEATTIE approached an undercover police officer means he cannot have committed an offence.

C The fact that the officer could not actually supply drugs means BEATTIE cannot commit an offence.

D BEATTIE can commit the offence, it would be possible for the officer to supply the drugs.

Question 3.12

DEEN was on holiday in Spain with his wife and while he was there, he became friendly with LAWRENSON. During a conversation one evening, DEEN told LAWRENSON that he was fed up with his wife and wished she were dead. LAWRENSON told DEEN that for a fee, he would see if he could locate someone who would do the job. They then discussed how they would meet again in the UK at a later time together with the person LAWRENSON knew would kill the wife. Unknown to them, their conversation was overheard by PAINTING, an off-duty police officer. Upon returning from holiday, PAINTING made a witness statement regarding the conversation to the local Crown Prosecution Service.

Could DEEN and LAWRENSON be prosecuted for an offence of conspiracy to commit murder in these circumstances?

A Yes, provided they return to this country to commit the substantive offence.

B Yes, whether or not they return to this country to commit the substantive offence.

C No, as neither DEEN nor LAWRENSON would actually carry out the offence.

D No, a person may only be guilty of conspiring in this country to commit an offence abroad.

Question 3.13

BOW, GREENE and BURGESS agree to be drug dealers for SCIMITER. They collaborate to ensure that the drugs SCIMITER supplies to them are then further supplied to drug users. They each select a particular area of the town they live in to be their 'turf', that is, the area for which they will be the main supplier of drugs. At the moment though, no actual drugs have been supplied to them by SCIMITER.

Are any of these persons guilty of statutory conspiracy to supply controlled drugs contrary to s. 1 of the Criminal Law Act 1977?

A All four are guilty, as each of them is aware of the overall common purpose to which they all attach themselves.

B BOW, GREENE and BURGESS are guilty as they are the ones with the joint agreement.

C SCIMITER only is guilty, as although there is a joint agreement only he will actually supply the drugs that are subject to the agreement.

D None of them is guilty as the intended recipients of the drugs to be supplied were the conspirators themselves.

ANSWERS

Answer 3.1

Answer **B** — The Serious Crime Act 2007, s. 44 states:

(1) A person commits an offence if—
 (a) he does an act capable of encouraging or assisting in the commission of an offence; and
 (b) he intends to encourage or assist its commission
(2) But he is not to be taken to have intended to encourage or assist the commission of an offence merely because such encouragement or assistance was a foreseeable consequence of his act.

This offence requires the defendant to intentionally encourage or assist an offence; answer D is therefore incorrect. As such, s. 44(2) makes it clear that foresight of a consequence is not sufficient to establish intention; answer A is therefore incorrect.

Section 49(1) of the Act states that offences can be committed regardless of whether or not the encouragement or assistance has the effect which the defendant intended or believed it would have; answer C is therefore incorrect.

Crime, para. 1.3.2

Answer 3.2

Answer **A** — Common law conspiracy to defraud involves:

an agreement by two or more [persons] by dishonesty to deprive a person of something which is his or to which he is or would or might be entitled [or] an agreement by two or more by dishonesty to injure some proprietary right [of the victim] ...

(*Scott* v *Metropolitan Police Commissioner* [1975] AC 819: *Crime*, para. 1.3.3.2)

Intent to defraud a victim must be shown (*R* v *Hollinshead* [1985] AC 975); answer B is therefore incorrect.

There is no requirement to prove that the end result would amount to the commission of an offence, simply that it would result in depriving a person of something under the specified conditions or in injuring his/her proprietary right; answers C and D are therefore incorrect.

Crime, para. 1.3.3.2

Answer 3.3

Answer **D** — A defendant cannot be convicted of a statutory conspiracy if the only other party to the agreement is:

- his/her spouse (or civil partner);
- a person under 10 years of age;
- the intended victim (Criminal Law Act 1977, s. 2(2)).

This does not include common law partners; answer A is therefore incorrect.

The victim here is the insurance company, not GORTON as it is a false burglary but a real fraud against the insurers; answers B and C are therefore incorrect.

Crime, para. 1.3.3.1

Answer 3.4

Answer **D** — The common law offence of conspiracy is defined in the leading case of *Scott* v *Metropolitan Police Commissioner* [1975] AC 819, where Viscount Dilhorne said:

> ...an agreement by two or more [persons] by dishonesty to deprive a person of something which is his or to which he is or would be or might be entitled [or] an agreement by two or more by dishonesty to injure some proprietary right of his suffices to constitute the offence...
>
> ...it suffices if there is a dishonest agreement to expose the proposed victim to some form of economic risk or disadvantage to which he would not otherwise be exposed.

Although the requirement for an agreement between at least two people is the same (answer C is therefore incorrect), this offence is broader than statutory conspiracy. There is no requirement to prove that the end result would amount to the commission of an offence, simply that it would result in depriving a person of something under the specified conditions or in injuring his/her proprietary right. The people who handed over the postal vote ballot slips lost their right to vote for who they wanted as KHAN used their votes for himself, the fact he didn't win the election is irrelevant; answers A and B are therefore incorrect (see *R* v *Hussain* [2005] EWCA Crim 1866).

Crime, para. 1.3.3.2

Answer 3.5

Answer **B** — Conspiracy to defraud involves:

> ...an agreement by two or more [persons] by dishonesty to deprive a person of something which is his or to which he is or would or might be entitled [or] an agreement by two or more by dishonesty to injure some proprietary right [of the victim]...

There are two principal variants of this offence, although these are not mutually exclusive. The first is defined in the previous paragraph in the leading case of *Scott* v *Metropolitan Police Commissioner* [1975] AC 819. There may or may not be an intent to deceive in such cases, and there may or may not be an intent to cause economic or financial loss to the proposed victim or victims, but it suffices if there is a dishonest agreement to expose the proposed victim to some form of economic risk or disadvantage to which he would not otherwise be exposed.

The second variant was also recognised in *Scott*, but has been more fully considered by the Privy Council in *Wai Yu-Tsang* v *The Queen* [1992] 1 AC 269. In this variant, there must be a dishonest agreement by two or more persons to 'defraud' another, by deceiving him into acting contrary to his duty.

Although the requirement for an agreement between at least two people is the same, this offence is broader than statutory conspiracy. There is no requirement to prove that the end result would amount to the commission of an offence, simply that it would result in depriving a person of something under the specified conditions or in injuring his or her proprietary right; answer C is therefore incorrect.

A good example of this offence can be found in *R* v *Hussain* [2005] EWCA Crim 1866 where the defendant pleaded guilty to conspiracy to defraud after a widespread abuse of the recently introduced postal voting system. In that case the defendant, an official Labour party candidate, collected uncompleted postal votes from households and completed them in his own favour. In that case it was shown that the end result was unlikely to have been affected by the defendant's actions, as it was likely he would have been elected in any case; however, this has no effect on the commission of the offence of conspiracy to defraud. The offence is complete when an agreement is reached (answer D is therefore incorrect) and is not limited to some dishonest *actus reus* like signing the forms fraudulently; answer A is therefore incorrect.

The *actus reus* of this offence is the agreement, the *mens rea* is the intent of the offender to defraud the victim (*R* v *Hollinshead* [1985] AC 975), and the dishonesty of the defendant as set out in *R* v *Ghosh* [1982] QB 1053.

Crime, para. 1.3.3.2

Answer 3.6

Answer **C** — Section 9 of the Criminal Attempts Act 1981 states:

(1) A person is guilty of the offence of vehicle interference if he interferes with a motor vehicle or trailer or with anything carried in or on a motor vehicle or trailer with the intention that an offence specified in subsection (2) below shall be committed by himself or some other person.

(2) The offences mentioned in subsection (1) above are—

    (a) theft of the motor vehicle or trailer or part of it;

    (b) theft of anything carried in or on the motor vehicle or trailer; and

    (c) an offence under section 12(1) of the Theft Act 1968 (taking and driving away without consent);

    and, if it is shown that a person accused of an offence under this section intended that one of those offences should be committed, it is immaterial that it cannot be shown which it was.

(3)–(4)...

(5) In this section 'motor vehicle' and 'trailer' have the meanings assigned to them by section 185(1) of the Road Traffic Act 1988.

The term 'interference' is not defined by the Criminal Attempts Act 1981; answer D is therefore incorrect.

This offence is one of specific intent and you must prove that the defendant interfered with the vehicle, etc. with one of the intentions listed. Although it is not necessary to show which particular intention, it has to be one of those intentions and not just intention to do 'something illegal', for instance an intention to commit criminal damage would not be covered by s. 9; answers A and B are therefore incorrect.

Crime, para. 1.3.4.1

Answer 3.7

Answer **C** — A person cannot be guilty of conspiracy if the only other party to the supposed agreement intends to frustrate or sabotage it. As the officer clearly will frustrate the agreement, answers A and D are incorrect. This was considered by the House of Lords in *Yip Chieu-Chung* v *The Queen* [1995] 1 AC 111, where N, the appellant's only fellow conspirator in a plan to smuggle heroin out of Hong Kong, was an undercover agent working with the knowledge of the authorities. The House of Lords held that if N's purpose had been to prevent the heroin being smuggled, no indictable conspiracy would have existed. Their Lordships said:

The crime of conspiracy requires an agreement between two or more persons to commit an unlawful act with the intention of carrying it out. It is the intention to carry out the crime that constitutes the necessary *mens rea* for the offence.... [A]n undercover agent who has no intention of committing the crime lacks the necessary *mens rea* to be a conspirator.

Conspiracy requires an agreement which will amount to or involve the commission of an offence. Where no such offence is likely, the offence is not made out. Common law conspiracy involves conspiracy to defraud only and therefore B is incorrect.

Crime, paras 1.3.3.1, 1.3.6.2

Answer 3.8

Answer **A** — Section 45 of the Serious Crime Act 2007 states:

Encouraging or assisting an offence believing it will be committed
(1) A person commits an offence if—
   (a) he does an act capable of encouraging or assisting the commission of an offence; and
   (b) he believes—
      (i) that the offence will be committed; and
      (ii) that his act will encourage or assist its commission.

So there are three elements that have to be fulfilled and we will examine those in relation to both STRUTHERS and his wife.

- There is an act capable of encouraging or assisting the commission of an offence.
  — Telling the burglar that the alarm is off is obviously such an act, both STRUTHERS and his wife are culpable here.
- The person must believe the offence will be committed.
  — Only STRUTHERS is culpable as he was keen to help his friend.
- The person must believe that his act will encourage or assist the commission of an offence.
  — Only STRUTHERS is culpable as only he wishes to encourage or assist in the offence.

All three elements must be present for the offence to be committed; therefore only STRUTHERS commits this offence; answers B, C and D are therefore incorrect.

Crime, para. 1.3.2

Answer 3.9

Answer **A** — Section 1(1) of the Criminal Attempts Act 1981 requires the accused to have committed an act which is 'more than merely preparatory' to the offence attempted. Where trial is on indictment, it is for the judge to determine whether there is evidence on which a jury could properly find that the accused's actions did go beyond mere preparation, but it is then for the jury to decide that question as one of fact; there is no specific formula used by the courts in interpreting this requirement.

Courts have accepted an approach of questioning whether the defendant had 'embarked on the crime proper' (*R* v *Gullefer* [1990] 1 WLR 1063) but there is no requirement for him or her to have passed a point of no return leading to the commission of the substantive offence. However, he must have passed the more than merely preparatory stage, which at this stage he has not; answers B, C and D are therefore incorrect.

Crime, para. 1.3.4

Answer 3.10

Answer **C** — The question of police entrapment is an emotive one. Where the line was drawn between legitimate police activity in undercover operations and the police acting as *agents provocateurs* was sometimes fuzzy. The House of Lords laid down the legal position in this issue in *R* v *Loosely; Attorney General's Reference (No. 3 of 2000)* [2001] 1 WLR 2060, where it was held, *inter alia*:

A useful guide is to consider whether the police did no more than present the defendant with an unexceptional opportunity to commit a crime. The yardstick for the purposes of this test is, in general, whether the police conduct preceding the commission of the offence was no more than might have been expected from others in the circumstances.

Was the officer enticing the accused to commit an offence he would not otherwise have committed? He was committing the offence of drug dealing, and was not entrapped there, but the officer goes beyond being a passive observer when he asks about the firearm. In *Loosely*, their Lordships stated:

The police must act in good faith. Having reasonable grounds for suspicion is one way good faith may be established. It is not normally considered a legitimate use of police power to provide people not suspected of being engaged in any criminal activity with the opportunity to commit crimes. The principle is that the police should prevent and detect crime, not create it.

So the fact the operation was authorised does not negate entrapment by an individual officer (answer B is therefore incorrect); nor does the fact that the accused seems keen to carry out the officer's request (answer A is therefore incorrect). What is also clear is that simply going beyond what is authorised is not necessarily entrapment; it depends on the officer's action—answer D is therefore incorrect. This area of law has guidelines set down, but ultimately it is for the judge to decide if actions amount to entrapment, and whether such entrapment should lead to a stay of proceedings or not, which is why answer C states 'may be entrapment'.

Crime, para. 1.3.6.1

Answer 3.11

Answer **D** — One of the arguments that is often raised by defendants who are caught by undercover officers is that they were induced or pressurised into committing the offence by the officers and that, as a result, either they should not be prosecuted or the evidence of the officer(s) should be excluded. This is mostly true where the approach is made by the officers to the suspect. And it is in this area only that entrapment is likely to occur; where the suspect approaches the officer, the officer cannot 'entrap' someone who voluntarily looks to commit an offence; answer A is therefore incorrect.

What of the situation where, rather than approaching others, an undercover police officer is approached to take part in a proposed offence? There are several types of situation where this may occur.

In relation to this activity, there is no need for the person encouraged to have any intention of going on to commit the offence. The Divisional Court has held that there is no requirement for 'parity of *mens rea*' between the parties (*DPP v Armstrong* [2000] Crim LR 379). In that case the defendant had approached an undercover police officer asking him to supply child pornography. At his trial, the defendant argued that, as the officer in reality had no intention of supplying the pornography, there was no offence of incitement (now encouraging/assisting an offence). On appeal by the prosecutor, the Divisional Court held that incitement, like conspiracies and attempts were auxiliary offences where criminal liability was attributed to the defendant where the full offence had not been committed. Consequently the intent of the person incited was irrelevant. The court also held that the issue of impossibility did not arise in circumstances such as Armstrong's because it had been 'possible' for the officer to supply the material; answers B and C are therefore incorrect.

Crime, para. 1.3.6.2

Answer 3.12

Answer **C** — Under s. 1(1) of the Criminal Law Act 1977, a person is guilty of conspiracy if he or she agrees with any other person(s) that a course of conduct will be pursued which, if the agreement is carried out in accordance with their intentions, either—

  (a) will necessarily amount to or involve the commission of any offence or offences by one or more of the parties to the agreement; or

  (b) would do so but for the existence of facts which render the commission of the offence or any of the offences impossible.

Offences may sometimes be tried in our country even though they were committed abroad. If the object of a conspiracy would amount to an offence under the jurisdiction of the relevant country *and* of England and Wales, the conspiracy may be tried under s. 1A of the Criminal Law Act 1977. In addition, it was held in *R v Manning* [1998] 2 Cr App R 461 that if people conspire abroad to commit offences in England and Wales they may, under certain circumstances, be indicted under English and Welsh law even if none of the conspirators enters the jurisdiction to do so. Answers A and D are therefore incorrect.

The 'end product' of the agreement must be the commission of an offence by one or more of the parties to the agreement; as this isn't the case answer B is therefore incorrect. When the next meeting is held, however, the offence is likely to be committed.

Crime, para. 1.3.3.1

Answer 3.13

Answer **B** — Section 1 of the Criminal Law Act 1977 states:

  (1) Subject to the following provisions of this part of this Act, if a person agrees with any other person or persons that a course of conduct will be pursued which, if the agreement is carried out in accordance with their intentions, either—

      (a) will necessarily amount to or involve the commission of any offence or offences by one or more of the parties to the agreement; or

      (b) would do so but for the existence of facts which render the commission of the offence or any of the offences impossible,

    he is guilty of conspiracy to commit the offence or offences in question.

For there to be a conspiracy there must be an agreement. Therefore there must be at least two people involved. Each conspirator must be aware of the overall common purpose to which they all attach themselves. If one conspirator enters into separate agreements with different people, each agreement is a separate conspiracy (*R v Griffiths* [1966] 1 QB 589).

A person can be convicted of conspiracy even if the other conspirators are unknown (as to the effect of the acquittal of one party to a conspiracy on the other parties, see s. 5(8) of the Criminal Law Act 1977).

However, a defendant cannot be convicted of a statutory conspiracy if the only other party to the agreement is:

- his or her spouse (or civil partner)
- a person under 10 years of age
- the intended victim

(Criminal Law Act 1977, s. 2(2)).

In this scenario SCIMITER has conspired to supply drugs to his co-conspirators; he therefore cannot be guilty of statutory conspiracy; answers A and C are therefore incorrect.

The other three have, however, conspired to supply controlled drugs to persons other than those who have conspired, and they are guilty; answer D is therefore incorrect.

Crime, para. 1.3.3.1

4 | General Defences

QUESTIONS

Question 4.1

GREEN is in debt to a drug dealer and when two persons wearing suits arrive at his door he believes them to be people sent by the drug dealer to injure him. GREEN then decides to push past the people at the door and in doing so one of the people falls backwards and suffers a serious head injury. The people were in fact Mormons.

If GREEN were to claim he was acting in self-defence due to mistaken belief, which of the following is correct?

A That the degree of force used was no more than necessary in the circumstances by reference to the circumstances as GREEN believed them to be.

B That the degree of force used was reasonable in the circumstances by reference to the circumstances as GREEN believed them to be.

C That the degree of force used was no more than necessary in the circumstances by reference to the circumstances as a reasonable bystander would believe them to be.

D That the degree of force used was reasonable in the circumstances by reference to the circumstances as a reasonable bystander would believe them to be.

Question 4.2

HIEN is at home one night when he hears a burglar break into his premises. He grabs a golf club and goes to tackle the burglar and finds him in the dining room. The burglar tries to run away but HIEN strikes him on the head with the golf club. The burglar falls but tries to get back up so HIEN strikes him again fracturing his skull.

Would HIEN be able to use the defence of self defence as he was defending his property?

A Yes, provided the degree of force used was reasonable in the circumstances by reference to the circumstances as HIEN believed them to be.

B Yes, provided HIEN could demonstrate that his actions were reasonable to defend his property in the prevention of crime.

C No, there is no defence in law to use force to defend property.

D No, the force used is disproportionate and it will not be regarded as being reasonable in the circumstances.

Question 4.3

There is no general defence of intoxication but what intoxication does is to potentially remove the necessary *mens rea* required for a defendant to commit an offence, so that there is, technically, a defence of intoxication. There are two types of intoxication, voluntary and involuntary.

For 'intent' which of the following is correct in relation to using intoxication as a defence?

A Voluntary intoxication can be raised in answer to a charge of an offence of specific intent but not basic intent; involuntary intoxication can be raised in answer to a charge of both specific *and* basic intent.

B Voluntary intoxication can be raised in answer to a charge of an offence of basic intent but not specific intent; involuntary intoxication can be raised in answer to a charge of both specific *and* basic intent.

C Voluntary intoxication can be raised in answer to a charge of an offence of specific intent but not basic intent; involuntary intoxication can be raised in answer to a charge of basic intent but not specific intent.

D Voluntary intoxication can be raised in answer to a charge of an offence of both specific *and* basic intent; involuntary intoxication can be raised in answer to a charge of specific intent but not basic intent.

Question 4.4

MAPLEY has been stopped by Constable MORRIS who was driving an unmarked police vehicle. The officer, although in uniform, did not have his warrant card with him. Constable MORRIS asked MAPLEY to take a breath test as he could smell alcohol on his breath; he refused when the officer could not produce his warrant card when asked by MAPLEY. The officer tried to grab hold of MAPLEY to arrest him; MAPLEY threw him off and drove away. MAPLEY later stated he did not believe that Constable MORRIS was a real police officer.

Considering the offence of assault with intent to resist arrest only, could MAPLEY avail himself of the defence of mistake?

A Yes, provided his belief that MORRIS was not a police officer was genuinely held.

B Yes, provided his belief that MORRIS was not a police officer was genuinely held and reasonable in the circumstances.

C No, the officer was in full uniform and was not under an obligation to produce a warrant card.

D No, the officer was in uniform; MAPLEY could never have any reasonable belief that MORRIS was not a police officer.

Question 4.5

GLOVER and his wife plan to kill his wife's mother to benefit from her will. They plan to poison her. However, before any action takes place GLOVER tells his wife he wants to back out of the plan for fear of being caught and sent to prison. His wife tells him that if he doesn't assist she will poison him as well; fearing his wife will carry out her threat he carries on poisoning his mother-in-law. However, they are caught doing this by GLOVER's sister-in-law and the police arrest GLOVER for attempting to murder his mother-in-law. He wishes to use the defence of duress.

Will GLOVER be able to use duress as a defence?

A Yes, provided he carried out the offence fearing death.

B Yes, provided he carried out the offence fearing death or serious injury.

C No, as he had agreed to commit the offence initially only later changing his mind.

D No, as duress is not a defence to a charge of attempted murder.

Question 4.6

BROOKS is married to a drug dealer; she has no criminal record at all and in fact has never committed a criminal offence. She is, however, legally searched by a police officer one day who finds a considerable amount of cocaine in her bag and she is arrested for possession with intent to supply. Although her husband was not with her at the time she was arrested, she claims she was carrying it on his behalf and that he had threatened to assault her if she didn't. She also states that she was asked to carry the drugs as she has no record and would be unlikely to be suspected of being a drug dealer.

Could BROOKS use the defence of marital coercion?

A Yes, provided she can show that she was threatened by her husband.

B Yes, provided she can show that she was coerced due to not having a criminal record.

C No, her husband was not present at the time she was arrested.

D No, as she had the opportunity to get rid of the drugs as her husband was not with her.

Question 4.7

SWANSON parks his car whilst he goes into a restaurant for a meal. He meets a friend and ends up drinking more than he had intended. Believing he would be over the legal limit for driving, SWANSON returns to his car to collect his laptop computer, fully intending to get a taxi. There is now a large gang near his car. The gang are very aggressive and SWANSON fears for his personal safety. As they charge at him, he jumps into his car and drives away. He stops about half a mile further down the road, and parks the car, intending to take a taxi. However, a police officer sees SWANSON and breathalyses him, the result of which is positive. SWANSON is charged with a drink driving offence.

Will SWANSON have a defence to this offence?

A Yes, he could claim duress.

B Yes, he could claim duress of circumstances.

C No, there is no defence to drink driving offences.

D No, general defences apply to criminal offences only.

Question 4.8

MULLALLY has suffered from domestic violence for several months and one evening she is subjected to significant threats. She fears violence from her husband and grabs the car keys to escape. She has been drinking heavily all evening. As she drives out of her driveway, the police arrive having been called by neighbours; they try to stop her leaving but she drives off. She is stopped by other officers about a mile away and fails the breath test. At court she claims the defence of duress of circumstances and claims that she knew the police were there but that they would have been unable to help her and that running away was her only option.

In relation to the defence of duress of circumstances, which of the following is correct?

A The defence will succeed as MULLALLY drove because she genuinely believed that if she did not do so death or serious injury to herself would result.

B The defence will succeed as MULLALLY drove because she genuinely believed, even if mistakenly, that if she did not do so death or serious injury to herself would result.

C The defence may not succeed as a sober reasonable person sharing the same characteristics would have stopped, knowing that the police had arrived to deal with the situation.

D The defence may not succeed as MULLALLY had the opportunity to neutralise the effects of the threat by stopping for the police officers who had attended her house.

Question 4.9

Constable CROWLEY is on the tactical firearms unit, and has been called to a hostage situation. Unfortunately, the incident ends when Constable CROWLEY fatally shoots RUSSELL, who was the assailant.

In relation to the lawfulness of CROWLEY's use of lethal force, what test will be applied?

A That he had an honestly held belief that it was necessary.

B That such force was reasonable in the circumstances.

C That such force was no more than absolutely necessary.

D That such force was necessary to protect the life of another.

Question 4.10

MARONEY was arrested and has been charged with an offence of assaulting a police officer who arrested her. The officer was in plain clothes at the time of the incident. MARONEY wishes to contest the matter stating she didn't know he was a police officer and had made a genuine mistake.

In relation to the defence of inadvertence and mistake which of the following is correct?

A The defence applies where there was a genuine and honest belief that was reasonably held.

B The defence applies where there was a reasonable and honest belief.

C The defence applies where there was a genuine and reasonable belief that was honestly held.

D The defence applies where there was a genuine and honest belief.

Question 4.11

OUDEKIRK, who is 65 years old, wakes up one night and finds someone in his lounge. Fearing he is about to be burgled he takes a golf club and hits the stranger on the head with it, fracturing his skull. Unfortunately the stranger is his daughter's new boyfriend who was sleepwalking. OUDEKIRK believed the force was necessary as he is an older man and the younger male was well over 6ft in height. He has also never met this boyfriend before.

Could OUDEKIRK use the defence of reasonable force for purposes of self-defence etc. under s. 76 of the Criminal Justice and Immigration Act 2008?

A Yes, as it applies to defence of property and he reasonably believed it was necessary force.

B Yes, as it applies to defence of property and although it was mistaken belief it was a reasonable mistake to make.

C No, this new defence does not apply to defence of property, defence of self or another only.

D No, as the amount of force used was disproportionate to the amount of force necessary in the defence of property.

Question 4.12

GYSLOR was found in possession of a shotgun and on the way to commit a burglary. When he was arrested and interviewed, however, he stated that his wife was being held captive by an armed gang who threatened to kill her if he did not commit the burglary. He also stated that it was his idea and not the gang's that he should take the shotgun; his intention was to use it to resist arrest and he felt his wife's life was in danger.

Considering that GYSLOR has committed an offence contrary to s. 18 of the Firearms Act 1968 (carrying a firearm or imitation firearm with intent to resist arrest), will he be able to claim the defence of duress?

A Yes, but only if he can show that the intention to resist arrest was as a result of duress.

B Yes, in these circumstances duress is available as a defence, as this was the reason he took the shotgun.

C No, duress is not available as he was only asked to carry out a burglary, the firearms offence was his idea.

D No, the defence of duress is not available if the threat is made against a third party, unless they are present at the time of the offence.

Question 4.13

In relation to the defence of duress of circumstances, the person accused of an offence must have acted in a certain way.

In relation to what caused the person to behave as they did which of the following is correct?

A The person must be impelled to behave as they did because they themselves actually feared a criminal act being committed.

B The person must be impelled to behave as they did because a reasonable person in those circumstances would fear a criminal act being committed.

C The person must be impelled to behave as they did because a criminal act was actually being committed there and then.

D The person must be impelled to behave as they did because they perceived a threat that in itself would not amount to a criminal act.

Question 4.14

WEDDON and HOPKINS have been jointly charged with an offence of aggravated burglary. It is alleged by the prosecution that during the burglary of a dwelling house, WEDDON and HOPKINS assaulted and seriously injured the elderly occupant. WEDDON is aged 10 and HOPKINS is aged 14.

Which of the following statements is correct, in relation to criminal liability of both defendants?

A Because of their ages, the prosecution *may* be asked by the court to adduce evidence to show that both knew that what they had done was seriously wrong, but only where challenged by the defence to do so.

B Both WEDDON and HOPKINS are criminally liable for the offence as charged, due to their ages.

C Because of his age, HOPKINS is criminally liable; however, the prosecution *may* be asked by the court to adduce evidence to show that WEDDON knew that what she had done was seriously wrong.

D Because of their ages, the prosecution *will always* be asked by the court to adduce evidence to show that both knew that what they had done was seriously wrong.

Question 4.15

NORSTER had driven his step-son to work although he was disqualified from driving. He claimed that he had done this because his wife had threatened to commit suicide unless he did so, as the boy was in danger of losing his job if he was late. The wife had suicidal tendencies and a doctor had told NORSTER that it was likely that she would carry out any threat to take her own life. In fact the wife had no intentions of killing herself that night; it was just her way of ensuring her son was not late for work.

In these circumstances would the defence of duress of circumstances be likely to succeed?

A Yes, as NORSTER had reasonable grounds to suppose his wife's threat was real due to the doctor's report.

B Yes, because NORSTER had an honestly held belief that his wife may carry out her threat.

C No, because there was no actual threat to NORSTER's life.

D No, because the threat made by the wife was not in fact true.

ANSWERS

Answer 4.1

Answer **B** — Section 3(1) of the Criminal Law Act 1967 provides that:

> A person may use such force as is reasonable in the circumstances in the prevention of crime, or in effecting or assisting in the lawful arrest of offenders or suspected offenders or of persons unlawfully at large.

Clarification of the law has come in the form of s. 76 of the Criminal Justice and Immigration Act 2008 which provides a gloss on the common law of self-defence and the defences provided by s. 3(1) of the Criminal Law Act 1967, which relate to the use of force in the prevention of crime or making an arrest. Section 76 aims to improve understanding of the practical application of these areas of law using elements of case law to illustrate how the defence operates. It does not change the current test that allows the use of reasonable force.

The question whether the degree of force used by the defendant was reasonable in the circumstances is to be decided by reference to the circumstances as the defendant believed them to be (s. 76(3)). So it is 'reasonable' and not 'no more than necessary'; answers A and C are therefore incorrect. And it is the defendant's belief not a reasonable bystander's belief; answer D is therefore incorrect.

Crime, para. 1.4.8.1

Answer 4.2

Answer **D** — Section 3(1) of the Criminal Law Act 1967 states reasonable force may be used in the prevention of crime. Therefore, if a person is acting in order to prevent a crime against his/her property, it follows that force can be used to protect property; answer C is therefore incorrect.

Whether such force is reasonable or not will be subject to the requirements of s. 76 of the Criminal Justice and Immigration Act 2008. However, it might be somewhat problematic (if not impossible) to reconcile reasonable force to protect property with the taking of a person's life or really serious injury. Here the burglar was trying to escape and yet was struck twice. This force would fall foul of s. 76(6) which states that if the force used is disproportionate then it will not be regarded as being reasonable in the circumstances; answers A and B are therefore incorrect.

Crime, para. 1.4.8.2

Answer 4.3

Answer **A** — There is no general defence of intoxication. If there were, a high proportion of criminal behaviour would clearly go unpunished. What intoxication does is to potentially remove the necessary *mens rea* required for a defendant to commit an offence. There are some statutory offences where specific provision is made for drunkenness (e.g. the Public Order Act 1986). Intoxication can be divided into two categories: voluntary intoxication (you got yourself in that condition) and involuntary intoxication (you are not responsible for getting in that condition). The distinction between the two types of intoxication is important when considering whether the offence the defendant is alleged to have commited is one of 'specific' or 'basic' intent (these terms were discussed at para. 1.1.3).

Where an offence is a specific intent offence, e.g. murder or theft, a defendant who was voluntarily intoxicated at the time the offence was committed may be able to show that he/she was so intoxicated that he/she was incapable of forming the *mens rea* required for the offence. An individual who is voluntarily intoxicated *would not* be able to say this if accused of an offence of basic intent as the courts have accepted that a defendant is still capable of forming basic intent even when completely inebriated (see *DPP* v *Majewski* [1977] AC 443).

Where the offence is a basic intent offence, e.g. a s. 47 assault, a defendant who was involuntarily intoxicated (perhaps because his/her drink had been spiked) at the time of the offence was committed may be able to say that they lacked the *mens rea* for that basic intent offence.

Therefore, voluntary intoxication can be raised in answer to a charge of an offence of specific intent but not basic intent; involuntary intoxication can be raised in answer to a charge of both specific *and* basic intent, you might have to look at the answers carefully, but this is option A; answers B, C and D are therefore incorrect.

Crime, para. 1.4.3

Answer 4.4

Answer **A** — The defence of mistake will only be used to negate the *mens rea* of the offence charged. In *R* v *Lee* [2001] 1 Cr App Rep 293, a case arising from an assault on two arresting police officers, the Court of Appeal reviewed the law in this area, reaffirming the following points:

- A genuine or honest mistake could provide a defence to many criminal offences requiring a particular state of mind, including assault with intent to resist arrest (*R v Brightling* [1991] Crim LR 364).
- A defence of mistake had to involve a mistake of fact, not a mistake of law.

Here MAPLEY is contesting a fact, not a point of law. The officer, although in uniform, did not produce a warrant card; MAPLEY would only have to show that he genuinely believed that the person who stopped him was not a police officer for the defence to succeed. The defendant need not even show that his belief was reasonable in the circumstances, only that he had no 'intent'; answer B is therefore incorrect.

It is immaterial what the officer's actions were and whether they were in uniform or not, all that is required is the honest mistake, and you would have to say that not being able to produce a warrant card 'gifts' this defence to MAPLEY; answers C and D are therefore incorrect.

Crime, para. 1.4.5

Answer 4.5

Answer **D** — Generally speaking, where a person is threatened with death or serious physical injury unless he or she carries out a criminal act, he or she may use the defence of duress. Note that this includes a threat of serious injury, not just death, therefore answer A is incorrect (see *R v Graham* [1982] 1 WLR 294). This defence is available to GLOVER even though he initially agreed to the crime as the intent he had formed when committing the offence could have been formed only by the threat so the defence could be available; answer C is therefore incorrect. However, the defence is not available in respect of an offence of murder (see *R v Howe* [1987] AC 417) or attempted murder (see *R v Gotts* [1992] 2 AC 412), as a principal or secondary offender; answer B is therefore incorrect.

Crime, para. 1.4.6

Answer 4.6

Answer **C** — Closely linked to the defence of duress is the defence of 'marital coercion' whereby a wife charged with any offence other than treason or murder, may raise the defence that she committed the offence in the presence and under the coercion of her husband (see the Criminal Justice Act 1925, s. 47 and *R v Shortland* [1996] 1 Cr App R 116).

The fact is here that her husband was not present when she was arrested therefore she cannot use that as a defence; answers A, B and D are therefore incorrect.

Crime, para. 1.4.6.1

Answer 4.7

Answer **B** — Duress of circumstances is available in traffic cases, so answers C and D are incorrect. SWANSON has to show that his actions were reasonable (*R* v *Martin* [1989] 1 All ER 652). Here his actions could be regarded as 'reasonable', as he feared for his safety. The fact he stopped soon after supports this claim, and the defence has succeeded in similar circumstances (*DPP* v *Bell* [1992] RTR 335). Contrast this with *DPP* v *Jones* [1990] RTR 33, where a similar defence failed because the accused drove all the way home, without even checking whether he was still being chased. The facts of this question would not support a defence of 'duress' as no threat has been made, which is a necessary component of that defence, which makes answer A incorrect.

Crime, para. 1.4.7

Answer 4.8

Answer **C** — The defence of duress of circumstances relates to times when circumstances leave the defendant no real alternative but to commit an offence. This type of duress should be distinguished from the defence of 'duress' where there is a threat made to the defendant compelling them to commit an offence; with duress of circumstances, there is no such threat being made. Answer D relates to 'duress' where there is an opportunity to neutralise the threat which means that the defence cannot be used and for that reason answer D is incorrect. In this question, the defendant drove away as she felt she had no real alternative.

In determining whether or not the defence of 'duress of circumstances' is available, the court held that the jury must ask two questions in relation to the defendant:

- Were they (or might they have been) impelled to act as they did because, as a result of what they reasonably believed, they had good cause to fear they would suffer death or serious injury if they did not do so?
- If so, would a sober person of reasonable firmness and sharing the same characteristics, have responded to the situation in the way that they did?

The answer to both questions must be yes; if not, the defence fails. In the circumstances of this question, answers A and B state that the defence will succeed and this is not the case; answers A and B are therefore incorrect. The fact is that the 'circumstances' changed when the police arrived and that there was an alternative to driving.

Crime, para. 1.4.7

Answer 4.9

Answer **C** — The law in relation to 'self-defence' has had some clarification in the form of s. 76 of the Criminal Justice and Immigration Act 2008 which provides a gloss on the common law of self-defence and the defences provided by s. 3(1) of the Criminal Law Act 1967, which relate to the use of force in the prevention of crime or making an arrest. Section 76 aims to improve understanding of the practical application of these areas of law using elements of case law to illustrate how the defence operates. It does not change the current test that allows the use of reasonable force.

Where such a defence is raised in relation to taking someone's life, the provisions of Art. 2 of the European Convention on Human Rights will apply. The requirements of Art. 2 are more stringent than under s. 3(1) of the Criminal Law Act 1967 and s. 76 of the Criminal Justice and Immigration Act 2008. Under Art. 2, the test will be whether the force used was no more than absolutely necessary and lethal force will be 'absolutely necessary' only if it is strictly proportionate to the legitimate purpose being pursued. In order to meet those criteria, regard will be had to:

- The nature of the aim being pursued;
- The inherent dangers to life and limb from the situation;
- The degree of risk to life presented by the amount of force employed.

The only circumstances in which lethal force might be permissible here are where the defendant was acting:

- in defence of any person from unlawful violence;
- in order to effect a lawful arrest or to prevent the escape of a person lawfully detained;
- in action lawfully taken for the purpose of quelling a riot or insurrection.

It is important to note that the taking of life in order to prevent crime is not mentioned in Art. 2.

So the test is 'no more than absolutely necessary'; answers A, B and D are therefore incorrect.

Crime, para. 1.4.8.1

Answer 4.10

Answer **D** — There are occasions where a defendant makes a mistake about some circumstance or consequence, but claims that a defendant 'made a mistake' or did something 'inadvertently' will only be an effective defence if they negate the *mens rea* for that offence. Therefore, if someone picks up another person's shopping at a supermarket till or wanders out of a shop with something they have yet to pay for, their mistake or inadvertence, in each case, might negative any *mens rea* of 'dishonesty'. As the requirement for the *mens rea* in such a case is *subjective* then the defendant's mistake or inadvertence will be judged subjectively. The same will generally be true for offences requiring subjective recklessness. It does not matter whether the mistake was 'reasonable' (*DPP* v *Morgan* [1976] AC 182); answers A, B and C are therefore incorrect. The appropriate test is whether the defendant's mistaken belief was an honest and genuine one. There are occasions where a genuine mistake on the part of the defendant may amount to a defence.

In *R* v *Lee* [2000] Crim LR 991, a case arising from an assault on two arresting police officers, the Court of Appeal reviewed the law in this area, reaffirming the following points:

- A genuine or honest mistake could provide a defence to many criminal offences requiring a particular state of mind, including assault with intent to resist arrest (*R* v *Brightling* [1991] Crim LR 364).
- A defence of mistake had to involve a mistake of fact, not a mistake of law (see later).
- People under arrest are not entitled to form their own view as to the lawfulness of that arrest. They have a duty to comply with the police and hear the details of the charge against them (*R* v *Bentley* (1850) 4 Cox CC 406).
- Belief in one's own innocence, however genuine or honestly held, cannot afford a defence to a charge of assault with intent to resist arrest under s. 38 of the Offences Against the Person Act 1861.

A defendant attempted to argue that his honest and reasonable mistake as to the *facts* of his arrest (as opposed to the law) after he was lawfully arrested for a public order offence was different from the decision in *Lee*. The Divisional Court did not agree with him (see *Hewitt* v *DPP* [2002] EWHC 2801 (Admin)).

Crime, para. 1.4.5

Answer 4.11

Answer **B** — Section 76 of the Criminal Justice and Immigration Act 2008 has not radically altered existing legislation, merely added gloss to it. Section 3(1) of the Criminal Law Act 1967 states reasonable force may be used in the prevention of crime. Therefore, if a person is acting in order to prevent a crime against their property, it follows that force can be used to protect property; answer C is therefore incorrect. Whether such force is reasonable or not, however, will be subject to the requirements of s. 76 of the Criminal Justice and Immigration Act 2008.

In deciding whether or not the degree of force used was reasonable in the circumstances, s. 76(7) requires certain considerations to be taken into account:

- that a person acting for a legitimate purpose (the purposes of the defences to which s. 76 applies) may not be able to weigh to a nicety the exact measure of any necessary action; and
- that evidence of a person's having only done what the person honestly and instinctively thought was necessary for a legitimate purpose constitutes strong evidence that only reasonable action was taken by that person for that purpose.

This does not mention force being necessary, only that it was done in circumstances such that the person using that force believed it was necessary; answer A is therefore incorrect.

This does not prevent other matters from being taken into account where they are relevant in deciding whether the degree of force used was reasonable in the circumstances. Section 76 retains a single test for self-defence and the prevention of crime (or the making of an arrest) which can be applied in each of these contexts. The law has been developed in line with case law regarding self-defence and the use of force, most notably the case of *Palmer* v *The Queen* [1971] AC 814. The defence will be available to a person if he honestly believed it was necessary to use force and if the degree of force used was not disproportionate in the circumstances as he viewed them. The section reaffirms that a person who uses force is to be judged on the basis of the circumstances as he perceived them, that in the heat of the moment he will not be expected to have judged exactly what action was called for, and that a degree of latitude may be given to a person who only did what he honestly and instinctively thought was necessary. A defendant is entitled to have his actions judged on the basis of his view of the facts as he honestly believed them to be. This does not therefore define what force will be proportionate or not; answer D is therefore incorrect.

Crime, para. 1.4.8.1

Answer 4.12

Answer **A** — First, let's consider the offence under s. 18 of the Firearms Act 1968 which states:

(1) It is an offence for a person to have with him a firearm or imitation firearm with intent to commit an indictable offence, or to resist arrest or prevent the arrest of another, in either case while he has a firearm or imitation firearm with him.

It is important to note that the offence asked of him is different from the offence he stands accused of; this does not mean *per se* that he cannot use the defence of duress. However, where applicable intent is a fundamental element of an offence, the accused must show that he or she had, or could only have formed that intent by reason of that duress. Without showing that the only compelling factor in the formation of the relevant intent is duress, then the defence will fail (*R* v *Fisher* [2004] EWCA Crim 1190); answer C is therefore incorrect. Note the relevant intent here is that of resisting arrest, not possession of the shotgun; therefore answer B is incorrect.

The question is whether the threat has to be directed at the accused or whether threats to third parties, especially close relatives, can suffice. There seems to be consensus amongst legal commentators on this point and certainly in principle threats to third parties should be capable of constituting duress. Even the bravest man may be prepared to risk his own neck whilst baulking at subjecting his loved ones to serious peril. Indeed there is Australian authority recognising threats to the accused's common law wife, and in *R* v *Ortiz* (1986) 83 Cr App R 173 threats to the accused's wife or family appear to have been considered to be sufficient; answer D is therefore incorrect.

Crime, para. 1.4.6

Answer 4.13

Answer **D** — As well as cases where a person receives a direct threat in order to make them commit an offence, there may be times when circumstances leave the defendant no real alternative. In *R* v *Cairns* [1992] 2 Cr App R 137 the court held that the jury must ask two questions in relation to this 'necessary action':

* Was he (or might he have been) impelled to act as he did because, as a result of what he reasonably believed, he had good cause to fear he would suffer death or serious injury if he did not do so?
* If so, would a sober person of reasonable firmness and sharing the same characteristics, have responded to the situation in the way that he did?

If each question were answered with a 'yes', the defence would be made out.

In the case of *R* v *Jones (Margaret) & Others* [2004] EWCA 1981, the Court of Appeal considered whether a case of necessity or duress of circumstances could be made out for a person who used force in the honestly held belief that in doing so he was protecting the property of others abroad from damage that would be caused by the executive's lawful exercise of the prerogative power to wage war. The court accepted that the defence of necessity was available if a defendant could show that he acted to prevent an act of greater evil but there was no requirement that the act of greater evil should be unlawful. This effectively means that a person can act in duress of circumstances where the threat (or perceived threat) does not amount to a criminal act. Therefore answers A, B and C are incorrect as they relate to criminal acts or perceptions of criminal acts.

Crime, para. 1.4.7

Answer 4.14

Answer **B** — Before the Crime and Disorder Act 1998, children under 14 years of age were subject to a presumption at common law to be 'incapable of evil' or *doli incapax*. The presumption of *doli incapax* in relation to children who were aged 10 or over but who had not yet reached 14 years of age was *rebuttable*. This meant that the prosecution could adduce evidence to show that the child defendant knew that what he or she had done was seriously wrong. If the evidence was accepted, the courts would regard that presumption as having been rebutted and the child defendant could be tried in much the same way as an adult. Some concern as to how appropriate such a presumption was in modern society led the House of Lords in *C (a Minor)* v *DPP* [1995] 2 WLR 383 to declare the rule to be outdated but adding that it was up to Parliament to change it. Section 34 of the Crime and Disorder Act 1998 did exactly that and abolished this second, rebuttable form of the presumption of *doli incapax*, effectively lowering the age of criminal responsibility to 10 years of age.

In relation to children under 10 years of age that presumption was, and still is, irrebuttable. Consequently, no evidence to the contrary will be entertained by a court and children under 10 cannot be convicted of a criminal offence.

Since both defendants are 10 or over, they are both criminally liable for their actions and therefore answers A, C and D are incorrect.

Crime, para. 1.4.10

Answer 4.15

Answer **B** — In *R* v *Martin* [1989] 1 All ER 652 Simon-Brown J stated that the principles of duress of circumstances may be summarised as:

- First, English law does in extreme circumstances recognise a defence of necessity. It can arise from objective dangers threatening the accused or others in which case it is conveniently called 'duress of circumstances'.
- Secondly, the defence is available only if, from an objective standpoint, the accused can be said to be acting reasonably and proportionately in order to avoid a threat of death or serious injury.
- Thirdly, assuming the defence to be open to the accused on his account of the facts, the issue should be left to the jury, who should be directed to determine these two questions:

  (1) Was the accused, or may he have been, impelled to act as he did because as a result of what he reasonably believed to be the situation he had good cause to fear that otherwise death or serious injury would result?

  (2) If so, may a sober person of reasonable firmness, sharing the characteristics of the accused, have responded to that situation by acting as the accused acted?

If the answer to both these questions was yes, then the jury would acquit: the defence of necessity would have been established. Further, the court in *Martin* was willing to contemplate the defence succeeding where an unqualified or disqualified driver took control of a car to get a person who had suffered a heart attack to hospital.

The important aspect to this defence then is that it will only avail the defendant as long as he or she is acting under compulsion of the prevailing circumstances when committing the offence. It appears that the defendant need only hold an *honest* belief that those circumstances exist without necessarily having *reasonable grounds* for that belief (see *DPP* v *Rogers* [1998] Crim LR 202) and there is no need for the threat to be 'real'. In other words there is no need for the doctor's report. Provided the defendant honestly believed his wife's threat (whether it was true or not), the defence could succeed; answers A and D are therefore incorrect.

The threat does also not have to be directed against the person who commits the unlawful act; answer C is therefore incorrect.

Crime, para. 1.4.7

5 | Homicide

QUESTIONS

Question 5.1

MEREDITH has been arrested at a football match and is placed in a holding area pending transport. He is violently sick and this is ignored by the private security staff looking after the facility. He is then placed in a police van to be transported to the custody suite at the police station. He is handcuffed and placed face down in the van where he vomits, asphyxiates and dies.

Considering corporate manslaughter, relevant duty of care, and s. 2 of the Corporate Manslaughter and Corporate Homicide Act 2007, which of the following is correct?

A Only the police officers who transported the prisoner may be liable if they failed in a relevant duty of care.

B Both the private security officers and the police officers may be liable if they failed in a relevant duty of care.

C Only the private security officers are liable as they failed to deal with the ill prisoner, a clear breach of the relevant duty of care.

D Neither the police officers nor the private security company will be liable as custodial deaths only relate to custody units or authorised remand centres.

Question 5.2

HOPKINS had many convictions for domestic violence against his wife. After yet another beating she takes a knife and stabs him through the heart instantly killing him. She is charged with murder.

In relation to 'loss of control' as defined by s. 54 of the Coroners and Justice Act 2009, which of the following is correct?

A She could use this defence provided her loss of control was sudden.

B She could use this defence provided someone of her age may have acted the same way in the same circumstances.

C She could not use this defence as it was a calculated act as she intended to stab him.

D She could not use this defence as it applies to manslaughter offences only.

Question 5.3

PIDGEON is a central heating engineer and is employed by a company. PIDGEON incorrectly fits a part when repairing a gas combi boiler and as a result it leaks carbon monoxide. Due to this leak the owner of the house dies of carbon monoxide poisoning. The company was aware that PIDGEON's work had not been up to scratch in the past, and had already issued two written warnings to him for errors in repairs he had done. Neither of the previous cases had led to any injuries though.

Considering the offence of manslaughter, which of the following is correct?

A PIDGEON could only be guilty of manslaughter by unlawful act, as due to his omission a person died unlawfully.

B PIDGEON could only be guilty of manslaughter by unlawful act, as due to his omission a person died unlawfully *or* manslaughter by gross negligence.

C PIDGEON could only be guilty of manslaughter by gross negligence due to the duty of care; the company are not culpable at all.

D PIDGEON could only be guilty of manslaughter by gross negligence due to the duty of care and the company guilty of corporate manslaughter.

Question 5.4

DE JONG is depressed and is contemplating suicide and confides in a friend, DEER-ING, of his wish to do so. DEERING decides to help his friend and goes to a drug dealer he knows and asks for a supply of very strong opiates. DEERING then gives DE JONG the drugs and leaves to allow him to commit suicide. DE JONG, however, changes his mind and does not take the drugs. In any case the drug dealer has duped DEERING as the opiates he supplied were in fact vitamin tablets.

Has DEERING committed an offence of encouraging or assisting suicide contrary to s. 2 of the Suicide Act 1961 as amended?

A Yes, as he has taken action that could assist or encourage another to commit suicide.

B Yes, as he has taken action that could assist or encourage another to commit suicide and the act was intended to so do.

C No, as DE JONG did not commit or attempt to commit suicide.

D No, as the actions could not have assisted or encouraged suicide as the pills could not have caused the death of DE JONG.

Question 5.5

IVY and his common law wife had been to the local pub where they had been drinking heavily and arguing. IVY returned to their flat where he chopped wood with an axe and drank more lager. His common law wife was still in a public house drinking. When she returned to the flat she picked up the axe and said she was going to put it in his head. In fear this would happen he took the axe from her and struck her seven or eight times with the axe, killing her, and is charged with murder.

IVY wishes to use 'loss of control' as a defence; for the purposes of this defence which of the following is correct in relation to what the defence would be based on?

A That a reasonable person with a normal degree of tolerance and self-restraint and in the same circumstances, might have reacted in the same way to IVY.

B That a reasonable person with a normal degree of tolerance and self-restraint and in the same circumstances, might have reacted in the same or in a similar way to IVY.

C That a person of IVY's sex and age, with a normal degree of tolerance and self-restraint and in the circumstances, might have reacted in the same way to IVY.

D That a person of IVY's sex and age, with a normal degree of tolerance and self-restraint and in the same circumstances, might have reacted in the same or in a similar way to IVY.

Question 5.6

NEWLEY and PROTHEROE were hunting fanatics. While hunting in the local woods, NEWLEY thought he would play a joke on PROTHEROE. NEWLEY pointed his rifle at PROTHEROE, believing there were no bullets in the chamber, and pulled the trigger. However, he had not checked the gun properly and PROTHEROE was hit by a bullet in the chest. PROTHEROE was taken to the local hospital, where he subsequently died.

In relation to any homicide offences committed by NEWLEY, which of the following is correct?

A NEWLEY is guilty of murder in these circumstances, as he was reckless in his actions.

B NEWLEY is guilty of manslaughter in these circumstances, as he was reckless in his actions.

C NEWLEY is not guilty of manslaughter by an unlawful act, as he had no intention to injure PROTHEROE.

D NEWLEY is guilty of manslaughter in these circumstances, as he was negligent in relation to his gun.

Question 5.7

KACIK had been bullying his college friend CROFT for several years. CROFT was terrified of KACIK and did everything he could to stay out of his way. CROFT was standing on the platform of the railway station when he saw KACIK walking towards him in a threatening manner. In panic he ran across the railway track, but stood on the electric rail which killed him outright. In fact KACIK had not seen CROFT on the platform, his threats were directed towards another person standing near CROFT.

Is KACIK guilty of manslaughter by unlawful act?

A Yes, as he was threatening someone, and as such committing an unlawful act, he will be guilty.

B Yes, as CROFT feared the application of immediate unlawful force, which is an unlawful act, KACIK is guilty.

C No, he did not have the relevant *mens rea* against CROFT.

D No, CROFT voluntarily stepped onto the tracks, thereby negating the unlawful intent of KACIK.

Question 5.8

BROTHERTON and his cousin are members of a right-wing political party and are concerned about the influence that Europe is having on UK policy. BROTHERTON telephones his cousin and proposes that his cousin goes to France and murders the President. BROTHERTON is serious about his proposal but his cousin thinks it is a joke.

Is this solicitation to murder?

A Yes, as it is sufficient to propose to any person the murder of any other person.

B Yes, as there was intention to propose to any person the murder of any other person.

C No, as the cousin was not in any way encouraged to commit murder.

D No as the intended victim was not a British subject and in fact is outside the United Kingdom.

Question 5.9

MALONE owned a taxi firm which was failing financially. MALONE owned the build-ing which contained the firm's office and decided to set fire to the building to claim from the insurance company. MALONE enlisted the help of a friend, LARIMY, who had no connection with the company, and one evening they went to the building with cans of petrol and matches. MALONE spread the petrol around the inside of the premises and lit a fire, while LARIMY stood near the door as the lookout. Unfortu-nately, when the petrol ignited there was an explosion which killed LARIMY and injured MALONE.

In relation to MALONE's liability for the offence of involuntary manslaughter, which of the following statements is correct?

A MALONE would be guilty of manslaughter by unlawful act in these circumstances as arson is an unlawful act.

B MALONE would be guilty of manslaughter by gross negligence in these circum-stances; he owns the property but was reckless as to the result of his actions.

C MALONE would not be guilty of either offence as he owns the building and did not commit an unlawful act and his actions were not grossly negligent.

D MALONE would not be guilty of either offence as he owns the building and did not commit an unlawful act and his actions were not grossly negligent as LARIMY was not an employee.

Question 5.10

SHIPLEY has been charged with an offence of murder and is due to appear in court. SHIPLEY intends pleading not guilty to murder and will ask the court to accept a plea of guilty to the offence of manslaughter on the grounds of diminished responsibility.

Which of the following is correct, in respect of the 'impairment of responsibility' that SHIPLEY must have suffered, in order to succeed with this approach?

A The mental impairment suffered must have been substantial and must also have been the sole cause of SHIPLEY's actions in committing the manslaughter.

B The mental impairment must have been substantial, and it must be shown that it contributed in some way to SHIPLEY's actions in committing the manslaughter.

C The mental impairment need not be substantial, provided it contributed in some way to SHIPLEY's actions in committing the manslaughter.

D The mental impairment need not be substantial, provided it can be shown that it was the sole cause of SHIPLEY's actions in committing the manslaughter.

Question 5.11

TILLY was aged 5 years and was on the at risk register for previous assaults on her by members of her family. She lived at home with her mother, and whilst her mother's boyfriend was a frequent visitor, he did not live there. TILLY's mother was aware that her boyfriend was violent particularly when drunk and had assaulted TILLY previously. One night after he returned home drunk from the pub the boyfriend was fed up with TILLY's crying and went up and shook her violently. TILLY died from injuries received from that shake.

Who could be charged with an offence contrary to s. 5 of the Domestic Violence, Crime and Victims Act 2004, causing or allowing the death of a child or vulnerable adult?

A Only TILLY's mother.

B TILLY's mother provided it could be established that she foresaw the attack on TILLY.

C Only the boyfriend.

D Both TILLY's mother and her boyfriend.

Question 5.12

Constable GREAVES from the road policing unit put his vehicle into the workshops as it had defective brakes and it was returned the following day from the workshop. After a short test drive he returned the car again claiming the brakes were not right. The workshop manager, HARDEN, told the officer the brakes were fine and there would be no more repairs made to it; he told the officer he was 'getting it in the neck' from the force's fleet manager to cut costs. The officer answered a call on the motorway and whilst travelling at 150 mph the brakes failed; the resulting collision killed the officer.

Which of the following is correct in relation to the Corporate Manslaughter and Corporate Homicide Act 2007?

A Both the force and the workshop manager could be charged with causing the officer's death.

B The force, the fleet manager and the workshop manager could be charged with causing the officer's death.

C Only the force could be charged with causing the officer's death.

D No one could be charged with causing the death as the decision was that of the workshop manager, who would not be 'senior management' as defined in the Act.

ANSWERS

Answer 5.1

Answer **B** — Section 2 of the Corporate Manslaughter and Corporate Homicide Act 2007 states:

(1) A 'relevant duty of care', in relation to an organisation, means any of the following duties owed by it under the law of negligence—
   (a) a duty owed to its employees or other persons working for the organisation or performing services for it;
   (b) a duty owed as occupier of premises;
   (c) a duty owed in connection with—
      (i) the supply by the organisation of goods or services (whether for consideration or not),
      (ii) the carrying on by the organisation of any construction or maintenance operations,
      (iii) the carrying on by the organisation of any other activity on a commercial basis, or
      (iv) the use or keeping by the organisation of any plant, vehicle or other thing;
   (d) a duty owed to a person who, by reason of being a person within subsection (2), is someone for whose safety the organisation is responsible.
(2) A person is within this subsection if—
   (a) he is detained at a custodial institution or in a custody area at a court or police station or customs premises;
   (aa) he is detained in service custody premises;
   (b) he is detained at a removal centre or a short-term holding facility;
   (c) he is being transported in a vehicle, or being held in any premises, in pursuance of prison escort arrangements or immigration escort arrangements;
   (d) he is living in secure accommodation in which he has been placed;
   (e) he is a detained patient.

The Act applies to deaths of persons owed a duty of care by virtue of: being detained at a custodial institution, or in a custody area at a court or police station, at a removal centre or short-term holding facility, transported in a vehicle or being held in any premises in pursuance of prison escort arrangements or immigration escort arrangements, living in secure accommodation in which the person has been placed, or if the person is a detained patient.

This means that both the police officers and the private security officers are culpable as it extends to short-term holding facilities and transportation; answers A, C and D are therefore incorrect.

Crime, para. 1.5.5.1

Answer 5.2

Answer **B** — Section 54 of the Coroners and Justice Act 2009 sets out the criteria which need to be met in order for the partial defence of loss of self-control to be successful, those being:

- the defendant's conduct resulted from a loss of self-control;
- the loss of self-control had a qualifying trigger; and
- a person of the defendant's sex and age with an ordinary level of tolerance and self-restraint and in the circumstances of the defendant might have acted in the same or similar way to the defendant.

Section 54(2) clarifies that the loss of control need not be sudden. Under the previous partial defence of provocation, the courts had held that the loss of self-control must be sudden; answer A is therefore incorrect.

A qualifying trigger is defined as:

- The defendant's fear of serious violence from the victim against the defendant or another identified person.
- To a thing or things done or said (or both) which constituted circumstances of an extremely grave character and caused the defendant to have a justifiable sense of being seriously wronged.
- A combination of the previous two factors.

This will apply even where a 'calculated' act takes place; answer C is therefore incorrect. The defence applies only to murder charges, not manslaughter; answer D is therefore incorrect.

Crime, para. 1.5.3.2

Answer 5.3

Answer **C** — In order to determine whether an act constitutes the offence of gross negligence manslaughter, the prosecution must establish that:

- there was a duty of care owed by the accused to the deceased;
- there was a breach of the duty of care by the accused;
- death of the deceased was caused by breach of the duty of care by the accused;
- the breach of the duty of care by the accused was so great as to be characterised as gross negligence and therefore a crime.

In the circumstances of the question the only part that remains unanswered is the last part. The actions of PIDGEON 'could', and in a case in Cwmbran in South Wales did, lead to a conviction for gross negligence manslaughter.

So PIDGEON could be guilty of gross negligence manslaughter, but what about manslaughter by unlawful act? In order to prove manslaughter by an unlawful act (constructive manslaughter), you must prove an unlawful act by the defendant, that is, an act which is *unlawful in itself*, irrespective of the fact that it ultimately results in someone's death. The act must be inherently unlawful. An act that only becomes unlawful by virtue of the way in which it is carried out will not be enough. Clearly fitting or repairing a gas boiler is not an unlawful act; answers A and B are therefore incorrect.

It is accepted that it is possible for a company to be prosecuted for gross negligence manslaughter, so-called corporate manslaughter. However, there are a number of difficulties which need to be addressed if a company is to be prosecuted successfully.

For a company to be guilty of manslaughter, it is necessary to identify a 'controlling mind', who is also personally guilty of manslaughter. This person must have acted 'as the company' to the extent that his or her identification 'is the mind of the company', and will therefore hold a senior position in the company. That individual or individuals will usually be prosecuted but there may be particular circumstances in which they are not. Even then the prosecution must still be able to demonstrate that the named individual is guilty of the offence. Therefore before the prosecution can even start to consider 'corporate manslaughter', it must first be able to identify an individual who has committed the offence.

So although in these circumstances the directors of the company may have been grossly negligent in employing someone who was clearly a danger to their customers, that negligence did not extend to an act that actually led to the death of the person, so they cannot be liable for 'corporate manslaughter'; answer D is therefore incorrect.

Crime, paras 1.5.4.1, 1.5.4.2, 1.5.5

Answer 5.4

Answer **B** — Section 2 of the Suicide Act 1961 (as amended) states:

(1) A person ('D') commits an offence if—
   (a) D does an act capable of encouraging or assisting the suicide or attempted suicide of another person, and
   (b) D's act was intended to encourage or assist suicide or an attempt at suicide.
(1A) The person referred to in subsection (1)(a) need not be a specific person (or class of persons) known to, or identified by, D.
(1B) D may commit an offence under this section whether or not a suicide, or an attempt at suicide, occurs.

So that act has to be done, and done with the intention of assisting/encouraging suicide; answer A is therefore incorrect.

This offence is an alternative verdict on a charge of murder/manslaughter (Suicide Act 1961, s. 2(2) as amended). The person committing the offence need not know, or even be able to identify, the other person. So, for example, the author of a website promoting suicide who intends that one of more of his/her readers will commit suicide is guilty of an offence, even though he/she may never know the identity of those who access the website. The offence applies whether or not a person commits or attempts suicide; answer C is therefore incorrect.

Section 2A of the Suicide Act 1961 (as amended) states:

(1) If D arranges for a person ("D2") to do an act that is capable of encouraging or assisting the suicide or attempted suicide of another person and D2 does that act, D is also to be treated for the purposes of this Act as having done it.
(2) Where the facts are such that an act is not capable of encouraging or assisting suicide or attempted suicide, for the purposes of this Act it is to be treated as so capable if the act would have been so capable had the facts been as D believed them to be at the time of the act or had subsequent events happened in the manner D believed they would happen (or both).
(3) A reference in this Act to a person ("P") doing an act that is capable of encouraging the suicide or attempted suicide of another person includes a reference to P doing so by threatening another person or otherwise putting pressure on another person to commit or attempt suicide.

These are 'new' subsections inserted into the Suicide Act 1961 and elaborate on what constitutes an act capable of encouraging or assisting suicide.

Section 2A(1) creates a liability when a defendant arranges for another to encourage or assist suicide so that responsibility cannot be avoided by using a third party as a conduit to commit the offence. Note that that third party must actually do the 'act', i.e. they must encourage or assist the suicide.

Section 2A(2) has the effect that an act can be capable of encouraging or assisting suicide even if the circumstances are such that it was impossible for the act to actually encourage or assist suicide. An act is therefore treated as capable of encouraging and assisting suicide if it would have been so capable had the facts been as the defendant believed them to be at the time of the act (e.g. if pills provided with the intention that they will assist a person to commit suicide are thought to be lethal but are in fact harmless), or had subsequent events happened as the defendant believed they would (e.g. if lethal pills which were sent to a person with the intention that the person would use them to commit or attempt to commit suicide get lost in the post), or both; answer D is therefore incorrect.

Crime, paras 1.5.7, 1.5.7.1

Answer 5.5

Answer **D** — Section 54 of the Coroners and Justice Act 2009 states:

(1) Where a person ('D') kills or is a party to the killing of another ('V'), D is not to be convicted of murder if—
   (a) D's acts and omissions in doing or being a party to the killing resulted from D's loss of self-control,
   (b) the loss of self-control had a qualifying trigger, and
   (c) a person of D's sex and age, with a normal degree of tolerance and self-restraint and in the circumstances of D, might have reacted in the same or in a similar way to D . . .

Section 54 sets out the criteria which need to be met in order for the new partial defence of loss of self-control to be successful, those being:

- the defendant's conduct resulted from a loss of self-control;
- the loss of self-control had a qualifying trigger (which is defined in s. 55—see later); and
- a person of the defendant's sex and age with an ordinary level of tolerance and self-restraint and in the circumstances of the defendant might have acted in the same or similar way to the defendant.

This is no longer the 'reasonable person'; answers A and B are therefore incorrect. It is also acted in the same or similar way, not just the same; answer C is therefore incorrect.

Crime, para. 1.5.3.2

Answer 5.6

Answer **C** — Like most offences, homicide requires that the defendant had the required *mens rea* for the relevant 'unlawful act', which for homicide offences would lead to the death of a victim. If the defendant did not have that *mens rea*, the offence of manslaughter will not be made out and therefore answers A, B and D are incorrect. In the case of *R* v *Lamb* [1967] 2 QB 981, the defendant pretended to fire a revolver at his friend. Although the defendant believed that the weapon would not fire, the chamber containing a bullet moved round to the firing pin and the defendant's friend was killed. As the defendant did not have the *mens rea* required for an assault his conviction for manslaughter was quashed.

Crime, para. 1.5.4.1

Answer 5.7

Answer **C** — Unlawful act manslaughter is the effect of the old felony/murder rule and is often known as constructive manslaughter—at common law it is manslaughter to kill in the course of committing an unlawful act just as it was murder to kill in the course of committing a felony. This felony/murder rule was repealed by s.1 of the Homicide Act 1957 but the constructive malice rule is still with us.

For unlawful act manslaughter, the requirements are that:

- the accused must have *caused* the death of another; *and*
- the killing must have occurred in the course of the accused's *unlawful* act; *and*
- that unlawful act must have also been *dangerous* i.e. exposing the victim to a risk of harm; *and*
- the defendant had the required *mens rea* for the relevant 'unlawful act'.

Note the '*and*': all four factors have to be present.

Did KACIK cause the death of CROFT? Arguably, yes, he did. Was it an unlawful act? If the threat amounted to a public order offence, then yes. Was the threat dangerous? It depends on the threat but again it could be. Did the defendant have the required *mens rea*? Here is where a 'weak' case dies.

There is no *mens rea*, and therefore no offence; answers A and B are therefore incorrect.

Note if all the other factors were present, a voluntary act by the victim would not exculpate the accused. Had the accused stepped towards the victim carrying a knife, with malicious intent, and the accused had tried to escape by running over the tracks and met a similar fate to CROFT, a charge of manslaughter may well have ensued; answer D is therefore incorrect.

Crime, para. 1.5.4.1

Answer 5.8

Answer **A** — Section 4 of the Offences Against the Person Act 1861 states:

> Whosoever shall solicit, encourage, persuade or endeavour to persuade, or shall propose to any person, to murder any other person, whether he be a subject of Her Majesty or not... shall be guilty of a misdemeanour...

The offence is made out even with a proposal and intent does not form part of the offence; answer B is therefore incorrect.

The proposed victim may be outside the United Kingdom and it does not matter whether or not the person is in fact encouraged to commit murder; answers C and D are therefore incorrect.

Crime, para. 1.5.8

Answer 5.9

Answer **A** — In order to prove manslaughter by an unlawful act (also called constructive manslaughter), you must prove:

- an unlawful act by the defendant, that is, an act which is unlawful in itself, irrespective of the fact that it ultimately results in someone's death. The act must be inherently unlawful;
- that the act involved a risk of bodily harm. That risk will be judged objectively, that is, would the risk be apparent to a reasonable and sober person watching the act.

Clearly setting fire to a building using accelerants carries a risk but is the act unlawful? The building is leased and arson does not have the protection that simple damage to your own property has; answers C and D are therefore incorrect.

A charge of manslaughter may be brought where a person, by an instance of gross negligence, has brought about the death of another. The ingredients of this offence were reviewed and restated by the Court of Appeal and essentially consist of death resulting from a negligent breach of a duty of care owed by the defendant to the victim in circumstances so reprehensible as to amount to gross negligence (*R* v *Misra and Srivastava* [2004] EWCA Crim 2375). There is no duty of care owed to the victim and therefore answers B and D are incorrect.

Crime, paras 1.5.4.1, 1.5.4.2

Answer 5.10

Answer **B** — Under s. 2 of the Homicide Act 1957, a defendant may be acquitted of murder, but be liable instead for manslaughter, if the person is able to show the court that he or she was suffering from such abnormality of mind (whether arising from a condition of arrested or retarded development of mind or any inherent causes or induced by disease or injury) as *substantially* impaired his/her mental responsibility for his or her acts or omissions in doing or being a party to the killing. The mental impairment suffered must be substantial and minor lapses of lucidity will not be enough. Answers C and D are therefore incorrect.

In the case of *R* v *Dietschmann* [2003] 1 AC 1209, the House of Lords accepted that a mental abnormality caused by a grief reaction to the recent death of an aunt with whom the defendant had had a physical relationship could suffice. In that case their Lordships went on to hold that there is no requirement to show that the 'abnormality of mind' was the sole cause of the defendant's acts in committing the killing. Answers A and D are therefore incorrect.

Crime, para. 1.5.3.1

Answer 5.11

Answer **D** — Section 5 of the Domestic Violence, Crime and Victims Act 2004 states:

(1) A person ('D') is guilty of an offence if—
   (a) a child or vulnerable adult ('V') dies or suffers serious physical harm as a result of the unlawful act of a person who—
      (i) was a member of the same household as V, and
      (ii) had frequent contact with him,
   (b) D was such a person at the time of that act,
   (c) at that time there was a significant risk of serious physical harm being caused to V by the unlawful act of such a person, and
   (d) either D was the person whose act caused V's the death or serious physical harm—
      (i) D was, or ought to have been, aware of the risk mentioned in paragraph (c),
      (ii) D failed to take such steps as he could reasonably have been expected to take to protect V from the risk, and
      (iii) the act occurred in circumstances of the kind that D foresaw or ought to have foreseen.

This seems very complicated at first reading, so it is important to break it down.

You will need to answer yes to all the following questions for the offence to be made out.

- Was the victim a child or vulnerable adult? Yes.
- Was the defendant a member of the same household? For these purposes a person will be a member of a particular household if they visit it so often and for such periods of time that it is reasonable to regard them as a member of it, even if they do not actually live there, so yes.
- Was there a significant risk of serious physical harm being caused to the victim by the unlawful act of such a person? Yes.
- Was the defendant the person who caused the victim's death? Yes.
- Was the defendant also—although not the person who caused the death—a member of the household? Yes.
  — If yes, were they aware of that risk? Yes.
  — Did they fail to take steps to protect the victim from that risk? Yes.
  — Did the act occur where it was foreseen or ought to have been foreseen? Yes.

As can be seen by all the yes answers the offence is made out for both the mother and the boyfriend, the mother being culpable even in circumstances where she ought to have foreseen the attack; answers A, B and C are therefore incorrect.

Crime, para. 1.5.6

Answer 5.12

Answer **C** — Section 1 of the Corporate Manslaughter and Corporate Homicide Act 2007 states:

(1) An organisation to which this section applies is guilty of an offence if the way in which its activities are managed or organised—
   (a) causes a person's death, and
   (b) amounts to a gross breach of a relevant duty of care owed by the organisation to the deceased.
(2) The organisations to which this section applies are—
   (a) a corporation;
   (b) a department or other body listed in Schedule 1;
   (c) a police force;
   (d) a partnership, or a trade union or employers' association, that is an employer.
(3) An organisation is guilty of an offence under this section only if the way in which its activities are managed or organised by its senior management is a substantial element in the breach referred to in subsection (1).

The offence is concerned with the way in which an organisation's activities were managed or organised. Under this test, the courts will examine management systems and practices across the organisation, and whether the adequate standard of care was applied to the fatal activity.

The threshold for the offence is gross negligence. The way in which the activities were managed or organised must have fallen far below what could reasonably have been expected.

The failure to manage or organise activities properly must have caused the victim's death.

A duty of care is an obligation that an organisation has to take reasonable steps to protect a person's safety. These duties exist, for example, in respect of the systems of work and equipment used by employees, the condition of worksites and other premises occupied by an organisation and in relation to products or services supplied to customers. The duty must be a relevant one. Relevant duties are set out in s. 2 of the Act and include:

- Employer and occupier duties.
- Duties connected to:
  — supplying goods and services;
  — commercial activities;
  — construction and maintenance work;
  — using or keeping plant, vehicles or other things.
- In relation to policing and law enforcement in the Act, there are some exceptions to the relevant duty of care obligation (s. 5 of the Act), these are in:
  — operations for dealing with terrorism, civil unrest or serious disorder, that involve the carrying on of policing or law-enforcement activities where officers or employees of the public authority in question come under attack, or face the threat of attack or violent resistance, in the course of the operations;
  — activities carried out in preparation for, or directly in support of, such operations above;
  — training of a hazardous nature or training carried out in a hazardous way in order to improve or maintain the effectiveness of officers or employees of the public authority with respect to such operations as noted previously.

Police services and authorities are still subject to the Act and could be prosecuted in matters where death relates to the organisation's responsibility as an employer (or to others working for the organisation) or as an occupier of premises.

The offence is concerned with the corporate liability of the organisation itself and does not apply to individual directors, senior managers or other individuals; answers

A and B are therefore incorrect. It is not possible to convict an individual of assisting or encouraging this offence (s. 18).

The term 'senior management' is defined in s. 1(4) of the Act to mean those persons who play a significant role in the management of the whole or of a substantial part of the organisation's activities. This covers those individuals in the direct chain of management as well as those in, for example, strategic or regulatory compliance roles, this would include both the fleet and workshop managers; answer D is therefore incorrect.

Crime, para. 1.5.5

6 | Misuse of Drugs

STUDY PREPARATION

Offences relating to the misuse of drugs require a sound knowledge both of the elements of the offences and the case law that supports them. You should also understand the elements of the statutory defences that apply, and how they affect the case in question. This chapter also covers the rather complicated power to enter, search and seize granted by s. 23 of the Misuse of Drugs Act 1971, and it is well worth taking your time over this section (if you've read it you'll know what we mean!). In addition to the more usual controlled drugs, this chapter also includes the law relating to intoxicating substances.

QUESTIONS

Question 6.1

TANVEER was in possession of a small box. He knew that the box contained a tin, and he suspected that the tin contained something. However he had no knowledge at all that the tin did actually contain something. The tin, in fact, contained several Ecstasy tablets.

Is TANVEER in possession of a controlled substance?

A Yes, as he suspected that the tin contained 'something'.

B Yes, as he knew he had the tin, and that tin did contain a controlled substance.

C No, he only knew that he possessed something inside the box, not inside the tin.

D No, he is in possession of the controlled substance but he did not know it was a controlled substance.

Question 6.2

HINDS has a bottle of vitamin tablets in her handbag. Unknown to her, her son had put three Ecstasy tablets in the bottle that morning. Before leaving the house HINDS checks that she has the bottle in her handbag.

Which of the following is correct?

A HINDS is in possession of a controlled drug, but may not be committing an offence.

B HINDS is in possession of a controlled drug and is committing an offence.

C HINDS is not in possession of a controlled drug as she did not put them in the bottle.

D HINDS is not in possession of a controlled drug as she has no knowledge of what the tablets are.

Question 6.3

Detective Constable FISCHER is a member of the National Crime Squad. She has been involved in an undercover operation in relation to drug trafficking. STROUER is a major drug dealer and has asked FISCHER to help in the supply of cocaine. FISCHER has provisionally agreed to this to maintain her cover. In fact FISCHER has no intention of illegally supplying drugs, and the arrest of STROUER is considered as necessary.

In relation to incitement under s. 19 of the Misuse of Drugs Act 1971, which of the following is correct?

A The offence is complete when STROUER asks FISCHER to supply the drugs.

B As FISCHER has no intention of supplying the drugs, the offence is not complete.

C The offence would be complete only if FISCHER actually supplied the drugs.

D The offence is complete only if STROUER receives the drugs, and supplying is complete.

Question 6.4

MORRISON is a self-employed chemist and her partner, OLDMAN, confessed to her that he was a heroin addict, although not registered as such. MORRISON was shocked by the news, but agreed to help OLDMAN break his addiction. MORRISON took some methadone from her storeroom, and gave it to OLDMAN.

In relation to MORRISON's actions, which of the following is incorrect?

A MORRISON has committed no offence in these circumstances, as she had lawful possession of the drug.

B Even though MORRISON would normally be entitled to lawfully possess a controlled drug, she has committed an offence by supplying it to OLDMAN.

C MORRISON has committed an offence in these circumstances.

D MORRISON has committed an offence from the time she took the drug from the surgery intending to supply it to OLDMAN.

Question 6.5

CARLOS found a bag containing white powder in her son's bedroom, which she believed was cocaine. CARLOS took the powder, intending to hand it in to the police. However, as a leader of the local youth club, CARLOS decided to keep the drugs to show other youth workers, so they will be able to recognise the drug should they find any.

Would CARLOS be able to claim a statutory defence to the offence of possession of a controlled drug, under s. 5(4) of the Misuse of Drugs Act 1971?

A Yes, providing it was her intent to destroy the drugs when she took possession of them to prevent her son from committing an offence.

B No, the defence would only apply if she took possession of the drugs and subsequently destroyed them.

C No, the defence would only apply if she took possession of the drugs and subsequently delivered them to a person lawfully entitled to possess them.

D No, the defence would only apply if she took possession of the drugs and either destroyed them or delivered them to a person lawfully entitled to possess them.

Question 6.6

An undercover police officer conducted several telephone conversations with PRIOR who was suspected of supplying heroin. PRIOR stated that although he had none with him at the times of the phone calls he would be happy to supply in the future. In fact PRIOR never did supply any drugs to the officer as he was arrested before that could happen. In relation to the offence under s. 4(3)(a) of the Misuse of Drugs Act 1971, offering to supply a controlled drug, PRIOR argues that he is not guilty of that offence as he is not really making a genuine offer to supply as the purchaser was an undercover police officer.

In relation to this which of the following is correct?

A PRIOR will be guilty as an offence was committed whether or not the offer was genuine.

B PRIOR will be guilty of that offence, provided the prosecution show he actually had the ability to supply the drugs.

C PRIOR will not be guilty of that offence as he did not actually have heroin at the time he made the offer.

D PRIOR will not be guilty of that offence as it was not a 'real' offer as the police officer could not accept the actual drugs.

Question 6.7

FLANDERS used his chemical knowledge to help his friends at their parties. He took equipment to the parties to make crack from cocaine in order that it could be vaporised and inhaled. Police officers arrested him at one such party and charged him with being involved in the production of a controlled drug contrary to s. 4(2) of the Misuse of Drugs Act 1971.

In relation to that which of the following is correct?

A FLANDERS is guilty of this offence merely by being in possession of the equipment from which the drug is produced.

B FLANDERS is guilty of this offence even though he is only producing one drug from another.

C FLANDERS is not guilty of this offence as he is not producing a controlled drug, he is only transforming one to another.

D FLANDERS is not guilty of this offence as essentially crack and cocaine are the same drug and FLANDERS did not 'produce' the cocaine.

Question 6.8

BOOYNET has long been suspected by the police of being involved in the supply of controlled drugs and a warrant has been obtained to search his premises. The police go to BOOYNET's house and, as they enter, BOOYNET takes various papers and shreds them. BOOYNET is unsure whether they are evidence or not, but is not willing to take a chance. These papers actually amounted to the only real evidence proving BOOYNET's involvement in the supply of controlled drugs.

Has BOOYNET committed an offence of obstruction under s. 23(4) of the Misuse of Drugs Act 1971?

A Yes, he was reckless as to whether the papers were evidence or not.

B Yes, he has obstructed the officers by destroying the evidence.

C No, as obstruction only applies to deliberate, physical obstruction of the officers themselves.

D No, as obstruction only applies to stop/searches in relation to drugs.

Question 6.9

Police suspect that STRONG is using her premises to allow persons to enter and smoke cannabis. Her neighbours have complained that the noise is continual, both day and night, and have asked the police if they can do something to stop the occurrence of the disorder associated with persons entering and leaving STRONG's house.

In relation to using the premises for the unlawful use, production or supply of a controlled drug which of the following is correct?

A A police officer not below the rank of superintendent may authorise the issue of a closure notice in respect of the premises in these circumstances.

B A police officer not below the rank of inspector may authorise the issue of a closure notice in respect of the premises in these circumstances.

C A closure notice can only be applied for by the local authority in these circumstances.

D No closure notice may be authorised in these circumstances.

Question 6.10

MITCHUM has a controlled drug in his pocket, which he intends to supply to someone else. Seeing a police officer in the distance, he hands the drugs to his friend, WAGNER, and says 'hold on to these for me and I will give you £20'. WAGNER agrees and takes possession of the drugs. The officer stops both men and carries out a lawful search and discovers the drugs that WAGNER has.

In relation to the controlled drugs, which offence(s) has WAGNER committed?

A Possession only as he did not return the drugs.

B Possession with intent to supply, as the drugs were meant by MITCHUM for supply.

C Possession with intent to supply as he was going to benefit from that supply.

D Possession with intent to supply as he intended returning the drugs; the money is irrelevant.

Question 6.11

McNIFF is 16 years old and works on Saturdays in his father's shop. He sells a bottle of solvent to his school friend whom he knows is 16 years old.

Under s. 1 of the Intoxicating Substances (Supply) Act 1985 (supply of an intoxicating substance), which of the following is correct in relation to the defences available to McNIFF?

A McNIFF has a defence owing to his age only.

B McNIFF has a defence as he was acting in the course of a business.

C McNIFF has a defence owing to his age and the fact that he was acting in the course of a business.

D McNIFF has no defence.

Question 6.12

SAUNDERS and TWEED are both drug addicts and bought a quantity of heroin together, which SAUNDERS carried back to a house. At the house, SAUNDERS divided the heroin equally and gave a share to TWEED. Unfortunately, TWEED had been drinking all day and fell asleep. SAUNDERS then injected TWEED with her own drugs while she was asleep.

At what point, if at all, does SAUNDERS commit the offence of supplying a controlled drug, under s. 4(3)(a) of the Misuse of Drugs Act 1971?

A When SAUNDERS divided the heroin and gave it to TWEED.

B Only when SAUNDERS injected TWEED with the heroin.

C On both occasions, when SAUNDERS divided the heroin and gave it to TWEED and later when TWEED was injected with the heroin.

D The offence is not committed at all, because the heroin was jointly purchased by SAUNDERS and TWEED.

Question 6.13

Travel restriction orders made under the Criminal Justice and Police Act 2001 restrict the travel of convicted drug traffickers.

For how long a period does this travel restriction order last?

A 2 years.

B 4 years.

C 10 years.

D Unlimited period; no set maximum.

Question 6.14

MAY was the sole tenant and occupier of a flat, which was raided by the police. They found MAY, along with seven others, and a number of items used for the smoking of drugs. They also found a quantity of cannabis resin. MAY admits he had given permission for drug smoking to take place. During the search of the premises the police could detect no smell of cannabis. MAY was charged with allowing the offence of permitting the smoking of cannabis, cannabis resin or prepared opium on premises under s. 8 of the Misuse of Drugs Act 1971.

Is MAY guilty of this offence?

A No, as he was not the owner of the premises.

B No, as there was no evidence actual smoking took place.

C Yes, as there was cannabis and drugs paraphernalia in the premises.

D Yes, as he admits that he gave permission for drug smoking.

Question 6.15

Police are considering a closure notice under s. 1 of the Anti-social Behaviour Act 2003, with regard to a club which has been used in connection with supplying Class A drugs.

In relation to the officer who can authorise this, and how long this individual can go back in relation to the club's activities (the officer is considering issuing the order today), which of the following is true?

A An officer of at least the rank of assistant chief constable (ACC) can authorise, and can consider the use of the club over the past month.

B An officer of at least the rank of superintendent can authorise, and can consider the use of the club over the past month.

C An officer of at least the rank of ACC can authorise, and can consider the use of the club over the past three months.

D An officer of at least the rank of superintendent can authorise, and can consider the use of the club over the past three months.

Question 6.16

Police officers have obtained a warrant to search a premises under s. 23 of the Misuse of Drugs Act 1971. When they enter the premises there are a number of persons present, including one who is clearly repairing the mashing machine.

Which of the following is true in relation to searching individuals on the premises?

A They can search all individuals in the premises under authority of the warrant.

B They can search all individuals in the premises under authority of the warrant, but only if it states individuals may be searched.

C They can search only individuals named on the warrant when using that warrant as authority to search.

D They could search everyone except those who are there for an ancillary purpose.

Question 6.17

Drug squad officers have been watching a premises for two months that is being used to cultivate, and then sell skunk cannabis. There have been several instances of disorder in and around that premises and the local neighbourhood policing team have had to deal with several calls to the area around this particular premises for anti-social behaviour during that two months.

Can the police apply for a closure notice under s. 1 of the Anti-social Behaviour Act 2003?

A Yes, as there is unlawful drug activity which is accompanied by disorder.

B Yes, as there is unlawful drug activity which is accompanied by disorder or nuisance.

C No, as this notice only applies to Class A drug activity.

D No, as the problems have not been taking place for a three-month period.

Question 6.18

RIDDICK was approached by CRAWLEY and asked to deliver a package to a nearby address. CRAWLEY gave RIDDICK £200 for taking the package. RIDDICK was very drunk at the time he was asked to take the package and did not realise that he had been given so much money. He takes the package but is stopped by police officers who have had CRAWLEY, a known drug dealer, under surveillance. The package is found to contain a very large quantity of a Class A drug and RIDDICK is charged with possession of, and possession with intent to supply, a Class A drug.

Consider RIDDICK's use of the defence under s. 28(2) of the Misuse of Drugs Act 1971 (lack of knowledge of some alleged fact) due to the fact he was drunk and he had no 'reason to suspect' what he was doing.

Which of the following is correct?

A The defence could be used for possession of the drugs, but not for the intention to supply.

B The defence could *not* be used for either charge as 'reason to suspect' is a factual test and not subject to individual peculiarities.

C The defence could be used for either charge as 'reason to suspect' is subject to individual peculiarities and is not a factual test.

D The defence could be used for intention to supply but not for mere possession of the drugs.

Question 6.19

EWINGS is a drug dealer who supplies drugs from his girlfriend's flat. Police have been watching the premises and when his girlfriend arrives in a car. the police strike. In the car there is a large quantity of heroin. The car belongs to EWINGS and the girlfriend states she was just delivering the drugs to EWINGS and is not involved in, and does not gain any benefit from, the supplying that EWINGS commits.

For what offence(s) under the Misuse of Drugs Act 1971 will the girlfriend be liable?

A Possession of a controlled drug only.

B Possession of a controlled drug and possession with intent to supply.

C Possession of a controlled drug and being concerned in the supply of a controlled drug.

D Possession of a controlled drug and being concerned in the supply of a controlled drug and possession with intent to supply.

ANSWERS

Answer 6.1

Answer **B** — What you have to recognise here is what you are being asked to answer. The lead-in to this question is 'Is TANVEER in possession of a controlled substance?'. To answer that question you have firstly to establish physical control.

A good starting point in understanding 'possession' is to realise that it is a neutral concept, not implying any kind of blame or fault. This is the key feature to understand first before going on to consider specific offences under any legislation. In order to be in possession of anything, the common law requires physical control of the object plus knowledge of its presence. This requirement is particularly problematic where containers of some sort (whether they be boxes, handbags, cigarette packets or whatever) are involved or where the person claims not to have realised what it was that he/she 'possessed'. In such cases, the common law makes the same requirements; you need to show that the person had physical control of the container together with a knowledge that it contained something. Once you have established possession, you then need to show that the substance/object/material possessed was in fact proscribed by the relevant statute.

In *R* v *Forsyth* [2001] EWCA Crim 2926, the defendant argued that there was a distinction between a person carrying something in a container and a person carrying something inside something else in a container! In that particular case, the defendant was found in possession of a box which contained a safe; inside the safe was a significant quantity of a controlled drug. The defendant argued that this type of possession should be differentiated from the situation where someone simply had possession of a box with drugs in it. The Court of Appeal ruled that there was no difference and the issues of proof were the same; answer C is therefore incorrect.

If a person has a container with him/her and that container is found to have controlled drugs in it, he/she is in possession of those drugs provided he/she knew that there was something in the container that was in fact a controlled substance; answers A and D are therefore incorrect. That does not mean that, at this point, the person necessarily commits an offence (and he/she may still have a statutory defence); it means that he/she was in 'possession' of the drugs. So as in *Forsyth*, TANVEER is in possession, although he may not be committing an offence.

Crime, paras 1.6.3.1, 1.6.3.2

Answer 6.2

Answer **A** — Common law outlines possession as physical control plus knowledge of the presence of the drugs. This becomes problematical where the person in possession claims not to realise what they possessed. In these cases it needs to be shown that the person had physical control of the container together with knowledge that it contained something. HINDS knew she had a container and that it contained tablets (answers C and D are therefore incorrect). This simply means that HINDS was in possession of controlled drugs, not that she was committing an offence under the 1971 Act, therefore answer B is incorrect. It is clear from various case authorities that the basic elements are that a person 'knows' that they are in possession of something which is in fact a controlled substance. As answer B states that she is committing an offence for simply possessing the drugs, it is incorrect. She may commit an offence, as outlined in answer A; however, she could avail herself of the statutory defences available.

Crime, paras 1.6.3.1, 1.6.3.2, 1.6.3.3

Answer 6.3

Answer **A** — The definition of this offence under s. 19 of the Misuse of Drugs Act 1971 is that it is an offence for a person to incite another to commit an offence under any other provisions of this Act. This clearly covers all sections, not just supplying.

On the arguments in *DPP* v *Armstrong* [2000] Crim LR 379, it would seem that a person inciting an undercover police officer may commit an offence under this section even though there was no possibility of the officer actually being induced to commit the offence, and therefore answer B is incorrect. As the offence is committed at the time the incitement is made and is not conditional on either the supply or receipt of the controlled drugs, answers C and D are incorrect.

Crime, para. 1.6.14

Answer 6.4

Answer **A** — Section 5 of the Misuse of Drugs Act 1971 states:

(3) Subject to section 28 of this Act, it is an offence for a person to have a controlled drug in his possession, whether lawfully or not, with intent to supply it to another in contravention of section 4(1) of this Act.

It is important to note that the lawfulness or otherwise of the possession is irrelevant; what matters here is the lawfulness of the intended supply. If a vet, or a police officer or some other person is in lawful possession of a controlled drug but they intend to supply it unlawfully to another, this offence will be made out.

This is a crime of specific intent and the intention to supply would have to be proven, as it is in the question. Consequently, MORRISON commits an offence, making answers B, C and D actually correct in law. The question, though, asks you what is incorrect, and therefore answer A is actually the correct answer.

Crime, para. 1.6.3.7

Answer 6.5

Answer **D** — Defences are provided by s. 5(4) of the Misuse of Drugs Act 1971, which states:

> In any proceedings for an offence under subsection (2) above in which it is proved that the accused had a controlled drug in his possession, it shall be a defence for him to prove—
>
> (a) that, knowing or suspecting it to be a controlled drug he took possession of it for the purpose of preventing another from committing or continuing to commit an offence in connection with that drug and that as soon as possible after taking possession of it he took all such steps as were reasonably open to him to destroy the drug or to deliver it into the custody of a person lawfully entitled to take custody of it;
>
> (b) that, knowing or suspecting it to be a controlled drug he took possession of it for the purpose of delivering it into the custody of a person lawfully entitled to take custody of it and that as soon as possible after taking possession of it he took all such steps as were reasonably open to him to deliver it into the custody of such a person.

It can be seen from this that once CARLOS had taken possession of the drugs, she would then be expected *either* to destroy them *or* deliver them to a person lawfully entitled to possess them—answers B and C are incorrect, because the defence is available to a person who does either of these things.

The issue of intent under s. 5(4)(b) was examined in the case of *R* v *Dempsey and Dempsey* [1985] 82 Cr App R 291. In this case it was held that the defendant must prove that it was his or her *sole* intention at the time of taking possession of the drug to deliver it to a person lawfully entitled to possess it. However, even though it was CARLOS's intent to hand the drugs in to the police when she actually took possession of the drugs, she later changed her mind and did not do so. From the point that she changed her mind, she was in unlawful possession of the drugs and would not be able to rely on the defence provided by s. 5(4). Answer A is therefore incorrect.

Crime, para. 1.6.3.8

Answer 6.6

Answer **A** — Section 4 of the Misuse of Drugs Act 1971 states:

(3) Subject to section 28 of this Act, it is an offence for a person—
    (a) to supply or offer to supply a controlled drug to another in contravention of sub-section (1) above; or
    (b) to be concerned in the supplying of such a drug to another in contravention of that subsection; or
    (c) to be concerned in the making to another in contravention of that subsection of an offer to supply such a drug.

The offence of offering to supply a controlled drug is complete when the offer is made. It is irrelevant whether or not the defendant actually has the means to meet the offer or even intends to carry it out (see *R* v *Goodard* [1992] Crim LR 588); answers B and C are therefore incorrect. If the offer is made by conduct alone (i.e. without any words), it may be difficult to prove this offence. If words are used, the defence under s. 28 does not appear to apply (see *R* v *Mitchell* [1992] Crim LR 723). If the offer is made to an undercover police officer, the offence is still committed and the defendant cannot claim that such an offer was not a 'real' offer (*R* v *Kray* [1998] EWCA Crim 3211); answer D is therefore incorrect.

Crime, para. 1.6.4

Answer 6.7

Answer **B** — Section 4 of the Misuse of Drugs Act 1971 states:

(2) Subject to section 28 of this Act, it is an offence for a person—
    (a) to produce a controlled drug in contravention of subsection (1)...; or
    (b) to be concerned in the production of such a drug in contravention of that subsection by another.

'Produce' means producing by manufacture, cultivation or any other method and 'production' has a corresponding meaning (Misuse of Drugs Act 1971, s. 37). This is further than merely possessing the equipment to match such a production; answer A is therefore incorrect.

Converting one form of a Class A drug into another has been held to be 'producing' (*R* v *Russell* (1991) 94 Cr App R 351). So although crack and cocaine are essentially the same drug, it is production to change powdered cocaine into rock crack; answers C and D are therefore incorrect.

Crime, para. 1.6.7

Answer 6.8

Answer **B** — This offence is complete where the person obstructs someone carrying out stop/search procedures and also executing a warrant, and therefore answer D is incorrect. In *R* v *Forde* (1985) 81 Cr App R 19, it was held that a person only committed this offence if the obstruction was intentional, that is to say the act viewed objectively, through the eyes of a bystander, did obstruct the constable's search, and viewed subjectively, that is to say through the eyes of the accused himself, was intended so to obstruct. BOOYNET knew he was intentionally obstructing the officers and, even though he was unsure of the outcome, recklessness does not apply (answer A is therefore incorrect). Section 23(4)(b) of the Misuse of Drugs Act 1971 states that the offence includes a person who 'conceals from a person acting in the exercise of his powers under subsection (1) above any such books, documents...'. So, as books and documents are included, answer C is incorrect.

Crime, para. 1.6.17.2

Answer 6.9

Answer **D** — Section 1 of the Anti-social Behaviour Act 2003 states:

This section applies to premises if a police officer not below the rank of superintendent (the authorising officer) has reasonable grounds for believing—
(a) that at any time during the relevant period the premises have been used in connection with the unlawful use, production or supply of a Class A controlled drug, and
(b) that the use of the premises is associated with the occurrence of disorder or serious nuisance to members of the public.

As can be seen closure notices only apply to circumstances surrounding the unlawful use, production or supply of a Class A controlled drug, and as cannabis is not Class A in these circumstances a closure notice cannot be authorised; answers A, B and C are therefore incorrect.

Although in relation to the drug usage it is the police who authorise closure notices this must be done in consultation with the local authority (s. 1(2)(a)); there is also a general power for local authorities to make a closure order in relation to noise and nuisance being caused in connection with the use of premises under s. 40 of the 2003 Act.

Crime, para. 1.6.12

Answer 6.10

Answer **D** — WAGNER has possession of the drugs and knows what they are. He is therefore in possession of them, but what is his intention?

The start-out intent for the drugs is not relevant. MITCHUM had them with intent to supply, however that intent does not transfer to WAGNER (after all he may well decide just to keep them); answer B is therefore incorrect.

So, if someone leaves drugs with a third person temporarily, what criminal liability is incurred by the third person? This situation was faced by the House of Lords in *R v Maginnis* [1987] AC 303. In that case their Lordships decided that Maginnis would have been 'supplying' the controlled drug had he returned it to the drug trafficker who had left a package of cannabis resin in Maginnis's car. Therefore he was in possession with intent to supply and so committed an offence under s. 5(3) of the Misuse of Drugs Act 1971. In another case when found in possession of the drugs, the defendant claimed the defence of duress and said that he had only been an 'involuntary custodian' of them, intending to return them at a later date. The Court of Appeal decided that it was irrelevant whether a person was a voluntary or involuntary custodian of the drugs and that an intention to return them to their depositor amounted to an 'intention to supply' (*R v Panton* [2001] EWCA Crim 611), so the fact he would benefit from their return was immaterial, the fact he intended to return them would suffice; answers A and C are therefore incorrect.

Crime, para. 1.6.4

Answer 6.11

Answer **D** — Section 1 of the Intoxicating Substances (Supply) Act 1985 defines the defence in subs. (2) as:

> in proceedings against any person for an offence under subsection (1) above it is a defence for him to show that at the time he made the supply or offer he was under the age of 18 and was acting otherwise than in the course or furtherance of a business.

So on the one hand McNIFF does have a defence in that he is 16; but this does not stand alone as the statute says 'under the age of 18 *and*'—that 'and' makes answer A incorrect. The second part of the subsection concerns 'acting otherwise than in the course or furtherance of a business' and as McNIFF was acting in the course of or in furtherance of a business, he is not afforded this defence and therefore answers B and C are incorrect.

Crime, para. 1.6.19

Answer 6.12

Answer **A** — It is an offence under s. 4(3)(a) of the Misuse of Drugs Act 1971 to supply a controlled drug to another. It has been held that dividing up controlled drugs which have been jointly purchased *will* amount to 'supplying' (*R v Buckley* (1979) 69 Cr App R 371).

Further, injecting another with his or her own controlled drug has been held *not* to amount to 'supplying' in a case where the defendant assisted pushing down the plunger of a syringe that the other person was already using. Parker CJ's comments in that case suggest that simply injecting another person with their own drug would not amount to 'supplying' (*R v Harris* [1968] 1 WLR 769). It may, however, amount to an offence of 'poisoning' under s. 23 of the Offences Against the Person Act 1861.

Answers B, C and D are therefore incorrect.

Crime, paras 1.6.4

Answer 6.13

Answer **D** — The introduction of ss. 33 to 37 of the Criminal Justice and Police Act 2001 allows any criminal court (but effectively, given the sentencing restriction, this means the Crown Court) to impose a travel restriction order on an offender who is convicted of a drug trafficking offence. The offender has to have been sentenced by that court to a term of imprisonment of four years or more (s. 33(1)). The effect of the order is to restrict the offender's freedom to leave the United Kingdom for a period specified by the court, and it may require delivery up of his passport. The minimum duration of a travel restriction order is two years, starting from the date of the offender's release from custody. There is no maximum period prescribed in the legislation, therefore answers A, B and C are incorrect. The court must always consider whether such an order should be made and must give reasons where it does not consider such an order to be appropriate (s. 33(2)).

Crime, para. 1.6.16

Answer 6.14

Answer **B** — Section 8 of the Misuse of Drugs Act 1971 states:

> A person commits an offence if, being the occupier or concerned in the management of any premises, he knowingly permits or suffers any of the following activities to take place on those premises, that is to say:

(a) producing or attempting to produce a controlled drug in contravention of section 4(1) of this Act;

(b) supplying or attempting to supply a controlled drug to another in contravention of section 4(1) of this Act, or offering to supply a controlled drug to another in contravention of section 4(1);

(c) preparing opium for smoking;

(d) smoking cannabis, cannabis resin or prepared opium.

As can be seen, it applies to occupiers and not just owners; answer A is therefore incorrect. It does, however, require that it was necessary to establish that the activity of smoking had taken place and not merely that the permission had been given (*R v Auguste* [2003] EWCA Crim 3929); answer D is therefore incorrect. It is also not sufficient that the drugs and paraphernalia were present—it seems the police may have timed their raid a bit too soon as no smoking had taken place; answer C is therefore incorrect.

Crime, para. 1.6.11

Answer 6.15

Answer **D** — Section 1 of the Anti-social Behaviour Act 2003 deals with premises where drugs are used unlawfully:

(1) This section applies to premises if a police officer not below the rank of superintendent (the authorising officer) has reasonable grounds for believing—

(a) that at any time during the relevant period the premises have been used in connection with the unlawful use, production or supply of a Class A controlled drug, and

(b) that the use of the premises is associated with the occurrence of disorder or serious nuisance to members of the public.

So it is a superintendent who authorises, not an assistant chief constable (ACC); therefore answers A and C are incorrect. The relevant period over which the officer can consider the use of the club is also defined in the Act by s. 1(10): 'The relevant period is the period of three months ending with the day on which the authorising officer considers whether to authorise the issue of a closure notice in respect of the premises'. So three months, and not one month, is the appropriate period; answer B is therefore incorrect.

Crime, para. 1.6.12

Answer 6.16

Answer **B** — The Misuse of Drugs Act 1971, s. 23 is a very wide statutory provision granting authority for a broad range of enforcement measures in connection with controlled drugs.

Particular care will need to be taken when drafting the application for a warrant under s. 23. Where police officers are on premises under the authority of such a warrant it will be important to have established the precise extent of the warrant. If such a warrant authorises the search of premises only, that in itself will not give the officers authority to search people found on those premises unless the officer can point to some other power authorising the search (see *Hepburn* v *Chief Constable of Thames Valley Police* [2002] EWCA Civ 1841); answers A and C are therefore incorrect.

However, where the warrant authorises the search of premises and people, the Divisional Court has held that it is reasonable to restrict the movement of people within the premises to allow the search to be conducted properly (see *DPP* v *Meaden* [2003] EWHC 3005 (Admin)); answer D is therefore incorrect.

Crime, para. 1.6.17.1

Answer 6.17

Answer **C** — Section 1 of the Anti-social Behaviour Act 2003 relates to closure notices. The police have power to close down premises being used for the supply, use or production of Class A drugs where there is associated serious nuisance or disorder. The activity period is in fact three months but the fact that the drug activity relates to a non-Class A drug means the closure notice cannot be applied for; answers A, B and D are therefore incorrect.

Crime, para. 1.6.12

Answer 6.18

Answer **B** — Section 28(2) allows a defence where the defendant did not know, suspect or have reason to suspect the existence of some fact which is essential to proving the case. In relation to this defence RIDDICK could discharge the evidential burden by showing that he neither knew, nor suspected that the package contained a controlled drug, and that he neither knew nor suspected that he was supplying it to another. Both of these elements would be facts, which the prosecution would have to allege in order to prove the offence.

However, external factors can impact on this defence. For example if RIDDICK knew the person to be a local drug dealer, or the reward for his errand was suspiciously big (say £200!), then he may not be able to discharge this, albeit evidential, burden.

However, it has been held that the test for 'reason to suspect' is an objective (factual) one (*R* v *Young* [1984] 1 WLR 654). Consequently, where a 'reason to suspect' was not apparent to a defendant because he or she was too intoxicated to see it, the defence will not apply. So if you're offered a package to deliver whilst drunk …

Consequently answers A, C and D are incorrect.

Crime, para. 1.6.9.1

Answer 6.19

Answer **B** — Well, obviously there is possession of the drugs but is there supply?

In *R* v *Maginnis* [1987] AC 303, the House of Lords held that 'supply' involves more than a mere transfer of physical control of the item from one person to another but includes a further concept, namely that of 'enabling the recipient to apply the thing handed over to purposes for which he desires or has a duty to apply it'—in other words, the person to whom the drug is given must derive some benefit from it. Clearly, in further supplying the drugs EWINGS receives benefit so therefore although the girlfriend does not benefit, the person she supplies to does therefore it fits the offence.

There is no actual 'supplying' or being concerned in the supplying as the drugs were intercepted prior to supply; answers C and D are therefore incorrect. But there is possession with intent to supply; answer A is therefore incorrect.

Crime, paras 1.6.4, 1.6.4.1

7 Firearms and Gun Crime

STUDY PREPARATION

Definitions play a big role in this chapter, and the first few pages are devoted to this area. You must understand these definitions, particularly 'firearm', 'shotgun' and 'imitation firearm' before you move on to the offences. Also, the familiar definitions of 'possession' and 'has with him' appear frequently throughout the legislation and their elements must be known.

There are several offences involving the criminal use of firearms with which you should familiarise yourself. This can be a confusing area, as some offences appear to cross over. Pay particular attention to those offences that may or may not be committed with an imitation firearm.

Police powers under the Firearms Act 1968 are wide ranging, and some offences carry their own power of entry and search. Do not ignore the various powers under the Act.

Ages also play a significant part in this legislation, and you should familiarise yourself with these.

In tackling questions on firearms, establish exactly what type of weapon is involved. Is it real or imitation? Is it an air weapon? Then, you will need to know whether the relevant offences carry a power of arrest.

Significant changes were made to this area of legislation with the introduction of the Violent Crime Reduction Act 2006.

QUESTIONS

Question 7.1

BREEM has a realistic imitation firearm in his possession which he sells to GRIER who is 17 years of age.

Under s. 40 of the Violent Crime Reduction Act 2006 which of the following is correct?

A Only BREEM commits an offence as he has sold the weapon to a person under 18 years of age.

B Both BREEM and GRIER commit an offence in these circumstances.

C Both BREEM and GRIER commit an offence as it is a 'realistic imitation firearm' and not just an 'imitation firearm'.

D Only BREEM commits this offence as he has sold a 'realistic imitation firearm' to a person under 18 years of age.

Question 7.2

BENTHAM was stopped by Constable RUBY while driving a motor vehicle. Constable RUBY stood outside the vehicle and conducted a radio check which revealed that the vehicle had just been circulated for its involvement in an armed robbery at a petrol station less than an hour previously. BENTHAM overheard Constable RUBY calling for assistance and got out of the car. BENTHAM placed his hand in his pocket and with his fingers extended, pretended that he had a pistol in his pocket and told the officer to back away. Constable RUBY was not fooled by BENTHAM's attempt and told him so. BENTHAM then gave up without resisting the officer.

Would BENTHAM be guilty of an offence under s. 17(1) of the Firearms Act 1968 (using a firearm/imitation firearm to resist arrest) in these circumstances?

A No, holding his fingers like this will not amount to an imitation firearm.

B No, because he did not have with him something which had been adapted or altered so as to resemble a firearm.

C No, because the officer was not fooled by his attempt.

D Yes, because his fingers had the appearance of a firearm.

Question 7.3

OWEN owned a rifle, for which he had a firearms certificate. He bought another rifle from his friend, VOYLE, whose own certificate had expired. OWEN did not have enough room in his own cabinet and asked VOYLE if he could keep the rifle for him until OWEN bought a new cabinet. OWEN intended applying for an extension to his certificate when he had the rifle in his home.

Which person, if either, would commit an offence in these circumstances?

A Only OWEN, as he has taken possession of the weapon.

B Only VOYLE, as OWEN has not yet taken possession of the weapon.

C Both people, from the time OWEN bought the rifle.

D Only VOYLE, as only one person may be in possession at any one time.

Question 7.4

In relation to any offences relating to firearms, the basic definitions, particularly those of firearm, ammunition and imitation firearm are important.

Which of the following is the definition of a 'firearm' as per s. 57 of the Firearms Act 1968?

A A barrelled weapon of any description from which any shot, bullet or other missile can be discharged.

B A lethal barrelled weapon of any description from which any shot or bullet can be discharged.

C A lethal barrelled weapon of any description from which any shot, bullet or other missile can be discharged.

D A barrelled weapon of any description from which any shot or bullet can be discharged.

Question 7.5

BROWN's marriage has broken up because his wife had an affair with MEADE. BROWN was very upset and went to MEADE's home, where his wife was staying, with a shotgun and ammunition. BROWN intended to threaten them both into ending the affair. BROWN left the shotgun in the car and was let into the house; however, his wife was upstairs, refusing to see him. BROWN said to MEADE, 'Tell her to come down, or I'll get my shotgun from the car and I'll take it upstairs to shoot her'. BROWN's intent was genuine if his wife did not speak to him.

In relation to proof required that a person has committed an offence under s. 16 of the Firearms Act 1968 (endangering life), which of the following statements is correct?

A This offence will be complete if MEADE believed that a life was endangered.

B This offence is incomplete, as BROWN's threat was conditional.

C This offence is incomplete, as BROWN did not have the shotgun with him at the time of making the threat.

D This offence is complete as BROWN's intent to carry out the threat was genuine.

Question 7.6

SANSOME has recently acquired a plastic toy gun, which has the appearance of a real pistol. SANSOME approached SAIF, who owes him money, and used the gun to threaten him, intending that SAIF would fear he would be shot unless he repaid the debt.

Has SANSOME committed an offence under s. 16A of the Firearms Act 1968?

A No, this offence may not be committed with an imitation firearm.

B Yes, provided SANSOME intended to use violence against SAIF.

C No, because the toy cannot be readily converted into a s. 1 firearm.

D Yes, the offence is complete in these circumstances.

Question 7.7

SHATTOCK owed KUSACK money. KUSACK drove to SHATTOCK's house with a shotgun in the boot of the car. On arriving, KUSACK left the shotgun in the car and approached SHATTOCK. KUSACK threatened SHATTOCK with violence if the money was not paid back. SHATTOCK was in fear that KUSACK would use violence and paid the money. Even though the shotgun was left in the car, KUSACK fully intended using it if SHATTOCK failed to pay the money.

Has KUSACK committed an offence under s. 16A of the Firearms Act 1968?

A Yes, provided SHATTOCK feared that KUSACK would use violence.

B No, SHATTOCK was not aware that KUSACK was in possession of the shotgun.

C Yes, even though SHATTOCK was not aware that KUSACK was in possession of the shotgun.

D No, the shotgun was not in KUSACK's physical possession at the time the threats were made.

Question 7.8

Constable CHAVEZ stopped PETERS in his car. When he conducted a Police National Computer (PNC) check Constable CHAVEZ found that PETERS was wanted for attempted robbery, having threatened a garage cashier with a knife. Constable CHAVEZ searched the car and discovered a firearm in the boot. There was no evidence to show that PETERS was in possession of a firearm at the time of the original offence.

Would PETERS be guilty of an offence contrary to s. 17(2) of the Firearms Act 1968 (possession at time of committing/being arrested for a sch. 1 offence)?

A No, he was not in possession of the firearm during the original offence.

B Yes, because he has attempted to commit an indictable offence.

C No, because he did not commit the full offence of robbery.

D Yes, because he has been arrested for attempting to commit a sch. 1 offence.

Question 7.9

MAYER was in a public house and went upstairs to look to steal something. He found a loaded air rifle in a bedroom, and decided to take it with him; but he heard a noise downstairs and thought the licensee was coming so he put the gun back.

At the time he had the air rifle, has MAYER committed an offence under s. 20 of the Firearms Act 1968 (trespassing with a firearm)?

A Yes, provided he entered the private part of the pub as a trespasser and then took possession of the firearm.

B Yes, as he was in the private part of the premises as a trespasser, and then picked up the firearm.

C No, he was only in possession of an air weapon.

D No, as he did not leave the private part of the pub with the firearm.

Question 7.10

SAUNDERS, a drug dealer, keeps a handgun in his house for protection. One day he drove to a local shop, where he entered and stole goods. As he was leaving the shop, he was stopped by a store detective. SAUNDERS punched the store detective and ran to his car and escaped. The handgun remained in his house during the incident.

Has SAUNDERS committed an offence relating to the handgun, under s. 18 of the Firearms Act 1968, in these circumstances?

A No, he did not have the firearm with him at the time of committing the offence.
B Yes, he was in possession of a firearm at the time of committing the offence.
C Yes, he was in possession of a firearm, while resisting arrest for the offence.
D No, as it cannot be shown that he committed an indictable offence.

Question 7.11

TIMKINS is aged 14 and he is in his back garden with his cousin MARR who is 22 years of age; they are firing MARR's legally held air rifle. One of the shots fired by TIMKINS however strays over the garden fence onto a public street narrowly missing a passer by.

In relation to s. 21A of the Firearms Act 1968 (firing an air weapon beyond premises) which of the following is correct?

A An offence is committed by TIMKINS and he would have no defence.
B An offence is committed by TIMKINS but only as he is under the age of 16 and he would have no defence.
C An offence is committed by TIMKINS; however he would have the defence that he was acting under the control or direction of a person aged 21 years or over.
D An offence is committed by MARR; as he is over 21 years of age he is responsible for the control and direction of TIMKINS.

Question 7.12

WATKINS is a drug dealer and is seeking to take over the drugs market in a large town. WATKINS has acquired a Samurai sword and intends using it to threaten other dealers. WATKINS has been tipped off that the police are about to execute a warrant at his home in the next few days. WATKINS has persuaded his friend MAYO, who is aged 18, to hide the sword in his house until the police lose interest in him.

Could WATKINS be guilty of an offence under s. 28(1) of the Violent Crime Reduction Act 2006 (using another to look after etc. a dangerous weapon)?

A No, this offence can only be committed in relation to a firearm.
B Yes, this offence can be committed in relation to a firearm or an offensive weapon.
C No, this offence can only be committed when the person looking after the weapon is under 18.
D Yes, this offence can be committed in relation to a firearm, including an air weapon, or an offensive weapon.

Question 7.13

DENCH is 18 years of age and owns an air rifle. DENCH was at home in the garden and was firing air pellets at targets that had been set up on a fence. After a while, DENCH realised that some of the pellets were passing through the fence into the garden next door. DENCH knew that the people next door were at work and believed they would not mind as no damage was being caused. DENCH carried on firing at the targets.

Has DENCH committed an offence under s. 21A of the Firearms Act 1968 (firing an air weapon beyond premises), in these circumstances?

A No, because DENCH is not under 17 years of age.

B Yes, regardless of DENCH's age.

C Yes, but DENCH may have a defence because of a reasonable belief that the neighbour would have consented.

D No, because DENCH is 18 years of age, or older.

Question 7.14

DE'SOUZA is 18 years of age and has recently been released from a young offenders' institution, having served 2 years of a 3 years and 6 months sentence of detention.

What restrictions, if any, are placed on DE'SOUZA being in possession of a firearm?

A He may only possess a firearm after 5 years from the date of his release.

B He may not possess a firearm at any time from the date of his release.

C He may only possess a firearm after 3 years from the date of his release.

D There are no restrictions, as he was not sentenced to a term of imprisonment.

Question 7.15

KEETLEY owns a shotgun, which he keeps at GRIFFITHS' farm. He has a current shotgun certificate for the weapon and only uses it to shoot clay pigeons with GRIFFITHS on the farm, which is not open to members of the public. KEETLEY attended the farm one Saturday afternoon to shoot clay pigeons with GRIFFITHS; however, he had been to the local pub before he arrived and was intoxicated. KEETLEY took his shotgun out of the cabinet, but before he was able to load it, GRIFFITHS realised the state he was in and refused to allow him to use any cartridges.

Would KEETLEY commit an offence under s. 12 of the Licensing Act 1872 (possession of a firearm when drunk) in these circumstances?

A   No, as he was not in a public place.

B   No, as the shotgun was not loaded.

C   Yes, regardless of whether or not he was in a public place.

D   Yes, regardless of whether or not the shotgun was loaded.

Question 7.16

Constable PEARCE attended a noisy house party. As Constable PEARCE arrived, one of the party-goers, BELSHAW, was leaving the party. BELSHAW told Constable PEARCE that he had seen ERNEST, the house owner, with what appeared to be a real pistol. Also, BELSHAW had overheard ERNEST and another man discussing a robbery that was to take place in an all-night petrol station that night.

What powers, if any, would be available to Constable PEARCE under the Firearms Act 1968?

A   No power under the Act, as ERNEST was not in a public place.

B   Power to enter the premises without warrant and arrest ERNEST for an offence under the Act.

C   Power to enter and search the premises without warrant, but only if Constable PEARCE suspects an offence has been committed.

D   Power to enter the premises without warrant and search for the weapon.

Question 7.17

MARTIN owns a s. 1 firearm and holds a certificate allowing its possession. MARTIN has decided to sell the firearm because it has not been used for a number of months.

What obligation does MARTIN now have, in respect of the sale of the firearm, under s. 32(2) of the Firearms (Amendment) Act 1997?

A   MARTIN must notify the chief officer of police within 24 hours.

B   MARTIN must notify the chief officer of police within 72 hours.

C   MARTIN must notify the chief officer of police within seven days.

D   MARTIN must notify the chief officer of police within 21 days.

ANSWERS

Answer 7.1

Answer **B** — Sections 36 to 41 of the Violent Crime Reduction Act 2006 introduced measures to deal with the misuse of firearms.

Section 40 inserted a new s. 24A into the Firearms Act 1968 and makes it an offence to sell an imitation firearm to a person under 18. It also makes it an offence for a person under 18 to purchase an imitation firearm (answer A is therefore incorrect). The term 'realistic imitation firearm' is not mentioned in this section; answer C is therefore incorrect.

The 2006 Act introduced the term 'realistic imitation firearm' and it is an offence to sell one, but this is not age restrictive; answer D is therefore incorrect.

Crime, para. 1.7.14

Answer 7.2

Answer **A** — Section 17(1) of the Firearms Act 1968 states:

> It is an offence for a person to make or attempt to make any use whatsoever of a firearm or imitation firearm with intent to resist or prevent the lawful arrest or detention of himself or another person.

The issue of whether a person's fingers could be an imitation firearm was examined in the case of *R v Bentham* [2005] 1 WLR 1057. The Court of Appeal held that holding your fingers inside a jacket and threatening to shoot someone could amount to an offence involving an imitation firearm. However, the House of Lords overturned this decision, finding that the definition of an imitation firearm under s. 57 of the Firearms Act 1968 requires the defendant to carry a 'thing' which is separate and distinct from him or herself and therefore being capable of being possessed. Holding your fingers under your coat will *not* amount to an imitation firearm for the relevant offences, because an unsevered hand or finger is part of oneself and therefore could not be 'possessed'. Answer D is therefore incorrect.

The 'imitation' must have the appearance of a firearm but it is not necessary for any object to have been constructed, adapted or altered so as to resemble a firearm (*R v Williams* [2006] EWCA Crim 1650). Answer B is therefore incorrect. (Further, in *K v DPP* [2006] EWHC 2183 (Admin) it was held that in some circumstances a realistic toy gun, in this case a plastic ball bearing gun, could become an imitation firearm.)

The offence allows for a person to make or attempt to make use of a firearm or imitation firearm; therefore answer C is incorrect.

Crime, paras 1.7.9.1, 1.7.2.4

Answer 7.3

Answer **C** — Under s. 1 of the Firearms Act 1968, it is an offence for a person to have in his or her possession, or to purchase or acquire a firearm, without holding a certificate in force at the time or otherwise than as authorised by such a certificate.

The Act allows for a person to possess more than one firearm, but he or she must apply for any new firearm to be included on his or her certificate.

As VOYLE has retained possession of the rifle after his certificate has expired, he clearly commits an offence (which is why answer A is incorrect).

It remains to be proved that OWEN is also in possession of the weapon. There is no requirement to prove that he had the weapon *physically* in his possession— possession has a wider meaning than 'has with him'.

It is possible for one person to be in possession, even though some other person has physical control; for example, in *Sullivan v Earl of Caithness* [1976] QB 966, it was held that a person can remain in possession of a firearm even if someone else has custody of it. It is also possible for more than one person to be in possession of the same article, which is why answers B and D are incorrect.

Crime, para. 1.7.4.3

Answer 7.4

Answer **C** — In s. 57 of the Firearms Act 1968 the expression 'firearm' means a lethal barrelled weapon of any description from which any shot, bullet or other missile can be discharged. This is answer C; answers A, B and D are incorrect as they vary in some way from this definition.

Crime, para. 1.7.2.1

Answer 7.5

Answer **D** — It is an offence under s. 16 of the Firearms Act 1968 for a person to have in his or her possession, a firearm or ammunition with intent by means thereof to endanger the life of another. There is no requirement to show that a person had the firearm/ammunition 'with him'. The offence refers to possession, which is a wider requirement (which is why answer C is incorrect).

This is a crime of 'specific intent' and the prosecution would have to show an intention by the defendant to behave in a way that he or she knows will in fact endanger the life of another (*R* v *Brown and Ciarla* [1995] Crim LR 328). Therefore, the important factor is the defendant's belief, not some other person's and therefore answer A is incorrect.

That intent does not have to be an immediate one and it may be conditional (e.g. intent to shoot someone if they do not do as they are asked—see *R* v *Bentham* [1973] QB 537). Answer B is therefore incorrect.

Crime, para. 1.7.9.1

Answer 7.6

Answer **D** — This question tests understanding of two areas: the definition of imitation firearms and s. 16A of the Firearms Act 1968.

There are two types of imitation firearms: 'general imitations' (those which have the appearance of a firearm); and 'imitations of s. 1 firearms' (those which have the appearance of a s. 1 firearm, and which can be readily converted into one).

The weapon in the scenario would fall within the first part of the definition, which is why answer C is incorrect.

Under s. 16A of the 1968 Act, a person commits an offence if he or she has in his or her possession a firearm or imitation firearm, with intent by means thereof to cause any person to believe that unlawful violence would be used against him or another.

Because the offence can be committed with an imitation firearm, answer A is incorrect. There is no requirement to show that the person using the firearm actually intended to use violence against another, merely that he or she intended the other person to believe unlawful violence would be used. Answer B is therefore incorrect.

Crime, para. 1.7.9.2

Answer 7.7

Answer **B** — Under s. 16A of the Firearms Act 1968, a person commits an offence if he or she has in his or her possession a firearm or imitation firearm, with intent by means thereof to cause any person to believe that unlawful violence would be used against him or another. There is no need to prove the person had the firearm in his or her physical possession—therefore answer D is incorrect.

There is no requirement to prove that the victim actually feared that violence would be used against him or her; it is the intention of the suspect to cause that fear that is important and for that reason answer A is incorrect.

While there is no need for a firearm/imitation firearm to be produced or shown to anyone, possession of a firearm/imitation firearm while making a general threat to someone who does not know of its presence is unlikely to fall within this section. Therefore, even though KUSACK was in possession of a firearm and made a threat of violence towards SHATTOCK, the firearm did not provide the 'means' of the threat and consequently answer C is incorrect.

Crime, para. 1.7.9.2

Answer 7.8

Answer **D** — Under s. 17(2) of the Firearms Act 1968, a person is guilty if he is in possession of a firearm (or imitation) at the time of committing or being arrested for either committing or attempting an offence listed in sch. 1.

There is a list of offences in sch. 1 and some of these are indictable offences. However, as not all the offences mentioned in sch. 1 are indictable, answer B is incorrect.

Answer A is incorrect because the offence may be committed by possessing the firearm while being arrested for a sch. 1 offence regardless of any timescales between the arrest and the original offence (or whether the offender even had the firearm with him when that offence was committed).

The offence includes attempting to commit a sch. 1 offence and therefore answer C is incorrect.

Crime, para. 1.7.9.5

Answer 7.9

Answer **B** — Section 20 of the Firearms Act 1968 states:

(1) A person commits an offence if, while he has a firearm or imitation firearm with him, he enters or is in any building or part of a building as a trespasser and without reasonable excuse (the proof whereof lies on him).

So it is irrelevant whether he entered as a trespasser; if he enters and then becomes a trespasser this offence can still be committed; answer A is incorrect as it states that entry as a trespasser is required. It is possession in the building that makes the offence, not leaving the building with the firearm; answer D is therefore incorrect.

Air weapons are covered by this legislation; if the relevant firearm is an imitation or an air weapon, the offence is triable summarily; answer C is therefore incorrect.

Crime, para. 1.7.10.2

Answer 7.10

Answer **A** — This offence is similar to s. 17(2) of the Firearms Act 1968 (possession while committing or being arrested for a sch. 1 offence), and the person would be guilty of an offence under that section. However, an offence under s. 18 requires a person to have with him a firearm either at the time of committing an indictable offence, or when resisting arrest or preventing the arrest of another for such an offence. 'Have with him' may include nearby in his car, but would not include in a house as it would not be readily available to him. In *R* v *Bradish* [2004] LTL 2 April, the Court of Appeal held that the defendant did not have a firearm 'with him' when it was in his house a few miles away from the scene. Answers B and C are incorrect because this offence does not include being in 'possession', which has a wider meaning than 'has with him'.

Answer D is incorrect, as 'indictable offence' will include offences which are triable either way.

Crime, para. 1.7.9.4

Answer 7.11

Answer **A** — Section 21A of the Firearms Act 1968 states:

(1) A person commits an offence if—
   (a) he has with him an air weapon on any premises; and
   (b) he uses it for firing a missile beyond those premises.
(2) In proceedings against a person for an offence under this section it shall be a defence for him to show that the only premises into or across which the missile was fired were premises the occupier of which had consented to the firing of the missile (whether specifically or by way of a general consent).

This makes it an offence for a person of any age to fire an air weapon beyond the boundary of premises; answer B is therefore incorrect. It is the 'firer' who commits the offence, not the responsible adult; answer D is therefore incorrect.

The defence would not be available where the missile ended up on a public street; answer C is therefore incorrect.

Crime, para. 1.7.7.1

Answer 7.12

Answer **B** — Under s. 28(1) of the Violent Crime Reduction Act 2006, a person is guilty of an offence if he or she uses another to look after, hide or transport a dangerous weapon for him or her, and he or she does so under arrangements or in circumstances that facilitate, or are intended to facilitate, the weapon's being available to him or her for an unlawful purpose.

A 'dangerous weapon' includes a firearm *other than* an air weapon or a component part of, or accessory to, an air weapon. Answer D is therefore incorrect.

Also included are weapons to which ss. 141 and 141A of the Criminal Justice Act 1988 apply. These include specified offensive weapons, such as knuckledusters, stealth knives and a host of other weapons (s. 141). Answer A is therefore incorrect.

One of the reasons this offence was introduced was to prevent adults from using children to hide weapons. Using a minor to mind a dangerous weapon is an aggravating factor, attracting a harsher sentence. However, this does not mean that the offence is incomplete when the weapon is being looked after by another adult and the offence is complete in these circumstances alone. Answer C is therefore incorrect.

Crime, para. 1.7.9.6

Answer 7.13

Answer **B** — Under s. 21A(1) of the Firearms Act 1968, a person commits an offence if—

(a) he has with him an air weapon on any premises; and
(b) he uses it for firing a missile beyond those premises.

This offence was inserted by the Violent Crime Reduction Act 2006 to close a loophole in the law by making it an offence for a person of *any* age to fire an air weapon beyond the boundary of premises. Prior to the introduction of this section the offence only related to persons under the age of 17. Answers A and D are therefore incorrect.

Under s. 21A(2) of the Act, it shall be a defence for a person to show that the only premises into or across which the missile was fired were premises the occupier of which had consented to the firing of the missile (whether specifically or by way of a general consent). In this question, the neighbour had not consented specifically or generally and DENCH's belief (reasonable or otherwise) that they would have consented is not covered in this defence; therefore answer C is incorrect.

Crime, para. 1.7.7.1

Answer 7.14

Answer **B** — Under s. 21 of the Firearms Act 1968, a person who has been sentenced to life imprisonment or three years' imprisonment (which includes detention in a youth offender institution) must not at any time have a firearm in his or her possession.

Note that the restriction applies to a person sentenced, and therefore it is immaterial that DE'SOUZA did not serve his whole sentence.

Answer A would be correct if DE'SOUZA had been sentenced to less than three years' detention (also covered by s. 21 of the Act). Answer C is merely a false statement and therefore incorrect.

As detention in a young offenders' institution is included, answer D is incorrect.

Crime, para. 1.7.11

Answer 7.15

Answer **B** — Under s. 12 of the Licensing Act 1872, it is an offence to be in possession of any loaded firearm, while drunk. Therefore, since KEETLEY did not load a cartridge into the shotgun, he would not be liable for this offence (and therefore answer D is incorrect). There is no requirement for the person to be in a public place for this offence to be made out. Therefore it may be committed on private premises (answer A is therefore incorrect). Had KEETLEY loaded the shotgun, he would have committed an offence, and answer C would have been correct. Since he did not, answer C is incorrect.

Crime, para. 1.7.12

Answer 7.16

Answer **D** — Two powers are provided under s. 47 of the Firearms Act 1968. First, a constable may require a person in a public place to hand over a firearm for examination (the purpose being to detect offences).

A further power is provided by s. 47 to examine a weapon from a person elsewhere than in a public place—provided the officer has reasonable cause to suspect the person is committing or is about to commit a relevant offence (offences in ss. 18 and 20 of the Act apply). Consequently, answers A and C are incorrect.

Answer B is incorrect because the power is provided to enter premises to search for or examine a firearm only—not to arrest (although an arrest may well be necessary if a firearm is found).

Crime, para. 1.7.13

Answer 7.17

Answer **C** — Section 32(2) of the Firearms (Amendment) Act 1997 requires that any person who is the holder of a certificate or permit who is involved in selling, letting on hire, lending or giving a s. 1 firearm or ammunition (which includes lending a shotgun for a period of more than 72 hours) to another must, within seven days of the transfer, give notice to the chief officer of police who granted the certificate or permit (s. 33(2)).

Answers A, B and D are therefore incorrect.

Crime, para. 1.7.15

8 | Racially and Religiously Aggravated Offences

STUDY PREPARATION

This chapter deals with those offences which are racially and religiously aggravated offences; these offences were introduced by the Crime and Disorder Act 1998. The 1998 Act does not create new offences but takes existing offences and sets out circumstances in which those existing offences become racially or religiously aggravated. The 'aggravated' form of the offence carries a higher maximum penalty than the ordinary form of the offence.

Students will have to be aware of when certain assault, public order, criminal damage and harassment offences become racially or religiously aggravated.

QUESTIONS

Question 8.1

Constable MURPHY is an Asian officer and is foot patrol when he comes across a group of youths. They start shouting and swearing at him calling him a 'Paki terrorist'. Their behaviour amounts to an offence contrary to s. 5 of the Public Order Act 1986.

The behaviour demonstrated by the offenders amounts to racial or religious hatred. In relation to that, which of the following is correct?

A In these circumstances the offenders can *only* be charged with the public order offence as it is only offences under s. 4 and s. 4A that can be racially aggravated.

B In these circumstances the offenders can *only* be charged with the public order offence as no public order offence can be racially aggravated.

C The offenders can be charged with a racially aggravated s. 5 offence as the offence is made out.

D The offenders can be charged with a racially aggravated s. 5 offence provided the officer gave the statutory warning.

Question 8.2

PARLAND went to a local kebab shop following a night out with his friends. Having purchased a kebab he feared he had been overcharged and asked for a refund, which was refused. The owner of the kebab shop then asked him to leave or the police would be called. Grudgingly PARLAND went outside and walked away; after about 20 yards he kicked a parked car and was heard to say 'bloody immigrants' as he did so. The car was damaged. The owner of the kebab shop was in fact not an immigrant, having been born in England, and the car did not belong to him.

Has PARLAND committed racially aggravated criminal damage?

A Yes, as the offence committed was aggravated by racism.

B Yes, as the hostility shown was based on the shop owner's membership or presumed membership of a racial or religious group.

C No, as the offence committed was not aggravated by racism, merely accompanied by it.

D No, as the victim was not the subject of the membership or presumed membership of a racial or religious group.

Question 8.3

SPEIGHT has a hatred of Muslims. He sees PATHAN in the street one day and assaults him occasioning actual bodily harm. When questioned he states he assaulted him because he thought he was a Muslim based on the colour of his skin. In fact PATHAN is an agnostic of Indian origin.

Would this be a religiously aggravated assault?

A Yes, as the hostility was based on the victim's presumed membership of a religious group.

B Yes, as the hostility was based on the colour of the victim's skin.

C No, as PATHAN is not a member of the religious group against whom the hostility was meant.

D No, as PATHAN is not a member of any religious group.

Question 8.4

Constable GOUGH is investigating a criminal damage offence; red paint has been poured all over the car of an Asian family. They claim that it was done because they recently bought out a local shop and that had caused local friction. Police identified the suspect, the previous shop owner, and when they arrest him several days later he said 'Fucking Paki, ought to go home and stop stealing our jobs'.

Is this a racially aggravated offence?

A Yes, as there is clear hostility towards the Asian family based on their race.

B Yes, at the time the offence was committed there was a racial motive.

C No, the racial comment was not made at the time the offence was committed.

D No, as the comment made on arrest does not refer to the offence committed directly.

Question 8.5

GRIFFIN is a white male Rastafarian. One day he returns home to find 'Hope you die, you Devil worshiper' daubed in paint all over his front door. A suspect is identified and arrested; he claims he believes all Rastafarians to be of the Devil as they don't believe in God.

Is this a case of religiously aggravated criminal damage?

A Yes, as at the time the damage was committed there is clear hostility.

B Yes, as the offender admits that there was a religious motive to the crime.

C No, as Rastafarians are not a specific religious group as they have no religious views.

D No, as there is no evidence of hostility carried out immediately before or after the offence was committed.

Question 8.6

SWEENEY is appearing in Crown Court for causing grievous bodily harm to KHAN. The prosecution hopes to prove that the assault was racially motivated by relying on evidence from witnesses who overheard SWEENEY boasting the following day, 'I'm glad I did it, somebody's got to sort these Arabs out'. However, the prosecution is not able to present witness evidence of SWEENEY making any such statements before or during the assault.

In these circumstances, are SWEENEY's actions likely to pass the test for 'racial aggravation' as outlined in s. 28 of the Crime and Disorder Act 1998?

A Yes, if the prosecution can show that the offence was motivated by hostility towards KHAN's racial group.

B Yes, the offence is made out on these facts alone.

C No, because SWEENEY did not make the statement immediately after the assault.

D No, because SWEENEY did not make the statement during the assault, or immediately before or immediately afterwards.

Question 8.7

WOODS appeared in court charged with a racially aggravated assault against ADAMS, a door supervisor, who had refused him entry into a night club. It is alleged that at the time of assaulting ADAMS, WOODS shouted, 'Let me in, you black bastard'. WOODS did not deny assaulting ADAMS, or uttering the words, but contested the racially aggravated element of the offence, stating he was motivated by frustration rather than racism when he uttered the words. When giving evidence in court, ADAMS said that he was not personally upset by what WOODS had said, stating that he suffered such abuse frequently in his job.

What facts should the court take account of, when considering the racially aggravated element of the offence, as set out in s. 28(1) of the Crime and Disorder Act 1998?

A WOODS' motivation when he uttered the words.

B ADAMS' own perception of the words, and whether he was personally upset by the situation.

C Neither WOODS' motivation nor ADAMS' own perception of the words.

D Whether ADAMS or an innocent bystander would have been personally upset by the words.

ANSWERS

Answer 8.1

Answer **C** — Racially and religiously aggravated offences are a product of the Crime and Disorder Act 1998. The Act does not create new offences but takes existing offences and sets out circumstances in which those existing offences become racially or religiously aggravated.

The offences that can become racially or religiously aggravated can be grouped in four categories:

Assaults

- wounding or grievous bodily harm—Offences Against the Person Act 1861, s. 20;
- causing actual bodily harm—Offences Against the Person Act 1861, s. 47;
- common assault—Criminal Justice Act 1988, s. 39 (see chapter 1.9).

Criminal Damage

- 'simple' criminal damage—Criminal Damage Act 1971, s. 1(1) (see chapter 1.16).

Public Order

- causing fear or provocation of violence—Public Order Act 1986, s. 4;
- intentional harassment, alarm or distress—Public Order Act 1986, s. 4A;
- causing harassment, alarm or distress—Public Order Act 1986, s. 5.

Harassment

- harassment—Protection from Harassment Act 1997, s. 2;
- putting people in fear of violence—Protection from Harassment Act 1997, s. 4;
- stalking—Protection from Harassment Act 1997 s. 2A and s. 4A.

So, s. 5 POA 1986 is covered; answers A and B are therefore incorrect.

The statutory warning would not apply as long as the basic offence has been committed; answer D is therefore incorrect.

Crime, para. 1.8.2

Answer 8.2

Answer **D** — For simple criminal damage to be racially or religiously aggravated the circumstances as set out at s. 28(1)(a) of the Crime and Disorder Act 1998 apply, namely that the defendant demonstrates hostility towards the victim:

- at the time of, or
- immediately before or after

committing the offence, and that hostility is based on the victim's membership or presumed membership of a racial or religious group. The courts have shown that they are prepared to adopt a wide approach when interpreting this important legislation, however not wide enough to incorporate where the hostility is towards someone other than the actual victim of the offence. In this scenario the hostility was shown towards the kebab shop owner, however he was not the owner of the car and ultimately not the victim of criminal damage; answers A and B are therefore incorrect.

In *R v Rogers* [2005] EWCA Crim 2863 the Court of Appeal considered whether verbal abuse towards three Spanish women on the grounds of their being 'foreigners' constituted abuse towards a racial group under s. 28(4) of the Crime and Disorder Act 1998. The court agreed it was; however, it noted that the very wide meaning of racial group under s. 28(4) gives rise to a danger of aggravated offences being charged where mere 'vulgar abuse' had included racial epithets that did not truly indicate hostility to the race in question. Consequently, s. 28 should not be used unless the prosecuting authority is satisfied that the facts truly suggest that the offence was aggravated (rather than simply accompanied) by racism. This is a fine line, and police officers may have difficulty in distinguishing between the two; in this scenario had the car belonged to the shop owner would the defendant's actions have been seen to be aggravated by racism or merely accompanied by racism?

Thankfully on this occasion the distinction does not have to be made as the owner was not in fact the victim of the offence; and for this reason answer C is incorrect.

Crime, para. 1.8.3.6

Answer 8.3

Answer **A** — The test for racial or religious aggravation is set out at s. 28 of the Crime and Disorder Act 1998:

(1) An offence is racially or religiously aggravated for the purposes of sections 29 to 32 ... if—
    (a) at the time of committing the offence, or immediately before or after doing so, the offender demonstrates towards the victim of the offence hostility based on the victim's membership (or presumed membership) of a racial or religious group ...

In this extract, 'presumed' means presumed by the offender and as that is what the offender presumes here the offence is complete. Answer B would be correct if the offence was racially motivated but you were asked about religious motivation which makes that answer incorrect.

Irrespective of actual membership of a group the offence is complete where the accused presumes that membership; answers C and D are therefore incorrect.

Crime, para. 1.8.3

Answer 8.4

Answer **C** — The test for racial or religious aggravation is set out at s. 28 of the Crime and Disorder Act 1998:

(1) An offence is racially or religiously aggravated for the purposes of sections 29 to 32 ... if—
   (a) at the time of committing the offence, or immediately before or after doing so, the offender demonstrates towards the victim of the offence hostility based on the victim's membership (or presumed membership) of a racial or religious group; or
   (b) the offence is motivated (wholly or partly) by hostility towards members of a racial or religious group based on their membership of that group.

The hostility therefore would have to occur contemporaneously with the offence. In *DPP* v *Parry* [2004] EWHC 3112 (Admin) the defendant had caused damage to a neighbour's door by throwing nail polish over it. The police attended the scene some 20 minutes after the damage had occurred and spoke to the defendant who was, by that time, sitting in his own house. At this stage the defendant made comments demonstrating hostility based on the victim's membership of a racial group. The defendant was convicted of racially aggravated criminal damage but appealed against this decision—the appeal was upheld and the conviction was quashed. The court held that the wording of the statute meant that any hostility had to be demonstrated immediately before or immediately after the substantive offence and that the courts below (magistrates') had not been entitled to consider the retrospective effect of the comments made later by the defendant; answers A, B and D are therefore incorrect.

Crime, para. 1.8.3.1

Answer 8.5

Answer **A** — The key question here is was there religious hostility demonstrated immediately before or immediately after the substantive offence? In this case there clearly is as the words themselves demonstrate. Where there was just damage committed the 'hostility' could come from words said or actions done at the time, where that did not exist there could be only the basic offence, even if they were voiced later; answer B is therefore incorrect. However, here there is clear hostility based on religious grounds; answer D is therefore incorrect.

A purely religious group such as Rastafarians (who have been held not to be members of an ethnic group per se (*Dawkins* v *Crown Suppliers (Property Services Agency)* [1993] ICR 517) are covered by the aggravated forms of offences as they are a religious group. In reality, a number of racial groups will overlap with religious groups in any event—Rastafarians would be a good example. An attack on a Rastafarian might be a racially aggravated offence under s. 28 of the Crime and Disorder Act 1998 because it was based on the defendant's hostility towards a racial group (e.g. African-Caribbean) into which many Rastafarians fall. Alternatively, an attack might be made on a white Rastafarian based on the victim's religious beliefs (or lack of religious beliefs), i.e. his 'membership of a religious group'; answer C is therefore incorrect.

Crime, para. 1.8.3.7

Answer 8.6

Answer **A** — The test for racial or religious aggravation is set out at s. 28(1) of the Crime and Disorder Act 1998, which states that an offence is racially or religiously aggravated for the purposes of ss. 29 to 32 if—

(a) at the time of committing the offence, or immediately before or after doing so, the offender demonstrates towards the victim of the offence hostility based on the victim's membership (or presumed membership) of a racial or religious group; or

(b) the offence is motivated (wholly or partly) by hostility towards members of a racial or religious group based on their membership of that group.

Therefore, s. 28(1) outlines two tests—either that the crime was based on hostility demonstrated towards the victim immediately before, during or immediately after the incident, *or* that the offence is motivated (wholly or partly) by hostility towards members of a racial or religious group based on their membership of that group. Therefore provided the crime was motivated by hostility there is no need to show hostility at the time; answers C and D are therefore incorrect.

However, the prosecution must show that motivation prior to the offence taking place; answer B is therefore incorrect.

Crime, para. 1.8.3

Answer 8.7

Answer **C** — The test for racial or religious aggravation is set out at s. 28(1) of the Crime and Disorder Act 1998, which states that an offence is racially or religiously aggravated for the purposes of ss. 29 to 32 if—

(a) at the time of committing the offence, or immediately before or after doing so, the offender demonstrates towards the victim of the offence hostility based on the victim's membership (or presumed membership) of a racial or religious group; or

(b) the offence is motivated (wholly or partly) by hostility towards members of a racial or religious group based on their membership of that group.

In a case involving the abuse and assault of a doorman, the Administrative Court held that a racial insult uttered a few moments before an assault was enough to make the offence racially aggravated for the purposes of s. 29 of the Crime and Disorder Act 1998. The court also held that the *victim's own perception of the words used was irrelevant*, as was the fact that he *was not personally upset* by the situation. Similarly, the fact that the defendant might have been motivated to utter the words merely by frustration rather than racism was also irrelevant (*DPP* v *Woods* [2002] EWHC Admin 85).

Simply, under s. 28(1)(a), when the person has *demonstrated* hostility based on the victim's membership (or presumed membership) of a racial or religious group at the time of committing the offence, or immediately before or after doing so, the offence is complete regardless of his/her motivation or the perception of the victim (or some other bystander).

Answers A, B and D are therefore incorrect.

Crime, para. 1.8.3.1

9 | Non-Fatal Offences Against the Person

STUDY PREPARATION

This chapter deals with non-fatal offences against the person. It examines the definition of assault and battery; it also addresses the offences of common assault, actual and grievous bodily harm, and the differences between them. Of particular importance in this area is the required element of state of mind (*mens rea*) and how that differs between offences.

Specific confrontation in relation to police officers, designated and accredited persons is considered.

This chapter should be read in conjunction with CPS Charging Standards.

QUESTIONS

Question 9.1

Sergeant HEALY is custody officer when Constable MOORE brings in a prisoner who he has arrested for criminal damage. The prisoner claims that he has been unlawfully arrested as the property he damaged was his own, and this in fact is correct. During the booking in process the prisoner assaults Sergeant HEALY and during the investigation it becomes clear that the prisoner was unlawfully arrested by Constable MOORE.

Has an offence of 'assault police' contrary to s. 89 of the Police Act 1996 been committed in these circumstances?

A Yes, provided the custody officer at the time of the assault believed the arrest to be lawful.

B Yes, the custody officer is entitled to assume that the arrest has been lawful even if the original arrest turns out to have been unlawful.

C No, the custody officer should have made enquiries to establish the lawfulness of the arrest as the prisoner has alleged it was unlawful therefore she was not acting in the execution of her duty.

D No, as the original arrest was unlawful any detention would be unlawful and therefore the custody officer was not acting in the execution of her duty.

Question 9.2

FLAVIN throws a rock at the back of SINISGILLI, who turns round and sees the rock just before it hits him. He ducks and the rock flies over his head.

Has FLAVIN assaulted SINISGILLI?

A Yes, provided it can be shown that SINISGILLI was aware that the rock had been thrown at him.

B Yes, provided it can be shown that SINISGILLI apprehended immediate, unlawful violence.

C No, there was no direct application of force; the rock missed.

D No, as SINISGILLI did not see the rock when it was first thrown.

Question 9.3

BREWSTER attends at a blood donation centre. The nurse puts a needle in a vein in his arm to extract the blood, and BREWSTER consented to this as he wished to donate his blood. However the previous day the nurse had been struck off as she was also working as an escort girl.

Had the nurse assaulted BREWSTER?

A Yes, as consent has been obtained by fraud.

B Yes, as consent was obtained by misrepresentation.

C No, as he knew that he would be having a needle put in his arm.

D No, any medical treatment is deemed to be true consent.

Question 9.4

BRADLEY is in a night club and heavily intoxicated. He is sitting on a railing that looks over the dance floor which is about 10 feet below him. Due to his intoxication he falls off the railing and falls into a female who had been on the dance floor. She received serious injuries directly caused by BRADLEY.

Irrespective of the injuries caused which of the following is correct in relation to 'recklessness' and an 'assault' offence being committed?

A BRADLEY may have committed an assault if it was shown he jumped and did not just fall.

B BRADLEY has committed the assault as he was reckless as to whether he fell off the railing.

C BRADLEY has not committed the assault as there is no evidence of a deliberate or reckless act on his behalf.

D BRADLEY has not committed the assault as there was no deliberate application of force by him on the victim.

Question 9.5

Constable WILCE wishes to question BOON about an alleged assault. The officer attends at BOON's home address and tells him the nature of the incident. Believing that he is about to be arrested, BOON grabs hold of Constable WILCE's arm and pulls him into the doorway; he then slams the door on the officer's arm and makes good his escape. As a result of this attack, Constable WILCE's arm is broken in two places. When interviewed, BOON states that he did not intend to cause the injury, but accepts that his conduct presented a risk of some harm to the officer.

Which of the following statements is correct?

A This would not amount to a s. 18 assault, as there was no malice, i.e. premeditation.

B This would not amount to a s. 18 assault, as there was no intention to cause serious harm.

C This would amount to a s. 18 assault, as BOON intended to prevent his lawful arrest.

D This would not amount to a s. 18 assault, as BOON had not actually been arrested.

Question 9.6

BACHMAN has fallen out with his girlfriend following a heated argument. He sees her in town one afternoon with another man. BACHMAN's girlfriend is walking next to her 10-year-old child. BACHMAN punches his girlfriend on the nose, breaking it and making it bleed. The child bursts into tears fearful that he will be punched next; fearing for his life the other man runs off.

In relation to this action, which of the following is correct?

A BACHMAN has committed battery on his girlfriend and assaulted the child and the other male.

B BACHMAN has committed battery on his girlfriend and assaulted the child only.

C BACHMAN has committed battery on his girlfriend only.

D BACHMAN has committed battery on all three of them.

Question 9.7

CONTADINO is a child minder and as such is in *loco parentis* for the 4-year-old child she is minding. The child is hyperactive and CONTADINO smacks the child on the bottom resulting in reddening of the skin, which would be transient at the most. The child's father discovers this reddening and complains to the police who investigate.

In relation to this 'smacking' which of the following is correct?

A This could be charged as an assault and as CONTADINO only has *loco parentis* status she could not claim lawful chastisement.

B This could be charged as an assault and even though CONTADINO only has *loco parentis* status she could claim lawful chastisement.

C This could not be charged as an assault as CPS charging standards for common assault do not include 'reddening of the skin'.

D This could not be charged as an assault as CPS charging standards for common assault do not include injuries that are transient at the most.

Question 9.8

BRUCE is angry with his neighbour for refusing to clear up mess outside his house. BRUCE tells the neighbour 'Clear up the mess or you know what is coming'; he then takes up a martial arts stance. BRUCE is a black belt in karate and his neighbour knows this. BRUCE intends his neighbour to believe that he would be seriously hurt if he didn't comply with the threat. The neighbour does not take the threat seriously at all in fact he laughs at it.

Considering the offence of threats to kill contrary to s. 16 of the Offences Against the Person Act 1861, which of the following is correct?

A BRUCE has committed this offence as it relates to threats to kill and threats to do serious harm.

B BRUCE has committed this offence as he intends the neighbour to believe that the threat will be carried out.

C BRUCE has not committed this offence as he never actually voiced a threat to kill the neighbour.

D BRUCE has not committed this offence as the neighbour did not take it seriously.

Question 9.9

KADAR is infected with the HIV virus, and has unprotected sex with a woman he met in a nightclub. The woman consents fully to have sex with KADAR, and it was her idea not to use a condom. She contracts HIV as a direct result of this sexual encounter with KADAR.

Has KADAR committed an offence under s. 20 of the Offences Against the Person Act 1861?

A Yes, in these circumstances the offence is made out.

B Yes, provided the prosecution can show that KADAR had the relevant intent.

C No, as the woman should have been aware of the risk of having unprotected sex.

D No, as the woman consented to have sex and to have it unprotected.

Question 9.10

BRIDEWELL is facing a criminal prosecution for assault at the Crown Court. The incident occurred while BRIDEWELL was playing rugby and was a prop forward. The scrum collapsed and BRIDEWELL's opposite number broke his neck. The referee decided that BRIDEWELL deliberately dropped the scrum and sent him off. The police became involved and charged BRIDEWELL with assault. BRIDEWELL has pleaded not guilty to the offence, his defence being that, by playing rugby, the injured person had 'consented' to harm being done to him or was accepting that there was a risk of serious injury through the nature of the game.

In relation to this which of the following is correct?

A BRIDEWELL will be guilty as his act was outside the rules of the game.

B BRIDEWELL may be guilty provided it can be shown he acted deliberately outside the rules of the game to injure someone.

C BRIDEWELL will be not guilty as the other player had implied consent when he took the field of play.

D BRIDEWELL will be not guilty as the other player accepted when he entered the field there was a risk of serious injury although accidental.

Question 9.11

The Children Act 2004 sets out to protect children from 'unreasonable punishment' by parents and carers.

Which of the following statements is correct, in relation to chastisement that *cannot* be justified as reasonable punishment under the Act?

A The battery of a child under 18 cannot be justified if the injuries amount to an offence under s. 18 or 20 of the Offences Against the Person Act 1861.

B The battery of a child under 16 cannot be justified if the injuries amount to an offence under s. 18 or 20, or under s. 47 of the Offences Against the Person Act 1861.

C The battery of a child under 16 cannot be justified if the injuries amount to an offence under s. 18 or 20 of the Offences Against the Person Act 1861.

D The battery of a child under 18 cannot be justified if the injuries amount to an offence under s. 18 or 20, or under s. 47 of the Offences Against the Person Act 1861.

Question 9.12

PLANTZ has been knocked over by a car and has sustained injuries as a result of this deliberate act.

In relation to a possible 'assault' charge contrary to the Offences Against the Person Act 1861 which of the following is correct?

A Although there are injuries, only relevant driving offences can be considered.

B An assault charge could be preferred as long as the injuries amounted to actual bodily harm (s. 47).

C An assault charge could be preferred as long as the injuries amounted to grievous bodily harm (s. 20).

D An assault charge could be preferred as long as the injuries amounted to grievous bodily harm with intent to do him grievous bodily harm (s. 18).

Question 9.13

PLEGGE and his girlfriend were having a stormy time in their relationship. PLEGGE was very upset when he discovered that she had been having an affair with her beauty therapist, who had helped manicure and keep her very long and polished nails. It had taken over two years to get her nails to the point where she thought they were perfect. Whilst she slept PLEGGE took some nail clippers and cut off one nail from each of his girlfriend's hands; needless to say she was less than happy and complained to the police that she had been assaulted.

In the circumstances outlined, would the actions of PLEGGE amount to an assault?

A This could only ever amount to a common assault, as she was asleep when the nails were cut.

B This could have amounted to assault occasioning actual bodily harm, but only if the girl had been awake and resisted the cutting.

C This could amount to assault occasioning actual bodily harm in these circumstances.

D This is not an assault at all; the nail beyond the cuticle is dead tissue, and in any event can be grown again.

Question 9.14

GREENDALE is driving along a road when he passes a white van parked in a lay-by that he believes to be a safety camera van carrying out speed enforcement. He starts flashing his headlights and puts his hand out of the window waving it up and down. His intention was to alert motorists driving towards the white van that a speed enforcement check was being carried out. In fact the van was just parked up at a burger bar and not carrying out speed enforcement checks at that time. Also there did not appear to be any cars driving on the road at excessive speeds.

In these circumstances has GREENDALE committed an offence of wilfully obstructing a constable contrary to s. 89 of the Police Act 1996?

A Yes, as he intended to obstruct the speed check; the fact he did not is irrelevant.

B Yes, as he took positive steps to make it more difficult for the officers to perform their duty by flashing his lights and waving his arm.

C No, as the officers were not performing their duty at the time.

D No, as there is no evidence that drivers are committing or about to commit the speeding offence.

Question 9.15

SELF separated from his wife when she became pregnant by another man three months ago. He has instructed a solicitor, TERRIGHTY, to represent him at divorce proceedings and has written a letter to TERRIGHTY. Part of the letter stated, 'I do not wish to take the child's life after it is born but…the Law will take its course after I get rid of it, and I hope prison won't be too bad'.

Which of the following statements is correct?

A This would be a threat to kill provided the solicitor feared it would be carried out.

B This would be a threat to kill provided SELF intended that it would be believed.

C This would not amount to a threat to kill, as the threat is not immediate or in the immediate future.

D This would not amount to a threat to kill, as the threat is merely implied and not direct.

Question 9.16

STOKES is a sergeant in the force firearms team and is carrying out an early morning raid to arrest an armed robber; the robber has been violent to officers in the past and threatened an old lady with a firearm during the robbery. Sergeant STOKES enters the bedroom where the robber is asleep in bed. The officer points his MP5 at the suspect and says 'No old women this time, big boys' games now, twitch and I'll waste you'. However the robber is not concerned about the threat and smiles at Sergeant STOKES.

Has the sergeant committed an offence of threats to kill contrary to s. 16 of the Offences Against the Person Act 1861?

A Yes, he has made a threat and pointed a firearm at the robber.

B Yes, provided he intended to scare the robber into thinking he might be shot.

C No, as the robber was unconcerned.

D No, as the officer was carrying out his lawful duty in executing a warrant of arrest.

ANSWERS

Answer 9.1

Answer **B** — Section 89 of the Police Act 1996 states:

(1) Any person who assaults a constable in the execution of his duty, or a person assisting a constable in the execution of his duty, shall be guilty of an offence...

This offence requires that the officer was acting in the execution of their duty when assaulted.

Where a prisoner is arrested and brought before a custody officer, that officer is entitled to assume that the arrest has been lawful. Therefore, if the prisoner goes on to assault the custody officer, that assault will nevertheless be an offence under s. 89(1) even if the original arrest turns out to have been unlawful (*DPP* v *L* [1999] Crim LR 752).

There is no need to believe or establish whether the original arrest was lawful as there is an automatic entitlement to assume it was lawful for the custody officer to still be acting in the execution of their duty; answer A, C and D are therefore incorrect.

Crime, para. 1.9.8.2

Answer 9.2

Answer **B** — Assault and battery are, strictly speaking, two separate things. What people generally think of as being an 'assault' (e.g. a punch on the nose) is a 'battery', that is, the infliction of unlawful force on someone else. While it would cover a punch on the nose, an 'assault' in its proper legal sense has a much wider meaning and includes any act whereby the defendant 'intentionally—or possibly recklessly—causes another person to apprehend immediate and unlawful personal violence' (*Fagan* v *Metropolitan Police Commissioner* [1969] 1 QB 439). Although the terms have distinct legal meanings they are often referred to as simply 'assaults' or 'common assault'.

The *mens rea* needed to prove a 'basic' assault is either:

- an intention to cause apprehension of immediate unlawful violence, or
- subjective recklessness (i.e. foresight) as to that consequence.

On the part of the victim, the state of mind is an 'apprehension' of immediate unlawful violence. If X threw a stone at Y, who has his/her back to X when the stone is thrown, and the stone sails past Y's head without Y noticing it, there would be no assault as Y did not 'apprehend' unlawful violence. However, if Y turns round and fears the rock will hit him/her, immediate unlawful violence, then there has been an 'assault'; answers A, C and D are therefore incorrect.

Crime, para. 1.9.3

Answer 9.3

Answer **C** — This question deals with situations where the consent of the victim has been obtained by fraud. In *R* v *Richardson* [1999] QB 444 a dentist (Diane Richardson), who had been suspended by the General Dental Council, continued practising dentistry. The suspension came to light and charges of assault were brought. Although initially convicted, the Court of Appeal quashed the conviction on the basis that fraud will only negate consent if it relates to the identity of the person or to the nature and quality of the act. Richardson did not lie about her identity (identity here does not relate to qualifications—your name is your identity) nor about the nature and quality of the act (the dentistry carried out). While her behaviour was reprehensible, it did not amount to an offence. In the question scenario there was no fraud in relation to having a needle put in the arm so consent was not obtained by fraud or misrepresentation; answers A and B are therefore incorrect.

This does not mean that a person without appropriate qualifications sneaking into a surgery and putting on a white coat and calling themselves 'Doctor' followed by their true name could avoid liability if they then made physical contact with another in the guise of providing treatment. While there is plainly no fraud as to identity, any treatment carried out would certainly be caught by a fraud in respect of the nature and quality of the act. Consent would also be negated if a genuine doctor indecently touched his patients on the basis that this was part of a routine medical examination when its true purpose was for sexual gratification (see *R* v *Tabassum* [2000] 2 Cr App R 328); answer D is therefore incorrect.

Crime, para. 1.9.5.1

Answer 9.4

Answer **C** — The *mens rea* needed to prove assault is either:

- an intention to cause apprehension of immediate unlawful violence, or
- subjective recklessness (i.e. foresight) as to that consequence.

When considering the *mens rea of* any assault, it is important to separate the assault or battery from *any further consequences caused by* that assault or battery. The *mens rea* needed for the assault/battery is set out previously. If a defendant's behaviour causes another to fear immediate and unlawful personal violence, he/she commits an 'assault' provided it can be shown that, at the time, the defendant *intended* to cause that fear or was *subjectively reckless* as to whether such a fear would result from his/her actions; answer D is therefore incorrect.

So what happens where the defendant's actions cause more than just fear, they cause more serious injury? This appears to depend on the extent of the injury and the wording of the offence charged. Among the more serious offences under the Offences Against the Person Act 1861 are causing 'actual bodily harm' (s. 47) and 'wounding' or inflicting/causing 'grievous bodily harm' (ss. 18 and 20). The *mens rea* required for an offence under s. 47, causing actual bodily harm, is the same as that required for the basic offence of assault (*R* v *Savage* [1992] 1 AC 699). This is because s. 47 makes no specific requirement for any greater degree of *mens rea* by the defendant and, in effect, the offence of causing actual bodily harm becomes simply an assault or battery with a more serious outcome. From the defendant's point of view this is really pot luck because there is no requirement for him/her to have intended or even foreseen the actual bodily harm.

So therefore in a 'battery' there has to be an application of force. What the prosecution will need to show is that the defendant either intended to do harm to the victim or that he/she *foresaw that harm* (though not the extent of that harm) *may be caused but nevertheless went on to take that risk*. In the scenario BRADLEY may have been reckless as to whether he would fall off the balcony, but that would not be enough to convict him of assault; answer B is therefore incorrect.

Even if BRADLEY had jumped and not fallen, there would have to be evidence that he intended harm or was reckless as to harm being caused; answer A is therefore incorrect.

Crime, para. 1.9.2.1

Answer 9.5

Answer **C** — 'Maliciously' does not need premeditation but rather amounts to subjective recklessness, and the suspect admits this. He accepts that there was a risk of harm. He does not have to foresee the degree of harm and therefore answer A is incorrect. This offence has two strands:

* an intention to cause serious harm; *or*
* an intention to resist or prevent lawful apprehension.

Where, in contrast, it is alleged that the defendant merely intended to resist arrest, etc., malice becomes an important further element to be proved, and therefore answer B is incorrect. It applies to intention to prevent as well as resist arrest, and not just when someone has actually been arrested, and therefore D is incorrect.

Crime, para. 1.9.7.3

Answer 9.6

Answer **A** — A battery requires the unlawful application of force upon the victim; an assault requires an act which caused the victim to apprehend the immediate infliction of unlawful force. So the girlfriend has been 'battered' and the other two assaulted; answers B, C and D are therefore incorrect.

Crime, para. 1.9.2.2

Answer 9.7

Answer **B** — Section 58 of the Children Act 2004 removes the defence of reasonable chastisement for parents or adults acting in *loco parentis* where the accused person is charged with assault occasioning actual bodily harm (s. 47 of the Offences Against the Person Act 1861), wounding or causing grievous bodily harm (s. 18 or 20 of the Offences Against the Person Act 1861) or child cruelty (s. 1 of the Children and Young Persons Act 1933). These offences all relate to acts committed against persons less than 16 years of age.

However, the reasonable chastisement defence remains available for parents and adults acting in *loco parentis* charged with common assault under s. 39 of the Criminal Justice Act 1988; answer A is therefore incorrect. CPS charging standards state that if an injury to a child amounts to no more than reddening of the skin, and the injury is transient and trifling, a charge of common assault may be laid against the defendant for whom the reasonable chastisement defence remains available; answers C and D are therefore incorrect.

Whether the actions of the defendant are 'reasonable' will be important; physical punishment where a child is hit (causing injury reddening to the skin) with an implement such as a cane or a belt may well be considered 'unreasonable'. It is important to note that the law does not rule out physical chastisement by parents etc., but that chastisement should only constitute 'mild smacking' rather than cause injuries subject to assault charges.

Crime, para. 1.9.6

Answer 9.8

Answer **C** — The Offences Against the Person Act 1861, s. 16 (amended by the Criminal Law Act 1977, s. 65, sch. 12) states:

> A person who without lawful excuse makes to another a threat, intending that that other would fear it would be carried out, to kill that other or a third person shall be guilty of an offence.

The proviso that the threat must be made 'without lawful excuse' means that a person acting in self-defence or in the course of his/her duty in protecting life (e.g. an armed police officer) would not commit this offence (provided that his/her behaviour was 'lawful').

You must show that the threat was made (or implied, *R v Solanke* [1970] 1 WLR 1) with the intention that the person receiving it would fear that it would be carried out. It is the intention of the person who makes the threat which is important in this offence. It does not matter whether the person to whom the threat is made does fear that the threat would be carried out. The threat may be to kill another person at some time in the future or it may be an immediate threat, but the threatened action must be directly linked with the defendant. Simply passing on a threat on behalf of a third person without the necessary intent would be insufficient for this offence.

It does not include threats to commit serious harm; answers A and B are therefore incorrect.

It is the intention of the person who makes the threat which is important in this offence. It does not matter whether the person to whom the threat is made does fear that the threat would be carried out; answer D is therefore incorrect.

Crime, para. 1.9.9

Answer 9.9

Answer **A** — Section 20 of the Offences Against the Person Act 1861 does not require intent to commit grievous bodily harm (GBH), that is a s. 18 offence, and the prosecution only have to show that the accused unlawfully and maliciously inflicted GBH; therefore answer B is incorrect. Certainly contracting HIV could be said to be an 'injury resulting in some permanent disability' and as such amounts to GBH; the issue here is consent. In *R v Dica* [2004] EWCA Crim 1103, it was held that recklessness to consent, as such, was not in issue. In *Dica* the defendant had unprotected sex with two women, knowing he was HIV positive. Although both women were willing to have sexual intercourse with the defendant, the prosecution's case was that their agreement would never have been given if they had known of the defendant's condition. The defendant stated that he told both women of his condition, and that they were nonetheless willing to have sexual intercourse with him. However, the judge ruled that whether or not the complainants knew of the defendant's condition, their consent, if any, was irrelevant and provided no defence, since *R* v *Brown* [1994] 1 AC 212 deprived the complainants of the legal capacity to consent to such serious harm. In *Brown* it was held that sado-masochistic acts which occurred in private and which were consented to could found charges under the 1861 Act, ss. 20 and 47, if the injuries, though not permanent, were neither transient nor trifling. So, irrespective of the victim's willingness to place herself at risk, or to consent to sexual activity, KADAR has committed the offence; answers C and D are therefore incorrect.

Crime, paras 1.9.5.2, 1.9.7.3

Answer 9.10

Answer **B** — The Court of Appeal examined the issue of 'consent to injury' in the case of *R* v *Barnes* [2004] EWCA Crim 3246. The case was similar to the circumstances in this question and, while accepting that the tackle was hard, the defendant claimed that it had been a fair challenge and that the injury was caused accidentally. The court held that, if the actions of the defendant had been within the rules of the game being played, it would be a firm indication that what had occurred was not criminal.

However, in relation to the *Barnes* case, the court held that the threshold level was an objective one to be determined by:

- the type of sport being played;
- the level at which it was being played;
- the nature of the 'act';
- the degree of force used;
- the extent of risk of injury to the participants; and
- the state of mind of the defendant.

Therefore what is important here is the nature of the act and the extent of the injury. Clearly, just going outside the rules of the game may not be an assault; answer A is therefore incorrect. And implied consent and acceptance of a risk taken by a player who takes part in sporting activity do not necessarily equate to acceptance of being deliberately injured; answers C and D are therefore incorrect.

Crime, para. 1.9.5.1

Answer 9.11

Answer **B** — Section 58 of the Children Act 2004 provides that the battery of a person under 16 years of age (not 18, therefore answers A and D are incorrect) cannot be justified on the ground that it constituted reasonable punishment in relation to an offence under s. 47, 18 or 20 of the Offences Against the Person Act 1861. Since all three of these offences are covered, answers A and C are incorrect.

Crime, para. 1.9.6

Answer 9.12

Answer **B** — The Court of Appeal held, in the case of *R v Bain* [2005] EWCA Crim 07, that there is nothing wrong in principle with charging a driver with causing grievous bodily harm as well as dangerous driving in appropriate circumstances; answer A is therefore incorrect. It follows that bringing about other forms of lasting or significant injury with a motor vehicle could also be so charged, leaving the starting point at actual bodily harm (s. 47); consequently answers C and D are incorrect.

Crime, para. 1.9.7.4

Answer 9.13

Answer **C** — It must be shown that 'actual bodily harm' was a consequence, directly or indirectly, of the defendant's actions. Such harm can include shock (*R v Miller* [1954] 2 QB 282) and mental 'injury' (*R v Chan-Fook* [1994] 1 WLR 689).

So what is 'actual bodily harm'? In *DPP v Smith* [1961] AC 290, it was noted that the expression needed 'no explanation' and, in *Chan-Fook*, the court advised that the phrase consisted of 'three words of the English language which require no elaboration and in the ordinary course should not receive any'. So actual bodily harm appears to mean what it says. But that is not necessarily as clear as it sounds.

In *DPP v Smith (Ross Michael)* [2006] EWHC 94 (Admin) the Divisional Court took the view that in light of there being no prior decisions directly in point, cutting off a person's hair can amount to actual bodily harm; answer D is therefore incorrect.

The court was of the view that:

> It is necessary to look at definitions because there is nothing to assist us in the decided cases. In ordinary language, 'harm' is not limited to 'injury', and according to the Concise Oxford Dictionary extends to 'hurt' or 'damage'. According to the same dictionary, 'bodily', whether used as an adjective or an adverb, is 'concerned with the body'. 'Actual', as

defined in the authorities, means that the bodily harm should not be so trivial or trifling as to be effectively without significance.

Sir Igor Judge (President of the Queen's Bench Division) stated in *Smith (Ross Michael)*:

In my judgment, whether it is alive beneath the surface of the skin or dead tissue above the surface of the skin, the hair is an attribute and part of the human body. It is intrinsic to each individual and to the identity of each individual. Although it is not essential to my decision, I note that an individual's hair is relevant to his or her autonomy. Some regard it as their crowning glory. Admirers may so regard it in the object of their affections. Even if, medically and scientifically speaking, the hair above the surface of the scalp is no more than dead tissue, it remains part of the body and is attached to it. While it is so attached, in my judgment it falls within the meaning of 'bodily' in the phrase 'actual bodily harm'. It is concerned with the body of the individual victim.

This case is identical to this scenario as nails would be said to be similar to hair in this regard. So although also being a common assault, there would be a case to answer for a s. 47 assault, and this is the case whether the person was asleep or awake; answers A and B are therefore incorrect.

Crime, para. 1.9.7.2

Answer 9.14

Answer **C** — Section 89 of the Police Act 1996 states:

(2) Any person who resists or wilfully obstructs a constable in the execution of his duty, or a person assisting a constable in the execution of his duty, shall be guilty of an offence.

To prove the obstruction of a constable in the execution of their duty there are three intrinsic points.

- Was there any obstruction of a constable?
- Was the constable acting lawfully in the execution of his duty?
- Was the obstruction intended to obstruct the constable in the execution of his duty?

So in answering the points in the scenario of the question:

- There was no obstruction of the constable (no one tried to steal the officer's burger!).
- No, the officer was not performing his duty.

- It was, but linked to this is the fact that the persons warned about the speed check must be actually committing or about to commit the speeding offence.

The first two points must be established first. Without those it does not matter what actions the driver took or what his intentions were; answers A and B are therefore incorrect.

Although answer D would be fatal to this offence it is incorrect as for it to be relevant the officer would first have to be performing duty which was not the case.

Crime, para. 1.9.8.2

Answer 9.15

Answer **B** — There are two factors to be proved in the offence of threats to kill contrary to s. 16 of the Offences Against the Person Act 1861: that the threat was made and that it was made with the intention that the person receiving it would fear that it would be carried out. It does not matter whether the person whose life is threatened so fears, or whether the person receiving the threat has such a fear; therefore answer A is incorrect. An implied threat will suffice (see the facts of *R v Solanke* [1970] 1 WLR 1) and therefore answer D is incorrect. The threat may be to kill another person at some time in the future and therefore answer C is incorrect. A threat to a pregnant woman in respect of her unborn child is not sufficient if the threat is to kill it before its birth. But if it is a threat to kill the child after its birth, then that would appear to be within the section (*R v Tait* [1990] 1 QB 290).

Crime, para. 1.9.9

Answer 9.16

Answer **B** — Section 16 of the Offences Against the Person Act 1861 (amended by Criminal Law Act 1977, s. 65, sch. 12) states:

> A person who without lawful excuse makes to another a threat, intending that that other would fear it would be carried out, to kill that other or a third person shall be guilty of an offence.

The proviso that the threat must be made 'without lawful excuse' means that a person acting in self-defence or in the course of his/her duty in protecting life (e.g. an armed police officer) would not commit this offence (provided that his/her behaviour was 'lawful'). The execution of the arrest warrant may have been lawful but were the sergeant's words lawful? Answer D is therefore incorrect.

You must show that the threat was made (or implied (*R v Solanke* [1970] 1 WLR 1)) with the intention that the person receiving it would fear that it would be carried out; answer A is therefore incorrect. It is the intention of the person who makes the threat which is important in this offence. It does not matter whether the person to whom the threat is made does fear that the threat would be carried out; answer C is therefore incorrect. So if the sergeant's intention was to make the robber scared that he may be shot, and his actions are not lawful, he may have committed this offence.

Crime, para. 1.9.9

10 Miscellaneous Offences Against the Person

STUDY PREPARATION

This chapter goes on to look at less frequently occurring, yet very serious offences. These are offences such as torture, kidnapping, poisoning and hostage taking.

You are tested on what the constituent parts of these offences are, together with what 'intent' is required to prove the offence has been committed.

You may only ever come across one of these offences on the pages of an examination booklet, but your understanding of them is never the less vital, if only for that one time you do come across them!

QUESTIONS

Question 10.1

MOORE stopped his car at a bus stop and told a lone woman waiting for the bus that the bus had broken down about half a mile down the road (this was not in fact true). He offered the woman a lift. She accepted, but then asked to be let out of the car after a short distance. MOORE refused and kept the woman in his car. He reached his house and forced her down into the basement.

At what point, if any, does MOORE 'kidnap' the woman?

A He does not kidnap her, she consents to get in the car.

B He kidnaps her when she first gets into the car.

C He kidnaps her when he refuses to let her out.

D He kidnaps her when he takes her into his house.

Question 10.2

WILSON sees a young couple out walking on the common. He approaches the girl and tells her that he is a police officer and is taking her to be searched for drugs. He tells the boyfriend to go home. He then walks her to his car about 25 metres away. Her boyfriend, suspecting something is not right, returns with two other friends and rescues the girl prior to WILSON putting her in his car. WILSON is not a police officer and had an unlawful purpose in mind.

Has WILSON committed the offence of kidnapping?

A Yes, as he has taken the girl away without her consent.
B Yes, as he has taken the girl away without her consent and had an unlawful purpose.
C No, as the girl went willingly with him.
D No, as he never really took her anywhere as they were still on the common.

Question 10.3

Constable MEALAMU used his pepper spray in arresting WOODCOCK, a violent individual, during a public order incident. However at court, WOODCOCK was found not guilty and the court questioned the legality of the arrest. WOODCOCK then makes an allegation that Constable MEALAMU has assaulted him and in particular committed an offence contrary to s. 23 of the Offences Against the Person Act 1861, of poisoning him by using the pepper spray. WOODCOCK alleges that the pepper spray seriously injured his eyes.

In relation to this allegation which of the following is correct?

A This offence may be complete provided the administering of the pepper spray was unlawful.
B This offence may be complete provided the administering of the pepper spray was unlawful and malicious.
C This offence may be complete provided the administering of the pepper spray was unlawful, malicious and with intention of causing injury.
D This offence may be complete provided the administering of the pepper spray was unlawful and malicious and actually did cause grievous bodily harm.

Question 10.4

Section 134 of the Criminal Justice Act 1988 states that a public official or person acting in an official capacity, whatever his nationality, commits the offence of torture if in the United Kingdom or elsewhere he intentionally inflicts severe pain or suffering on another in the performance or purported performance of his official duties.

In relation to this torture, which of the following statements is correct in relation to the pain and suffering?

A It is immaterial whether the pain or suffering is physical or mental or whether it is caused by an act or an omission.

B It is immaterial whether the pain or suffering is physical or mental and is caused by a physical act.

C The pain or suffering is physical only and is caused by an act or an omission.

D The pain or suffering is physical only and is caused by a physical act.

Question 10.5

WAUGH is an anti-vivisectionist who sends an envelope containing white powder to a scientific institute she believes to be involved in animal experimentation. She encloses a letter stating that the powder is anthrax and that it will affect the staff and any members of the public who visit the premises. The letter states that anyone who comes in contact with the powder is likely to die. The powder was in fact talcum powder. Only the staff in the post room are aware of the threat and they do not treat it seriously.

Has an offence of using noxious substances to cause harm or intimidation under s. 113 of the Anti-terrorism, Crime and Security Act 2001 been committed by WAUGH?

A Yes, as a noxious substance includes substances made to appear noxious and there was intention to intimidate the public.

B Yes, as the powder has or is likely to induce in members of the public the fear that the action is likely to endanger their lives or create a serious risk to their health or safety.

C No, as the powder was not actually a noxious substance.

D No, as no members of the public were in fear that the action is likely to endanger their lives or create a serious risk to their health or safety.

Question 10.6

DELCOURT is a French national living in Paris. He uses false pretences to get an admin assistant from the British Embassy to come to his flat where he detains her; he then phones the Embassy and states he will kill her unless the British government adopts the Euro as its currency. In fact he has absolutely no intention of harming the girl.

Considering s. 1 of the Taking of Hostages Act 1982, has this offence been committed?

A Yes, as soon as the girl was detained against her will.

B Yes, as soon as the threat to kill her was made.

C No, although this offence can be committed outside the UK it has to involve a citizen of the UK.

D No, as there is no intention to actually harm the girl.

Question 10.7

GILGRASS invited a cold caller into his house to discuss double glazing. Some time later the cold caller alleged that GILGRASS had held him unlawfully in the house and would not let him go. GILGRASS when questioned stated that the caller had picked up a knife, he believed he was a burglar so detained him to await police arrival; however the caller escaped.

Has GILGRASS committed an offence of false imprisonment contrary to Common Law?

A Yes, as he has falsely imprisoned another person.

B Yes, as he has falsely imprisoned another person with no power of arrest.

C No, as the caller voluntarily entered the house.

D No, as he had no reasonable belief that the caller was a burglar.

ANSWERS

Answer 10.1

Answer **B** — Kidnapping is defined at common law as 'the taking or carrying away of one person by another without the consent of the person so taken or carried away, and without lawful excuse'.

The issue here is consent, and certainly the woman consents to get into the car. However, the Court of Appeal held in *R v Cort* [2003] 3 WLR 1300, that if the consent is obtained by fraud, as it was here through the lies told, then this would not be true consent. Without such consent, the offence is made out when the woman gets in the car and, as MOORE has kidnapped her, therefore answer A is incorrect. Although he further detains her, this is more the offence of false imprisonment, and happens after she is kidnapped; answers C and D are therefore incorrect.

Crime, para. 1.10.5

Answer 10.2

Answer **A** — Kidnapping is defined at common law as follows:

> It is an offence at common law to take or carry away another person without the consent of that person and without lawful excuse.

The required elements of this offence are the unlawful taking or carrying away of one person by another by force or fraud (*R v D* [1984] AC 778). These requirements go beyond those of mere restraint needed for false imprisonment. Parents may be acting without lawful excuse, for instance if they are acting in breach of a court order in respect of their children.

The taking or carrying away of the victim must be without the consent of the victim. If the victim consents to an initial taking but later withdraws that consent, the offence would be complete. If the consent is obtained by fraud, the defendant cannot rely on that consent and the offence—or attempted offence—will be made out (see *R v Cort* [2003] 3 WLR 1300); answer C is therefore incorrect. There is no limit as to how far the taking should be; answer D is therefore incorrect.

There need only be a 'taking'; the purpose is irrelevant which makes answer B incorrect.

Crime, para. 1.10.5

Answer 10.3

Answer **D** — Section 23 of the Offences Against the Person Act 1861 states:

> Whosoever shall unlawfully and maliciously administer to or cause to be administered to or taken by any other person any poison or other destructive or noxious thing, so as thereby to endanger the life of such person, or so as thereby to inflict upon such person any grievous bodily harm, shall be guilty of [an offence] …

Other than the requirement for 'malice', this offence is mainly concerned with the consequences caused to the victim and not the defendant's intentions.

'Causing to be administered' would cover indirect poisoning or even inducing someone to poison themselves. 'Administering' is a very broad term which has been held to include the spraying of gas into another's face (*R* v *Gillard* (1988) 87 Cr App R 189). As such this would appear to include the use of CS spray by police officers but the 'administering' would also have to be shown to be both unlawful and malicious, not just unlawful; answer A is therefore incorrect. There is, however, a requirement to prove a consequence with this offence, namely the endangering of a person's life or the infliction of grievous bodily harm; answer B is therefore incorrect.

There is no requirement to prove intent with s. 23; answer C is therefore incorrect.

Crime, para. 1.10.3

Answer 10.4

Answer **A** — Section 134 of the Criminal Justice Act 1988 states:

(1) A public official or person acting in an official capacity, whatever his nationality, commits the offence of torture if in the United Kingdom or elsewhere he intentionally inflicts severe pain or suffering on another in the performance or purported performance of his official duties.

(2) A person not falling within subsection (1) above commits the offence of torture, whatever his nationality, if—

    (a) in the United Kingdom or elsewhere he intentionally inflicts severe pain or suffering on another at the instigation or with the consent or acquiescence—

        (i) of a public official; or

        (ii) of a person acting in an official capacity; and

    (b) the official or other person is performing or purporting to perform his official duties when he instigates the commission of the offence or consents to or acquiesces in it.

(3) It is immaterial whether the pain or suffering is physical or mental or whether is caused by an act or an omission.

Section 134(3) then is answer A; answers B, C and D are therefore incorrect.

Crime, para. 1.10.2

Answer 10.5

Answer **C** — As well as offences of poisoning under s. 23 and s. 24 of the Offences Against the Person Act 1861 there is a further, more extreme offence of using noxious substances to cause harm or intimidation under s. 13 of the Anti-terrorism, Crime and Security Act 2001. This offence, which carries 14 years' imprisonment on indictment, occurs where a person takes any action which:

- involves the use of a noxious substance or other noxious thing (answers A and B are therefore incorrect as the powder is not 'noxious');
- has or is *likely* to have an effect set out in the following list (answer D is therefore incorrect); and
- is designed to influence the government or to intimidate the public or a section of the public.

The effects are:

- causing serious violence against a person, or serious damage to property, anywhere in the world;
- endangering human life or creating a serious risk to the health or safety of the public or a section of the public; or
- inducing in members of the public the fear that the action is likely to endanger their lives or create a serious risk to their health or safety.

Crime, para. 1.10.3.1

Answer 10.6

Answer **B** — Section 1 of the Taking of Hostages Act 1982 states:

(1) A person, whatever his nationality, who, in the United Kingdom or elsewhere—
  (a) detains any other person ('the hostage'), and
  (b) in order to compel a State, international governmental organisation, or person to do or abstain from doing any act, threatens to kill, injure or continue to detain the hostage,
  commits an offence.

So as it is 'whatever his nationality', answer C is therefore incorrect.

The offence is committed when the threat is made, not when the taking is made; answer A is therefore incorrect.

Although this is a crime of specific intent, the intent relates to the threat not the intention to carry out the threat; answer D is therefore incorrect.

Crime, para. 1.10.6

Answer 10.7

Answer **A** — It is an offence at common law falsely to imprison another person.

The elements required for this offence are the unlawful and intentional/reckless restraint of a person's freedom of movement (*R* v *Rahman* (1985) 81 Cr App R 349); this is the case whether the person voluntarily entered the place they were being held or not; answer C is therefore incorrect. Where there is a power of arrest it is a defence, not a constituent part of the offence; answer B is therefore incorrect.

A person would have a defence to a charge of false imprisonment if he/she detained a person in the genuine belief that a person was a burglar—even if this genuine belief were unreasonable (*R* v *Shwan Faraj* [2007] EWCA Crim 1033). The court held that the principle of defence of property as a defence to a charge of false imprisonment was not dependent upon whether the defendant had reasonable grounds for suspecting that the complainant was a burglar. Such defence depended only on whether the defendant in fact believed that the complainant was a burglar; answer D is therefore incorrect.

Crime, para. 1.10.4

11 | Sexual Offences

STUDY PREPARATION

Sexual offences cover a wide range of activities. In answering these questions there is a real need first of all to identify who is doing what to whom. Usually the key to the offences that arise from such activities is to be found in:

- the ages of the parties;
- the intent of the offender;
- the consent of the victim;
- the accompanying circumstances.

Until fairly recently sexual offences were subject to an Act almost half a century old—ask yourself, have sexual activity and attitudes changed since then? The existing framework was described as 'archaic, incoherent and discriminatory'. The resulting Sexual Offences Act 2003 is a landmark statute that repealed almost all of the Sexual Offences Act 1956 and many other statutory provisions enacted since, delivering, in effect, a new criminal code of sexual offences. The Sexual Offences Act 2003 not only introduces a considerable number of new offences and criminalises certain types of conduct not previously subjected to the written law, it also substantially redefines many sex crimes, incorporating new terms and language deemed more appropriate to contemporary society.

QUESTIONS

Question 11.1

HILL goes on a blind date and as they get on so well he invites the girl back to his house. At the house the girl initially agrees to have sexual intercourse with him and they then both consume a lot of alcohol; the girl is very drunk. HILL goes to the bathroom to get a condom, and prior to his return the girl falls asleep on the bed. HILL has sex with her while she sleeps.

Has HILL committed rape?

A No, as she agreed to sex prior to falling asleep and never negated that consent.

B No, as her drunkenness was self-induced and she never negated consent to sex.

C Yes, even though she agreed when she was awake she may not agree at the time HILL had sex with her.

D Yes, but the onus is on the prosecution to prove beyond doubt that there was no consent.

Question 11.2

BAINES meets a woman and begins to have a full sexual relationship with her, but she calls off the relationship. BAINES starts sending texts to her threatening harm to her if she doesn't have sex with him again; she reports the matter to Constable THOMAS. The officer begins to investigate the matter; however BAINES sends the girl a text purporting to be from Constable THOMAS stating that she should continue to have sex with BAINES until she has concluded her investigation. The girl believes the text and has sex several more times with BAINES.

In these circumstances has BAINES committed rape?

A Yes, as the girl is deceived as to the nature of the act.

B Yes, as the girl is deceived as to the identity of the text sender.

C No, as the girl was not deceived by the nature of the intercourse.

D No, as the girl was not deceived by the identity of BAINES.

Question 11.3

STONE is walking through the park in the summer when he comes across a girl sunbathing wearing only her bikini bottoms, exposing her breasts. Seeing STONE staring at her she invites him over and says 'I can show you more', he nods and she pulls her pants aside and exposes her vagina. STONE thanks her and walks off. A female was also walking past and was distressed at this behaviour and informs the police. The girl exposed herself to STONE for her own sexual gratification.

In relation to exposure contrary to s. 66 of the Sexual Offences Act 2003, which of the following is correct?

A The girl has committed the offence of exposure by deliberately exposing her breasts.

B The girl has committed the offence of exposure by deliberately exposing her vagina.

C The girl has not committed the offence of exposure as STONE was clearly not alarmed or distressed.

D The girl has not committed the offence of exposure as when she did so she did not intend to cause anyone alarm or distress.

Question 11.4

WALSH is 15 years of age, but is a mature boy who looks older than he is. He has been infatuated with his neighbour's 18-year-old daughter for some time, and wishes to have sex with her. One night they are alone in WALSH's house and he asks to have oral sex, the girl agrees and he has oral sex with the girl.

Has the girl committed an offence contrary to s. 9 of the Sexual Offences Act 2003, sexual activity with a child?

A Yes, she commits this offence when she agrees to have oral sex with him.

B Yes, she commits this offence when she actually has oral sex with him.

C No, as she did not penetrate him, he penetrated her.

D No, as this offence is committed by a person over 18 years of age.

Question 11.5

McNALLY and his girlfriend, who are both 17 years of age, are in their bedroom and are joined by McNALLY's younger brother, who is 13 years of age. Whilst the brother watches, McNALLY and his girlfriend participate in mutual masturbation and oral sex. They both know the child is present, and both are getting sexual gratification from the fact they are being watched by the brother. The brother is not offended and enjoys watching.

Is this engaging in sexual activity in the presence of a child contrary to s. 11 of the Sexual Offences Act 2003?

A Yes, as they are over 17 years of age.

B Yes, because the brother is under 14 years of age.

C No, because they are not 18 years of age or over.

D No, because the child is not offended, nor forced to watch.

Question 11.6

TRITON invites GRAHAM, who is 19 and suffering from a severe mental disorder, back to his house. TRITON then asks GRAHAM to take all his clothes off, which he willingly does. Because of his mental disorder GRAHAM is unable to refuse involvement in sexual activity. TRITON then tries to penetrate GRAHAM anally, which GRAHAM has freely agreed to. TRITON only just manages to penetrate GRAHAM, then gives up and sends GRAHAM home.

In order to prove the offence of sexual activity with a person with a mental disorder (s. 30), what does the prosecution have to show?

A That TRITON knew GRAHAM suffered from a mental disorder.

B That TRITON knew GRAHAM suffered from a mental disorder and knew he was unlikely to refuse his advances.

C That TRITON used inducements to get GRAHAM to agree to the touching.

D That TRITON coerced GRAHAM into agreeing to the touching.

Question 11.7

McMANUS's computer was found to contain thousands of indecent images of children. Most had been downloaded via an Internet file-sharing system whereby members installed software allowing files, held in their shared folder, to be accessed and downloaded directly into shared folders of other members whilst connected to the Internet. Only six of all the files downloaded were found in the defendant's shared folder, in respect of which he was charged with six counts of possessing indecent photographs or pseudo-photographs of a child with a view to their being distributed or shown by himself or others, contrary to s. 1(1)(c) of the Protection of Children Act 1978.

The defendant contended that he did not intend to distribute or show the photographs to others and, once downloaded, he usually moved the files into folders not accessible to other members. The six files in the shared folder had not yet been moved due to the process he used to download and move images in bulk.

Considering the offence contrary to s. 1(1)(c) of the Protection of Children Act 1978, has McMANUS committed this offence?

A The images in the shared folder were possessed with a view to their being distributed, and he is guilty.

B The images are being held in a file that could be accessed by other members and McMANUS is aware of this, and therefore he is guilty.

C The images are stored with a view to moving them to a private folder and as such he is not guilty of this offence.

D The images are not stored with an intention of allowing the distribution of them and as such he is not guilty of the offence.

Question 11.8

CORNELIUS lives with his prostitute girlfriend and has recently encouraged her to go to work as a prostitute for DIBLEY, a local drug dealer. CORNELIUS hopes that in providing his girlfriend, DIBLEY will supply him with cheap drugs in the future, which is likely. CORNELIUS receives no money from DIBLEY for the deal. His girlfriend is happy with this arrangement, as she will make more money working for DIBLEY.

Has CORNELIUS committed an offence of controlling prostitution for gain under s. 53 of the Sexual Offences Act 2003?

A No, there has been no gain as yet, only future hopes of gain.

B No, as CORNELIUS's girlfriend is not forced into prostitution.

C Yes, as there will be future financial advantage.

D Yes, as the prostitute will make money and she lives with CORNELIUS.

Question 11.9

MOOLES and his female secretary, MAKINS, attended a conference in Blackpool. While they were in the bar, MOOLES asked his secretary if she wanted to try some new sex drug to aid her enjoyment, as she enjoyed being overpowered. She agreed and MOOLES put it in her drink. They went upstairs to MOOLES' bedroom and started to have consensual sex. However the drug she took stupefied MAKINS and she passed out. MOOLES continued until he ejaculated.

Has MOOLES committed rape if MAKINS were to make such a complaint?

A Yes, as MOOLES administered a substance which was capable of causing the complainant to be stupefied.

B Yes, as MAKINS was unconscious MOOLES should have stopped.

C No, as MAKINS agreed to take the drug that ultimately stupefied her.

D No, as clearly MAKINS had consented to sex prior to passing out.

Question 11.10

COLLIAS is very upset that his daughter's ex-boyfriend was unfaithful to her and plans revenge. COLLIAS finds out the email address of the ex and uses a messaging service to induce him to masturbate in front of his webcam. The ex-boyfriend believes, however, that he was masturbating for the gratification of a 20-year-old girl.

Has COLLIAS committed an offence of causing a person to engage in sexual activity without consent contrary to s. 4 of the Sexual Offences Act 2003?

A Yes, as he deceived the ex-boyfriend as to the purpose of the masturbation.

B Yes, as he deceived the ex-boyfriend as to the purpose of the masturbation and by impersonating someone else.

C No, as the ex-boyfriend was not deceived as to the actual sexual activity, he knew he was being asked to masturbate.

D No, as COLLIAS did not impersonate someone known personally to the ex-boyfriend.

Question 11.11

COMETSON who is 30 years of age and his wife adopted KATIE when she was 14 years of age. KATIE becomes infatuated with COMETSON over the time when she lives with her adopted family. On her 17th birthday they have consensual sex.

Have offences contrary to ss. 64 and 65 of the Sexual Offences Act 2003, having sex with a family member, been committed?

A Yes, both COMETSON and KATIE have committed this offence.

B Yes, but only COMETSON has committed this offence.

C No, as KATIE is over 16 years of age no offence has been committed.

D No, as KATIE was adopted and is now over 16 years of age no offence has been committed.

Question 11.12

BUTCHER is a man who wishes to pay a prostitute for sexual intercourse. He has never done this before and is a bit unsure of what to do. He gets into his car and drives to a residential area he believes, mistakenly, to be a well-known red light area. He notices a lone woman standing near a bus stop. He stops beside her and says, 'Are you doing business?' Not knowing what he means she says, 'No I'm waiting for a bus, what sort of business are you looking for?'. Confused, BUTCHER drives straight home.

Which of the following is correct?

A He has committed an offence of kerb-crawling as his behaviour is likely to cause annoyance to the woman.

B He has committed an offence of kerb-crawling as he has solicited the woman from his car.

C He has not committed an offence of kerb-crawling as the woman was not offended or annoyed.

D He has not committed an offence of kerb-crawling as he did not solicit the woman on more than one occasion.

Question 11.13

LINTERN has a 15-year-old daughter, FAY, who looks older than her age. LINTERN introduced FAY to his friend, GREGORIOUN, who is a pimp. Between them, LINTERN and GREGORIOUN persuaded FAY to become a prostitute. She agreed and went out with GREGORIOUN on weekends only, and solicited in the street for prostitution. FAY's mother was aware of what was happening to her daughter and encouraged her, but refused to accept any money from what the child earned.

In relation to offences under s. 48 of the Sexual Offences Act 2003 of causing or inciting child prostitution, which of the following is true?

A GREGORIOUN has committed the offence, but LINTERN has not.

B LINTERN has committed the offence, but GREGORIOUN has not.

C LINTERN and GREGORIOUN have committed the offence in these circumstances.

D LINTERN, GREGORIOUN and the child's mother have committed the offence.

Question 11.14

POTTER downloaded some pornographic pictures of children under the age of 16 from the Internet. He took them to work and lent them to his friend, BOYD, who returned them the next day.

Who has committed an offence in relation to the photographs?

A Both: POTTER for possessing and distributing photographs; BOYD for being in possession of them.

B Only POTTER, for possessing and distributing the photographs to another person.

C Both POTTER and BOYD for possession, as photographs cannot be distributed to just one person in this way.

D Both POTTER and BOYD for possession, as the offence of distributing does not include lending.

Question 11.15

Over a three-week period, ROWLING leaves several notes in lavatories asking for interested children to get in contact with him; that is all the notes say. A male finds the notes and is outraged at the content. He alerts the police who locate and arrest ROWLING; police find a diary with notes made by ROWLING that indicate a desire for sexual activity with boys and linking him with the notes.

In relation to outraging public decency contrary to common law, which of the following is correct?

A The offence is committed as a member of the public was outraged by the notes.

B The offence is complete as ROWLING intended to be lewd and obscene with children.

C The offence is not complete as ROWLING did not actually contact any children directly.

D The offence is not complete as the notes are not lewd or obscene.

Question 11.16

STREETER is very keen to have sexual intercourse with BETTY. She tells him she is only interested in his friendship and wants nothing more than that. One night STREETER decides that she will have sex with him if he forces the issue, so he hides outside her bedroom window on the ledge, intent on entering and having sex with BETTY. He intends to force her to have sex, although he honestly believes she wants to. He breaks the window and enters the house. However, she is not in the house.

Which of the following is true in relation to the Sexual Offences Act 2003, regarding STREETER's intent?

A STREETER commits an offence when he breaks the bedroom window.

B STREETER commits an offence when he hides outside the bedroom window.

C STREETER does not commit an offence, as he has an honest belief and no sex took place.

D STREETER does not commit an offence, as BETTY was not in the house.

Question 11.17

REYNOLDS, aged 48 years, owns a sweet shop, which he uses to further his paedophilic desires. He sees BEN, who is 12 years old, in the shop and has desires to touch him sexually. He arranges to meet BEN later in the local park. He has never met BEN before. He walks to the park at about 7 pm, and meets BEN by the swings. BEN realises something is wrong and runs off before REYNOLDS can touch him.

At what point, if any, does REYNOLDS commit an offence under s. 15 of the Sexual Offences Act 2003, on child grooming?

A When he arranges to meet the child.

B When he starts walking to meet the child.

C When he first meets the child in the park.

D He does not commit the offence as he has not previously communicated with the child.

Question 11.18

RICH is a biology teacher at the local high school, and ELAINE is a 16-year-old pupil in his class. They are very friendly and ELAINE adores RICH, and they converse frequently in an Internet chatroom. RICH sends indecent still photographs in an email to ELAINE's school computer terminal from his; they are very explicit pictures. ELAINE loves the pictures and is not in the least concerned by them. RICH receives sexual gratification from knowing that ELAINE looks at the pictures, and if questioned by the school he will say it is part of a sex education programme.

Has RICH committed an offence under s. 19 of the Sexual Offences Act 2003 an abuse of position of trust causing a child to watch a sexual act?

A Yes, but only because ELAINE is a pupil in his class.

B Yes, but only because of the sexual gratification he gets.

C No, this offence only applies to a child under 16 years of age.

D No, because they are still pictures and not a 'moving image'.

Question 11.19

FOWLER is the manager of a gym, and has recently been subject to a number of thefts of personal property from clients using the sunbeds. To combat this he gets permission from all the clientele to install a hidden camera in this area. The clients agree to the camera recording the activities in this area of the gym, and for it to be viewed by the police should a further theft occur. No permission was obtained for FOWLER to view the recording 'live'. All the clientele also agree to wear underwear during the time the camera is installed. A camera is installed and begins to record; unknown to the clientele FOWLER has a fetish about women walking round in their underwear and although his original intention was to try to catch the thief he now starts to watch the recording 'live' expressly for his own sexual gratification.

In these circumstances has FOWLER committed an offence of voyeurism contrary to s. 67 of the Sexual Offences Act 2003?

A No, as he has permission from the clients to film them and as such cannot commit this offence.

B No, as the persons using the sunbeds are wearing underwear and not exposing any part of their 'private' areas.

C Yes, although he had permission to film he did not have permission to view the video 'live'.

D Yes, as the clientele were unaware of the purpose formed after the camera was installed he commits this offence.

Question 11.20

WILIAMS is a 32-year-old female. She was walking down the street when a male, JONES, approached her and said 'any chance of a blow job darling?'. WILIAMS walked away, but was approached again by JONES who asked if she was shy or a lesbian. JONES then tried to pull WILIAMS towards him by grabbing at a pocket that was located at the side seam of WILIAMS's trousers. WILIAMS is greatly offended by this and she believes it to be sexual.

Is this an offence of sexual touching contrary to s. 3 of the Sexual Offences Act 2003?
A No, because JONES did not touch a part of the body itself as is required by the legislation.
B No, because JONES did not touch a sexual organ as is required by the legislation.
C Yes, because of the purpose of JONES' actions and 'touching' includes clothing.
D Yes, because WILIAMS thought that it was sexual and 'touching' includes clothing.

Question 11.21

STRACHAN receives an email from a friend that includes an attachment he knows contains pornographic images. He downloads and then opens the attachment, which is several pages long. He views adult females engaged in various sexual activities and then leaves the room where the computer is. On the page after the one he was look-ing at are several images of children that are indecent in content. STRACHAN is una-ware that there are sexually explicit pictures of children in the attachment, and has not seen them himself.

Has STRACHAN committed an offence contrary to s. 160 of the Criminal Justice Act 1988?
A Yes, because he downloaded images he knew would contain pornographic mate-rial, irrespective of his knowledge of its contents.
B Yes, because he has opened the attachment containing the pornographic images, irrespective of his knowledge of its contents.
C No, but only because he had not seen the images of the children.
D No, provided he had no cause to suspect it to be an indecent photograph of a child and he had not seen the images.

Question 11.22

BOUNEKHLA is travelling on a train in rush hour and is standing in a very crowded carriage. He is pressed up against a woman and his penis becomes erect. His penis is then touching the woman's back and BOUNEKHLA ejaculates in his trousers, but the semen does not go on the woman. The woman is completely unaware of this incident and, apart from putting his penis against her, BOUNEKHLA does not actually touch the woman.

Would this amount to sexual touching as defined in s. 79(8) of the Sexual Offences Act 2003?

A Yes, even though BOUNEKHLA never actually touched the woman.

B Yes, provided BOUNEKHLA's actions had a sexual intent when he put his penis against the woman.

C No, the woman is never aware of the incident and no semen is on her clothing.

D No, as BOUNEKHLA never touched the woman physically with any part of his body.

Question 11.23

KRUGER invites a girl back to his house and they begin to kiss, with full consent. KRUGER asks the young lady if she would mind him touching her toes through her stockings. She thinks this is amusing and fully allows him to do so. He rubs her toes for a bit and then lets out a large groan. The lady realises that he has just ejaculated and is horrified. She states she would never have let it happen if she had known there was a sexual motive.

Would this be 'sexual touching' and therefore a sexual assault committed by KRUGER?

A Yes, as KRUGER received sexual gratification from it and the lady would not have consented had she known the circumstances.

B Yes, as the lady believed the touching to be sexual and would not have consented had she known the circumstances.

C No, as touching toes is not sexual by its nature.

D No, as touching toes is not sexual by nature and cannot be made so even by the purpose of the person doing it.

Question 11.24

PARISH has recently had gender reassignment surgery where the penis was removed and replaced with a surgically constructed vagina. Whilst out in a pub PARISH meets a man she finds very attractive, and she invites him back to her flat.

They begin kissing and PARISH allows the male to digitally penetrate her vagina. The male then removes a small dildo from his back pocket and starts to use it to penetrate PARISH's vagina. She asks him to stop as she does not want to risk damaging her reconstructive surgery. She firmly tells him 'no', but he does so anyway, laughing.

Which of the following statements is correct in relation to a sexual assault contrary to s. 2 of the Sexual Offences Act 2003?

A A surgically constructed vagina is not included in this offence.

B This offence is only committed by using a body part for penetration, not an inanimate object.

C The offence here is not committed as PARISH agreed to digital penetration.

D The offence is committed as PARISH did not consent to penetration by the dildo.

Question 11.25

STEGMAN intends to rape a woman during a music festival. He hides inside her tent and intends then dragging her into the nearby woods where he intends committing the offence. He had spoken to the woman at the canteen and she had said to come back to her tent later. She meant when she was there, and STEGMAN never confirmed this.

Has STEGMAN committed the offence of trespass with intent to commit a relevant sexual offence contrary to s. 63 of the Sexual Offences Act 2003?

A Yes, provided it can be proved that he knows he is a trespasser and intends to commit a sexual offence.

B Yes, as he knows or is at least reckless as to whether he is a trespasser and intends to commit a sexual offence.

C No, as he does not intend to commit the offence in the tent.

D No, as he is not a trespasser in a building or part of a building or accommodation with a degree of permanence.

Question 11.26

BELENKI was found with an image on his computer of a woman and a dead horse. The woman had the horse's penis in her mouth.

Considering s. 63 of the Criminal Justice and Immigration Act (extreme pornographic images), which of the following is correct?

A This would be an offence if the 'reasonable person' looking at the image would think it was grossly offensive.

B This would be an offence provided it was produced solely or principally for the purpose of sexual arousal.

C This would not be an offence as the animal was dead at the time the photograph was taken.

D This would not be an offence as the animal was dead at the time the photograph was taken, and the 'reasonable person' looking at the image would think that the animal was dead.

Question 11.27

MARKU is involved in exploiting girls for prostitution. He accepts payment from CROSS for the services of a prostitute. MARKU then persuades a young illegal immigrant to have sex with CROSS and tells her that if she does he will ensure that she will get political asylum in the UK. MARKU has absolutely no way of being able to influence the immigration status of the girl; however he intends giving the girl half of the money paid by CROSS. CROSS has no idea that MARKU has used a deception on the girl.

Considering the offence of paying for sexual services of a prostitute subjected to force contrary to s. 53A of the Sexual Offences Act 2003 (as amended), which of the following is correct?

A Both MARKU and CROSS have committed this offence as CROSS has made payment and MARKU has benefited.

B Only CROSS has committed this offence as he has made payment; MARKU has not committed this offence at all.

C Only CROSS has committed this offence as he has made payment; MARKU has not committed this offence as he has offered to share the benefits with the prostitute.

D Only MARKU commits this offence as CROSS knows nothing about the exploitative conduct committed by MARKU.

ANSWERS

Answer 11.1

Answer **C** — The Sexual Offences Act 2003 still has consent as a key issue in rape. 'Consent' is defined by s. 74 as follows: 'For the purposes of this Part, a person consents if he agrees by choice, and has the freedom and capacity to make that choice.'

Sections 75 and 76 of the 2003 Act apply to rape, and s. 75 provides for presumptions that the person did not, in certain circumstances, consent *per se*:

(2) The circumstances are that—
    (a) any person was, at the time of the relevant act or immediately before it began, using violence against the complainant or causing the complainant to fear that immediate violence would be used against him;
    (b) any person was, at the time of the relevant act or immediately before it began, causing the complainant to fear that violence was being used, or that immediate violence would be used, against another person;
    (c) the complainant was, and the defendant was not, unlawfully detained at the time of the relevant act;
    (d) the complainant was asleep or otherwise unconscious at the time of the relevant act ...

This means that as the girl was asleep when intercourse took place, and HILL knew she was asleep, the complainant will be presumed *not* to have consented to the act and the defendant will be presumed *not* to have reasonably believed that the complainant consented.

Answer A is incorrect because, even though earlier consent was given, at the time of the act consent was presumed absent, even though the girl's condition was due to self-intoxication (which also makes answer B incorrect). This places an evidential burden upon the defendant, and not the prosecution, which makes answer D incorrect. The judge must be satisfied that the defendant can produce 'sufficient evidence' to justify putting the issue of consent before a jury; lack of such evidence will result in a direction to the jury to find the defendant guilty.

Crime, para. 1.11.3.3

Answer 11.2

Answer **C** — Rape requires the absence of consent and as such both ss. 75 and 76 of the Sexual Offences Act 2003 (evidential presumptions of consent) must apply. The scenario of this question relates to s. 76. It is important to emphasise the fact that s. 76 deals with situations where the defendant either:

(i) deceives the victim regarding the nature and purpose of the act; or
(ii) deceives the victim regarding the identity of the person who is carrying out the act.

If the deception does not relate to either of these aims then s. 76 has no application. For example, in *R* v *Jheeta* [2007] EWCA Crim 1699, the defendant deceived the complainant into having sex more frequently than she would have done otherwise. In these circumstances the conclusive presumptions under the Sexual Offences Act 2003 had no relevance as the complainant had not been deceived as to the nature or purpose of the sexual intercourse. She knew what the nature of the sexual act was and she knew who BAINES was; the deception as to the sender of the text is of no relevance. As she knew the nature of the act and the identity of the person carrying out the act this cannot be rape; answers A and B are therefore incorrect.

Even if the girl had known BAINES personally, had he stated that sex would improve her complexion then s. 76 would apply and it could be rape; answer D is therefore incorrect.

Crime, para. 1.11.3.4

Answer 11.3

Answer **D** — Section 66 of the Sexual Offences Act 2003 states:

(1) A person commits an offence if—
  (c) he intentionally exposes his genitals, and
  (d) he intends that someone will see them and be caused alarm or distress.

This offence requires only the intentional exposure of the genitals with the dual intention of them being seen by someone else and that this other person will be caused alarm or distress.

Without that intent this offence is not made out, even if someone is actually offended; answer B is therefore incorrect. However, it does not matter that someone is not distressed, provided the exposure was done with the relevant intent; answer C is therefore incorrect. A woman who exposes her breasts will not be guilty of an offence under s. 66; answer A is therefore incorrect.

Crime, para. 1.11.9.1

Answer 11.4

Answer **B** — Section 9 of the Sexual Offences Act 2003 makes it an offence for a person aged 18 or over (answer D is therefore incorrect) intentionally to engage in sexual touching of a child under 16.

It involves penetration of the victim's anus or vagina by a part of the defendant's body or anything else, of the victim's mouth with the defendant's penis, of the defendant's anus or vagina by a part of the victim's body or of the defendant's mouth by the victim's penis; answer C is therefore incorrect. It is not committed until the act actually takes place; answer A is therefore incorrect.

Crime, para. 1.11.5.1

Answer 11.5

Answer **C** — Section 11 makes it an offence for a person aged 18 or over intentionally to engage in sexual activity when a child under 16 is present, or in a place from which he can be observed by the child, the purpose of which is for obtaining sexual gratification from the presence of the child. 'Sexual' is defined by s. 78. The offence is met where the child is under 16 years of age, therefore answer B is incorrect; and is committed by those who are aged 18 or over, therefore answer A is incorrect. The offence is committed even where the child apparently consents to watching the sexual act, and does not need to cause offence; answer D is therefore incorrect.

This offence is intended to cover the situation where someone seeks sexual gratification not from the sexual act itself, but rather from the fact that he is performing that act in the presence or intended presence of a child. The motive of sexual gratification is a necessary safeguard intended to avoid capturing those who engage in sexual activity in front of a child for a legitimate reason. For example, a teacher who sexually kisses his partner just outside the school gates could be deemed to be engaging in sexual activity intentionally in front of a child, and might otherwise be caught by the offence. Note that in the circumstances of the question an offence contrary to s. 13 of the 2003 Act would have been committed as the assailant was under 18, but you were asked specifically about s. 11.

Crime, para. 1.11.5.2

Answer 11.6

Answer **B** — Sections 30 to 33 of the Act deal with offences where the victim is unable to refuse to engage in or to watch a sexual activity because of, or for a reason related to, a mental disorder. It is a requirement of these offences that the offender knew, or could reasonably have been expected to know, that the victim had a mental disorder *and* that because of it he was likely to be unable to refuse. Note the *and*, which means that both elements of the offender's guilty knowledge have to be shown, therefore answer A is incorrect. Section 30 makes it an offence intentionally to touch someone sexually when that person, because of, or for a reason related to, a mental disorder is unable to refuse. The s. 78 definition of 'sexual' applies, and touching means all physical contact, including touching with any part of the body, with anything else and through anything, for example, through clothing. It includes penetration (s. 79(8)). Using inducements and/or threats and deceptions are separate offences in themselves (ss. 34 to 37) and are not requirements for this offence; answers C and D are therefore incorrect.

Crime, para. 1.11.8.2

Answer 11.7

Answer **C** — Section 1(1)(c) of the Protection of Children Act 1978 states:

(1) Subject to sections 1A and 1B, it is an offence for a person—
   (c) to have in his possession such indecent photographs or pseudo-photographs, with a view to their being distributed or shown by himself or others …

In these days of computer integration the storing and sharing of indecent images has attracted the attention of the courts as the law attempts to decipher the purpose for which offenders have such images electronically stored. Note however that no specific intention to distribute is required, the requisite *mens rea* being 'a view to'; answer D is therefore incorrect.

Such IT issues were considered in *R* v *Dooley* [2005] EWCA Crim 3093 which mirrors the scenario of this question. The defendant maintained that he had intended to remove the pictures from the shared folder. The appeal turned on the judge's preliminary ruling on the meaning of 'with a view to' under s. 1(1)(c). The Court of Appeal agreed with the judge's ruling that there was a distinction between 'with the intention of' and 'with a view to'—where a defendant had knowledge that images were likely to be accessed by other people, any images would be downloaded 'with a view to distribute'. If one of the reasons the defendant left the pictures in the shared folder was so others could have access to them, he would be in possession of the images 'with a view to their being distributed'. However, as the court accepted that the defendant did not leave the pictures in the shared folder for that reason his conviction could not stand; answers A and B are therefore incorrect.

The court believed that 'with a view to' required more than the knowledge that the files could be accessed; as an analogy (although not a great one!) the court considered that 'a general may foresee the likelihood of his soldiers being killed in battle, but he surely does not send his troops into battle with a view to their being killed'.

Crime, para. 1.11.5.9

Answer 11.8

Answer **C** — Section 53 makes it an offence for a person intentionally to control another person's activities relating to prostitution, in any part of the world, where it is done for, or in the expectation of, gain for himself or a third party. Clearly COR-NELIUS is controlling his girlfriend's activity, even although she is happy to go along with it, and it was done with a view to gain, therefore answer B is incorrect. 'Gain' is defined by s. 54 of the Act as any financial advantage, including the discharge of a debt or obligation to pay, or the provision of goods or services (including sexual services) for free, or at a discount. It also covers the goodwill of any person likely to bring such a financial advantage. So this would cover CORNELIUS inciting his girlfriend to work as a prostitute for DIBLEY, where CORNELIUS expects this will lead to DIBLEY providing him with cheap drugs at a later date. This future gain therefore makes answer A incorrect. It is immaterial that CORNELIUS will be in a household with extra income due to his girlfriend's 'activities'; the offence is complete with the goodwill, and answer D is therefore incorrect.

Crime, para. 1.11.12.2

Answer 11.9

Answer **B** — Section 1 of the Sexual Offences Act 2003 states:

(1) A person (A) commits an offence if—
  (a) he intentionally penetrates the vagina, anus or mouth of another person (B) with his penis,
  (b) B does not consent to the penetration, and
  (c) A does not reasonably believe that B consents.

However, this has to be seen to be a continuing consent. Section 75 of the Sexual Offences Act 2003 states:

(1) If in proceedings for an offence to which this section applies it is proved—
  (a) that the defendant did the relevant act,
  (b) that any of the circumstances specified in subsection (2) existed, and

(c) that the defendant knew that those circumstances existed, the complainant is to be taken not to have consented to the relevant act unless sufficient evidence is adduced to raise an issue as to whether he consented, and the defendant is to be taken not to have reasonably believed that the complainant consented unless sufficient evidence is adduced to raise an issue as to whether he reasonably believed it.

Clearly initially the female consented to sex whilst conscious; however, when she became unconscious the parameters change and s. 75 kicks in again, in particular s. 75(2). These conditions are:

(d) the complainant was asleep or otherwise unconscious at the time of the relevant act;
(e) ...
(f) any person had administered to or caused to be taken by the complainant, without the complainant's consent, a substance which, having regard to when it was administered or taken, was capable of causing or enabling the complainant to be stupefied or overpowered at the time of the relevant act.

In relation to (f) this is not an issue as the complainant consented to taking the drug; however, when it affected her as it did (d) becomes effective. This is where the continuing consent applies, could MOOLES really state that MAKINS had consented to have sex whilst unconscious, and as such she could not make decisions about MOOLES ejaculating inside her. Without this evidence, continuing to have sex with a person who is asleep or unconscious may well be rape; answers A, C and D are therefore incorrect.

Crime, para. 1.11.3

Answer 11.10

Answer **A** — An offence of causing a person to engage in sexual activity without consent contrary to the s. 4 of Sexual Offences Act 2003, is committed where a person intentionally causes another person to engage in an activity, the activity is sexual, and the other person does not consent to engaging in the activity. This question only relates to 'consent' and to answer this we have to turn to s. 76 of the Sexual Offences Act 2003 which states that, if it is proved in some sexual offences (including s. 4) that the defendant did the relevant act and that he/she:

(a) intentionally deceived the complainant as to the nature or purpose of the relevant act or
(b) intentionally induced the complainant to consent to the relevant act by impersonating a person known personally to the complainant.

There will be a conclusive presumption both that the victim did not consent and also that the defendant did not believe she or he consented.

The 'or' between points (a) and (b) means that only one of the points applies, not both; answer B is therefore incorrect.

In *R* v *Devonald* [2008] EWCA Crim 527 (a case under s. 4 where the court held that s. 76 applied) the court held that it was open to the jury to conclude that the complainant was deceived into believing he was masturbating for the gratification of a 20-year-old girl via a webcam when in fact he was doing it for the father of a former girlfriend who was teaching him a lesson. Here 'purpose' has been given a wide meaning in that the deception was not as to sexual purpose, rather it was as to the purpose of the act of masturbation and, in particular, as to the identity of the observer. This ruling means answers C and D are incorrect, even though *Devonald* may seem out of step with *R* v *Jheeta* [2007] EWCA Crim 1699, where the defendant deceived the complainant into having sex more frequently than she would have done otherwise. In these circumstances the conclusive presumptions under the Sexual Offences Act 2003 had no relevance as the complainant had not been deceived as to the nature or purpose of the sexual intercourse.

Crime, paras 1.11.3.4, 1.11.4.3

Answer 11.11

Answer **B** — The Sexual Offences Act clarifies and extends a number of other sexual offences involving adult family members (see ss. 64 and 65). These replace the former offences of incest and generally create either-way offences punishable by up to two years' imprisonment. They can be committed by both parties where one relative (who is 16 or over) intentionally penetrates the vagina or anus of another relative (aged 18 or over) with anything, or penetrates their mouth with his penis and in each case the relative knows (or could reasonably be expected to know) that he/she is related to the other in the way described. The relatives are parent, grandparent, child, grandchild, brother, sister, half-brother, half-sister, aunt, uncle, nephew or niece.

The Criminal Justice and Immigration Act 2008 amended ss. 64 and 65 of the Sexual Offences Act 2003 so that the offences of sex with an adult relative are committed where an adoptive parent has consensual sex with their adopted child when he or she is aged 18 or over. The adopted person does not commit this offence unless he or she is aged 18 or over.

As KATIE is not over 18 she cannot commit this offence; answer A is therefore incorrect. The fact she is 16 years or over is irrelevant as she is an adopted person and is not aged 18 years or over; answers C and D are therefore incorrect.

Crime, para. 1.11.5.7

Answer 11.12

Answer **B** — Section 51A of the Sexual Offences Act 2003 (as amended) states:

(1) It is an offence for a person in a street or public place to solicit another (B) for the purpose of obtaining B's sexual services as a prostitute.
(2) The reference to a person in a street or public place includes a person in a vehicle in a street or public place.

This offence is applicable to both sexes.

Kerb-crawling or soliciting is punishable on the first occasion the activity takes place; answer D is therefore incorrect.

In the case of kerb-crawling, there is no requirement for the soliciting to be shown to be likely to cause nuisance or annoyance to others or to actually go on to cause nuisance or offence; answers A and C are therefore incorrect.

Crime, para. 1.11.12.5

Answer 11.13

Answer **D** — Section 48 makes it an offence for a person intentionally to cause or incite a child under 18 into prostitution or involvement in pornography in any part of the world. The prostitution or pornography itself does not need to take place for the offence to be committed. This offence is targeted at the recruitment into prostitution or pornography of a child who is not engaged in that activity at the time. The offence would be committed where a 'pimp' makes a living from the prostitution of others and encourages new recruits to work for him. It could also cover the situation where the defendant forces the victim to take part in child pornography for any reason.

Unlike the equivalent adult offence at s. 52, there is no requirement that the prostitution or pornography must be done for the gain of any of the persons involved, therefore FAY's mother is as culpable as the others. All three persons have incited the child, therefore answers A, B and C are incorrect.

Crime, para. 1.11.5.8

Answer 11.14

Answer **A** — There are two offences here. The first offence is under the Protection of Children Act 1978, of taking, making, distributing, showing, publishing, advertising and possessing with intent to distribute indecent photographs.

The second offence is committed under the Criminal Justice Act 1988, which added the offence of mere possession of such photography.

Therefore, offences would be committed in this scenario by the person distributing, POTTER, and the people possessing, both POTTER and BOYD (answer B is therefore incorrect).

The offence of distribution is to 'another person'; there is no requirement to distribute to more than one person (answer C is therefore incorrect).

Distributing *will* include lending, which is why answer D is incorrect.

Crime, para. 1.11.5.9

Answer 11.15

Answer **D** — It is an offence at common law to commit an act of a lewd, obscene or disgusting nature and outrage public decency.

This offence is committed by the deliberate commission of an act that is, *per se*, lewd, obscene or disgusting (*R v Rowley* [1991] 1 WLR 1020). If an act is not lewd, obscene etc. then the motives or intentions of the defendant cannot make it so; answer B is therefore incorrect. Therefore, where the defendant's acts involved leaving messages that were not in themselves obscene in public toilets, his motives (to induce young boys to engage in gross indecency with him) did not bring his actions under this offence (*Rowley*).

It is irrelevant that someone is actually outraged if the notes are not lewd; answer A is therefore incorrect. If the notes had been lewd then the offence would be complete even without actual contact with children; answer C is therefore incorrect.

Crime, para. 1.11.9.1

Answer 11.16

Answer **A** — There are two relevant offences where a person is premeditating a sexual offence. So what offence is intended? STREETER clearly intends (although he may not realise it) to commit rape. Under the 2003 Act, rape differs from the offence in the Sexual Offences Act 1956, in that it requires that the defendant does not have a 'reasonable belief' in consent, rather than that he does not have an 'honest belief' in consent. STREETER's belief is not reasonable, so he will commit rape; answer C is therefore incorrect.

There are two preparatory offences to consider: trespass with intent to commit a sexual offence (s. 63); and committing an offence with intent to commit a sexual offence (s. 62). For an offence under s. 63, the person must be 'on any premises where he is a trespasser'. Whilst STREETER is outside the bedroom window he is not a trespasser; answer B is therefore incorrect. When he breaks the window he has committed a criminal offence, and with the required intent an offence (s. 62) is committed regardless of whether or not the substantive sexual offence is committed; answer D is therefore incorrect.

Crime, paras 1.11.10.2, 1.11.10.3

Answer 11.17

Answer **D** — Section 15 makes it an offence for a person aged 18 or over to meet intentionally, or to travel with the intention of meeting, a child aged under 16 in any part of the world, if he has met or communicated with that child on at least two earlier occasions, and intends to commit a 'relevant offence' against that child either at the time of the meeting, or on a subsequent occasion. An offence is not committed if he reasonably believes the child to be 16 or over. The stumbling block to the offence in this question is the lack of a previous meeting. Had there been such previous meeting or communication then the offence would be complete as soon as REYNOLDS started travelling towards the meeting, and again when he actually does meet BEN. Note that simply arranging a meeting would not be captured by this offence; answer A is therefore incorrect. Because of the lack of two earlier communications, answers B and C are incorrect. The section is intended to cover situations where an adult establishes contact with a child through, for example, meetings, telephone conversations or communications on the Internet, and gains the child's trust and confidence so that he can arrange to meet the child for the purpose of committing a 'relevant offence' against the child ('relevant offences' are offences under Part 1 of this Act). The course of conduct prior to the meeting that triggers the offence may have an explicitly sexual content, such as entering into conversations with the child about the sexual acts he wants to engage in when they meet, or sending images of adult pornography. However, the prior meetings or communication need not have an explicitly sexual content and could, for example, simply involve giving the child swimming lessons or selling him sweets.

Crime, para. 1.11.5.4

Answer 11.18

Answer **B** — This offence mirrors that under s. 12 of causing a child to watch a sexual act, with the addition of the perpetrator being in a position of trust. There is a significant difference, however, in that for the abuse of position of trust offences, the child may be 16 or 17 (under 16 for the s. 12 offence); therefore answer C is incorrect.

A position of trust is defined by s. 21 of the Act, and in relation to someone in education subs. (5) states:

This subsection applies if A looks after persons under 18 who are receiving education at an educational institution and B is receiving, and A is not receiving, education at that institution.

'Receiving education at an educational institution' is defined by s. 22(4)(a) as:

... he is registered or otherwise enrolled as a pupil or student at the institution.

'Looks after persons under 18' is a wide caveat, which extends this section beyond the actual teacher/pupil relationship within a specific lesson; therefore answer A is incorrect.

Lastly, s. 12 outlines that it is an offence for a person aged 18 or over intentionally to cause a child, for the purposes of his own sexual gratification, to watch a third person engaging in sexual activity, or to look at an image of a person engaging in a sexual act. The act can be live or recorded, and there is no need for the child to be in close physical proximity to the sexual act. An example would be where he sends a child indecent images over the Internet. In order for an offence to be committed, the adult must act for his own sexual gratification. This ensures that adults showing children sex education material, either in a school or in another setting, will not be liable for this offence. However, this will not be an excuse if the act was done purely for sexual gratification. The term 'image' means a moving or still image, and includes an image produced by any means and, where the context permits, a three-dimensional image; therefore answer D is incorrect.

Crime, para. 1.11.5.5

Answer 11.19

Answer **D** — The offence of voyeurism is divided into three parts:

- The first offence involves a defendant observing another doing a private act with the relevant motive of gaining sexual gratification.
- The second offence deals with people operating equipment such as hoteliers or landlords using webcams to enable others to view live footage of their residents or tenants, in each case for the sexual gratification of those others.
- The third offence deals with the recording of the private act with the intention that the person doing the recording or another will look at the image and thereby obtain sexual gratification.

The three offences described require proof that the victim does not consent to the observing, recording or operating of the relevant equipment for the purpose of the defendant or another's sexual gratification. The accused must know that the victim does not consent to his recording the act with that intention. It follows that consent to recording given by the victims for another purpose will not avail the accused; answers A and C are therefore incorrect.

A 'private act' is defined as where they are in a place which, in the circumstances, would reasonably be expected to provide privacy, and:

- their genitals, buttocks or breasts are exposed or covered only with underwear;
- they are using a lavatory; or
- they are doing a sexual act that is not of a kind ordinarily done in public.

So the fact that the persons could be seen in underwear makes this a 'private act' and within the scope of s. 67; answer B is therefore incorrect.

Crime, para. 1.11.9.2

Answer 11.20

Answer **C** — New legislation usually takes time to find precedents; given the number in its predecessor it is not surprising that the Sexual Offences Act 2003 has already started!

The Court of Appeal in *R v H* [2005] EWCA Crim 732 has held that the touching of an individual's clothing was sufficient to amount to 'touching' under s. 3; answers A and B are therefore incorrect.

It also confirmed that where touching was not by its nature 'sexual' it was appropriate to ask the jury to consider two questions:

- Would the jury, as 12 reasonable people, consider that the touching could be sexual?
- Would the jury, as 12 reasonable people and in all the circumstances of the case, consider that the purpose of the touching had in fact been sexual?

An affirmative answer to both questions led to a finding that the touching, in similar circumstances to this scenario, was sexual and the accused properly convicted. It is the circumstances of this scenario, or JONES's purpose in relation to it, that is important in what is 'sexual', not the victim's belief (which would be important, of course, but not definitive). A conviction could arise where the victim felt that the act was not sexual applying the test in *H*; therefore answer D is incorrect.

Crime, para. 1.11.4.2

Answer 11.21

Answer **D** — Possession of indecent photographs of children is an offence contrary to s. 160 of the Criminal Justice Act 1988.

Section 160 of the 1988 Act penalises possession, even though the possessor does not intend that the photograph or pseudo-photograph be distributed. Clearly STRACHAN has the images in his possession.

However, a defendant has a defence to a charge under s. 160 if they can prove that they had a legitimate reason for having the photograph in their possession, or that they had not themselves seen the photograph, *and* neither knew nor had any reason to suspect that it was indecent, or that the photograph was sent to them without any prior request by them, and that they did not keep it for an unreasonable time.

A person who suspects that images in his possession are indecent but shows that he had no reason to suspect that they were images of children may rely on this statutory defence. So held the Court of Appeal in *R* v *Collier* [2004] EWCA Crim 1411.

Hooper LJ, in the reserved judgment of the court, said that the defence in s. 160(2)(b) would be made out if a defendant proved that he had not seen the indecent photograph of a child alleged in the charge against him *nor* had he had any cause to suspect it to be an indecent photograph of a child. Answer C is therefore incorrect. So, although knowing the general content of the attachment when downloading and opening it, not knowing its specific content permits the defence. Answers A and B are therefore incorrect.

Crime, para. 1.11.5.9

Answer 11.22

Answer **A** — Section 79(8)of the Sexual Offences Act 2003 states that touching includes touching:

* with any part of the body,
* with anything else,
* through anything,

and in particular, touching amounting to penetration.

'Touching' for the purposes of an offence under this section includes the touching of a victim's clothing. This is clear from the Court of Appeal's decision in *R* v *H* [2005] EWCA Crim 732. There it was held that it was not Parliament's intention to preclude the touching of a victim's clothing from amounting to a sexual 'assault'. Where touching was not automatically by its nature 'sexual', the test under s. 78(b) applies by answering two questions.

First, would the jury, as 12 reasonable people, consider that the touching could be sexual and, if so, whether in all the circumstances of the case, they would consider that the purpose of the touching had in fact been sexual.

Note this is not asking if an offence has been committed, but simply if it amounts to sexual touching. The man is touching the woman within the definition therefore answer D is incorrect. It is immaterial whether the woman was aware of the incident or not; answer C is therefore incorrect.

It is the jury's view of the incident and not the defendant's that decides if it is sexual touching and answer B is therefore incorrect.

Crime, para. 1.11.2.2

Answer 11.23

Answer **D** — Section 78 of the Sexual Offences Act 2003 provides that penetration, touching or any other activity will be sexual if a reasonable person would consider that:

(a) whatever its circumstances or any person's purpose in relation to it, it is sexual by its very nature, or

(b) because of its nature it *may* be sexual and because of its circumstances or the purpose of any person in relation to it, it is sexual.

Therefore, activity under (a) covers things that a reasonable person would always consider to be sexual (e.g. masturbation), while activity under (b) covers things that may or may not be considered sexual by a reasonable person depending on the circumstances or the intentions of the person carrying it out (or both). For instance, a doctor inserting a finger into a vagina might be sexual under certain circumstances, but if done for a purely medical purpose in a hospital, it would not be.

The essential definition of sexual touching therefore is not in the mind of either the assailant or the victim. If the activity would not appear to a reasonable person to be sexual, then it will not meet either criterion and, irrespective of any sexual gratification the person might derive from it, the activity will not be 'sexual'; answers A and B are therefore incorrect. Therefore weird or exotic fetishes that no ordinary person would regard as being sexual or potentially sexual will not be covered. It is whether the action is or may be sexual; answer C is therefore incorrect.

Crime, paras 1.11.2.1, 1.11.4.2

Answer 11.24

Answer **D** — As with rape, s. 79(3) of the Sexual Offences Act references to a vagina include a surgically constructed vagina; answer A is therefore incorrect. The penetration may be penetration with a part of the offender's body, for example, a finger or a fist, or with anything else, for example, a dildo or a sharp object (the term 'anything else' will include an animal or other living organism); answer B is therefore incorrect.

Consent is an on-going criterion; whilst she may have freely consented to one activity, on-going consent to that activity, or any other activity, can be withdrawn at any time. Failure to conform to withdrawal of consent would be an assault; answer C is therefore incorrect.

Crime, para. 1.11.4.1

Answer 11.25

Answer **C** — Section 63 of the Sexual Offences Act 2003 states:

(1) A person commits an offence if—
   (a) he is a trespasser on any premises,
   (b) he intends to commit a relevant sexual offence on the premises, and
   (c) he knows that, or is reckless as to whether, he is a trespasser.

A person is a trespasser if they are on the premises without the owner or occupier's consent, whether express or implied. Generally, the defendant ought to know whether he/she is trespassing or not and recklessness will be enough in that regard; answer A is therefore incorrect.

Premises here will include a structure or part of a structure (including a tent, vehicle or vessel or other temporary or movable structure)—s. 63(2)—which is wider than the term 'building' used in the Theft Act offence of burglary; answer D is therefore incorrect.

This offence is one of intention rather than consequence and so there is no need to prove that the substantive sexual offence took place. There is still considerable overlap between this offence and burglary and, if the person is caught going equipped for burglary and also has the intention of committing a relevant sexual offence at the time, he/she may commit the more general offence under s. 62.

Note that the defendant must intend to commit the relevant offence on the premises. As he does not this particular offence is not made out; answers A and B are therefore incorrect.

Crime, para. 1.11.10.3

Answer 11.26

Answer **B** — Section 63 of the Criminal Justice and Immigration Act 2008 states:

(1) It is an offence for a person to be in possession of an extreme pornographic image.

There are three elements to the offence. An image must come within the terms of all three elements before it will fall foul of the offence. Those elements are:

- that the image is pornographic;
- that the image is grossly offensive, disgusting, or otherwise of an obscene character; and
- that the image portrays in an explicit and realistic way, one of the following extreme acts:
  — an act which threatens a person's life (this could include depictions of hanging, suffocation or sexual assault involving a threat with a weapon);
  — an act which results in or is likely to result in serious injury to a person's anus, breasts or genitals (this could include the insertion of sharp objects or the mutilation of the breasts or genitals);
  — an act involving sexual interference with a human corpse (necrophilia);
  — a person performing an act of intercourse or oral sex with an animal (whether dead or alive) (bestiality);
- and a reasonable person looking at the image would think that the people and animals portrayed were real.

All three elements must be covered. It makes no difference whether the animal is alive or dead; answers C and D are therefore incorrect. The 'reasonable person' test does not apply to the image, it will be grossly offensive by design; answer A is therefore incorrect.

An 'extreme pornographic image' is an image which is both pornographic and an extreme image. An image is 'pornographic' if it is of such a nature that it must reasonably be assumed to have been produced solely or principally for the purpose of sexual arousal.

Crime, para. 1.11.7

Answer 11.27

Answer **B** — Section 53A of the Sexual Offences Act 2003 (as amended by the Policing and Crime Act 2009) states:

(1) A person (A) commits an offence if—
  (a) A makes or promises payment for the sexual services of a prostitute (B),

    (b) a third person (C) has engaged in exploitative conduct of a kind likely to induce or encourage B to provide the sexual services for which A has made or promised payment, and

    (c) C engaged in that conduct for or in the expectation of gain for C or another person (apart from A or B).

(2) The following are irrelevant—

    (a) where in the world the sexual services are to be provided and whether those services are provided,

    (b) whether A is, or ought to be, aware that C has engaged in exploitative conduct.

(3) C engages in exploitative conduct if—

    (a) C uses force, threats (whether or not relating to violence) or any other form of coercion, or

    (b) C practises any form of deception.

The Policing and Crime Act 2009 inserted a new offence, s. 53A, into the Sexual Offences Act 2003. The new section creates an offence which is committed if someone pays or promises payment for the sexual services of a prostitute who has been subject to exploitative conduct of a kind likely to induce or encourage the provision of sexual services for which the payer has made or promised payment. The person responsible for the exploitative conduct must have been acting for or in the expectation of gain for himself or herself or another person, other than the payer or the prostitute.

So only CROSS can commit this offence; answers A, C and D are therefore incorrect.

It does not matter where in the world the sexual services are to be provided. An offence is committed regardless of whether the person paying or promising payment for sexual services knows or ought to know or be aware that the prostitute has been subject to exploitative conduct. In other words, the offence is one of strict liability and no mental element is required in respect of the offender's knowledge that the prostitute was forced, threatened, coerced or deceived.

Crime, para. 1.11.12.3

12 | Control of Sex Offenders

STUDY PREPARATION

There is specific legislation made by Parliament for the control and monitoring of sex offenders. This chapter looks at these various control strategies including: risk of sexual harm orders, sexual offences prevention orders and the requirement on sex offenders to notify certain personal details to the police.

QUESTIONS

Question 12.1

MORTLEY, 22 years old, is a convicted child sex offender currently on parole. He is seen by concerned parents every day of the week standing outside a local primary school. He says or does nothing, but is always outside the school when the children are released.

What is the fullest extent to which a risk of sexual harm order (RSHO) may be made to protect children?

A To protect all the children at the school who are at risk from MORTLEY.

B To protect a particular child at the school who is at risk from MORTLEY.

C To protect any child in the locality who is at risk from MORTLEY.

D To protect any child anywhere who is at risk from MORTLEY.

Question 12.2

WILKINSON is a convicted paedophile, and notified police of his home address. He has stayed with a friend some 20 miles from his home address; he stayed with this friend for three days, two months ago, and now intends spending another five days with him.

Should he now notify police that he is staying with his friend?

A Yes he must notify police as he will now accumulate seven days.

B Yes, he must notify police as this is his second period at this address.

C No, he is not staying for seven days straight at this address.

D No, as the premises is within 50 miles of his home address.

Question 12.3

PROTHERO was a convicted sex offender who had notified the police of his home address. He has been having trouble at that address with hate mail and has decided he will move in with his mother for an unknown period.

Which of the following is correct in relation to notification requirements?

A PROTHERO will only have to notify a change of address if he intends being away from his home address for three months or more.

B PROTHERO will only have to notify a change of address if he intends being away from his home address for six months or more.

C PROTHERO must notify the police in the area in which his home address is situated of an intention to change address.

D PROTHERO may notify the police in the area into which he is moving of an intention to change address.

Question 12.4

PARFITT was charged with carrying out a number of sexual assaults against children; however due to a procedural error at Crown Court trial the judge rules that the charges against him are dismissed and directs the jury to find him not guilty. The police consider that a sexual offences prevention order should be made as PARFITT is a risk to the public.

In relation to this which of the following is correct?

A The court can now impose that order as it has dealt with him for a relevant (sch. 3) offence.

B The court can now impose that order even though it has found him not guilty of a relevant (sch. 3) offence.

C The police would have to apply to a Magistrates' Court for such an order now.

D An order could never be sought as he was found not guilty of the offence.

Question 12.5

A 17-year-old male has been made subject to a Notification Order by virtue of the Sexual Offences Act 2003 and the court has further ordered a parental direction. The young male has failed to comply with the order by not attending at the police station to report a change of address. His parents tried many times to get him to attend at the police station, even trying to physically take him there. The youth no longer lives with his parents.

Has an offence been committed by the parent made subject of the parental direction in relation to an offence of failure to notify contrary to s. 91 of the Sexual Offences Act 2003?

A Yes, the point of a parental direction is to make them responsible for ensuring their child complies with notification requirements; as they have not the offence is complete.

B Yes, as their child has failed to comply with notification requirements they should have attended the police station themselves or applied to the court to vary the order.

C No, as the male subject to the order no longer lives with the parents who were subject to the parental direction.

D No, as the offence is only committed by a person with no reasonable excuse and the parents are likely to have such excuse.

Question 12.6

GREENHAUGH was convicted of a sex offence in Northern Ireland and given a caution. The offence he committed would be subject to notification requirements as set out in sch. 3 to the Sexual Offences Act 2003. GREENHAUGH has moved into your local area.

In relation to notification requirements which of the following is correct?

A GREENHAUGH must fulfil the requirements as he was cautioned for a relevant offence; this applies to offences committed in England, Wales and Northern Ireland.

B GREENHAUGH must fulfil the requirements as he was cautioned for a relevant offence; this applies to offences committed anywhere in the United Kingdom.

C GREENHAUGH need not fulfil the requirements as this relates to offences committed in England and Wales only and subject to a caution therein.

D GREENHAUGH need not fulfil the requirements as this relates to convictions only and not cautions or conditional discharges.

Question 12.7

GREENING is a registered sex offender and the police are carrying out a risk assessment in relation to his re-offending. They have visited his address in order to carry out this risk assessment; however he has never been in. Apart from this it seems that GREENING has been acting in compliance with his notification requirements. The police are considering whether they have a power of entry into the address to carry out a risk assessment.

In relation to this which of the following is correct?

A They can apply for a search warrant provided there have been at least two failed attempts to enter a specified premises.

B They can apply for a search warrant provided there have been at least three failed attempts to enter a specified premises.

C They cannot apply for a search warrant as the person seems to be in compliance with his notification requirements.

D They cannot apply for a search warrant as there is no power to search the address to carry out a risk assessment.

ANSWERS

Answer 12.1

Answer **D** — A risk of sexual harm order (RSHO) is applied to protect children from an individual. The court can only make a RSHO if it is satisfied that the defendant committed an act outlined in s. 123(3) of the Sexual Offences Act 2003 on at least two occasions and that the order is necessary to protect children generally or any specific child from harm *from the defendant*. It goes beyond a risk to any child or all of the children that go to the school, so answers A and B are therefore incorrect. Indeed, such an order can extend beyond the locality where the person is, so answer C is therefore incorrect. Although a RSHO can be made to protect a particular child or a group of children, it extends to children in general (provided they are under 16 years of age) who may be at risk of sexual harm from MORTLEY.

Crime, para. 1.12.5

Answer 12.2

Answer **A** — Sections 80 to 92 of the Sexual Offences Act 2003 re-enact, with amendments, Part 1 of the Sex Offenders Act 1997, which established a requirement on sex offenders to notify certain personal details to the police. This process is commonly known as 'registration', often referred to loosely as creating a 'sex offenders register'.

Section 84 sets out the requirements on a relevant offender to notify the police of changes to notified details. Under s. 84(1)(c), an offender must notify the police within three days, of the address of any premises he has stayed at within the UK, besides his home address, for a 'qualifying period'. This place might be a friend's or relative's house, or a hotel where he has stayed. A qualifying period is defined by s. 84(6) as a period of seven days, or two or more periods, in any 12 months, which taken together amount to seven days—note it is the number of days, not the number of visits; answer B is therefore incorrect. It is an accumulative period of seven days, not seven days straight, therefore answer C is incorrect. There are no restrictions on distances, only on the 'qualifying period'; answer D is therefore incorrect.

Crime, para. 1.12.2.3

Answer 12.3

Answer **D** — Having registered correctly with the police in the area in which he lives he must then notify them of any change of address. If he is staying away from home for seven days or more (answers A and B are therefore incorrect) then he must notify this change of address or an advance change of address. In these circumstances there is no requirement to notify the police in the home address area and the offender may give the notification at a police station in the police area of the other address (Sexual Offences Act 2003, s. 87(2)); answer C is therefore incorrect.

Crime, para. 1.12.2.6

Answer 12.4

Answer **D** — Sexual Offences Prevention Orders (SOPOs) are civil law measures to prevent offending and protect the public. They have replaced the old sex offender orders and restraining orders (although someone who is still subject to those older orders remains under the relevant obligations contained in them).

A court can make a SOPO in a number of circumstances where it is satisfied that it is necessary to do so for the purpose of protecting the public (or any particular member(s) of the public) from serious sexual harm from the defendant. In summary, the SOPO can be made where:

- the court deals with (rather than simply 'convicts') a person for a sch. 3 offence (deals with, not dealt with as the trial is over this does not apply; answer A is therefore incorrect);
- the court decides that a defendant is not guilty of an offence listed in sch. 3 or sch. 5 by reason of insanity, or that he is under a disability and has done the act charged against him in respect of such an offence; this is broader than only sexual offences and answer C is therefore incorrect (found not guilty by technicality; answer B is therefore incorrect); or
- a chief officer applies for one in respect of a 'qualifying offender' and certain conditions are met.

Those conditions are:

- the person is a qualifying offender (basically this means he/she has been convicted of, cautioned for or found not guilty by reason of insanity or to have been under a disability, in respect of an offence under sch. 3 or 5 here or by a foreign court for an equivalent offence), and

- the person has, since the appropriate date (e.g. date of first conviction or caution) acted in such a way as to give reasonable cause to believe that it is necessary (rather than just desirable or a 'good idea') for such an order to be made.

Neither of these apply so answer C is also incorrect.

Crime, para. 1.12.3.1

Answer 12.5

Answer **D** — An offence is committed under s. 91 where the relevant person fails, without reasonable excuse, to comply with the notification requirements under the 2003 Act, the relevant person being the offender, and also the person who is subject to a parental direction and this is so even if the young person moves house; answer C is therefore incorrect. Under this direction the parent must ensure that the young offender attends at the police station with them when notification is being given. This does not mean that they can attend and give notification themselves, the person subject to the order must personally attend; answer B is therefore incorrect. Although they can ask the court to vary the order this is a continuing offence and takes place until such an order is varied.

Reasonable excuse will be a question of fact for the court, but it is more than likely that given the circumstances of this case the parents will have such excuse, having done all they can to ensure attendance of their son, and will therefore not have committed the offence; answer A is therefore incorrect.

Crime, para. 1.12.2.11

Answer 12.6

Answer **A** — The notification applies where:

- they are convicted of an offence listed in sch. 3—this covers most of the commonly occurring sex offences;
- they are found not guilty of such an offence by reason of insanity;
- they are found to be under a disability and to have done the act charged against them in respect of such an offence; or
- they are cautioned in respect of such an offence, not only in England and Wales but for an offence in Northern Ireland as well.

Note that Scotland is not included in this legislation and as it is part of the United Kingdom answer B is therefore incorrect. As can be seen it applies to cautions as well as convictions and does include Northern Ireland; answers C and D are therefore incorrect.

Crime, para. 1.12.2

Answer 12.7

Answer **A** — Section 96B of the Sexual Offences Act 2003 (inserted by s. 58 of the Violent Crime Reduction Act 2006) provides a power of entry and search to risk assess sex offenders subject to the notification requirements; answer D is therefore incorrect.

The power enables the police to gather all the information they need about a relevant offender for the purposes of assessing the risks he poses, even if he is in apparent compliance with the notification requirements (answer C is therefore incorrect) and there are insufficient grounds to believe he has committed a new substantive offence.

Under the section, the police are allowed to seek a warrant from a magistrates' court to enter and search, by force if necessary, the last notified address of a registered sex offender (or a place where there are grounds to believe the offender resides or can be regularly found) where there have been two failed attempts to enter a specified premises, for the purposes of assessing the risks he poses, note two and not three; answer B is therefore incorrect. The application must be made by a senior police officer, not below the rank of superintendent. The senior police officer should attend court in person to apply for the warrant.

A warrant will only be issued by a magistrate if they are satisfied that the following conditions have been met:

- that the offender is a relevant offender (i.e. an offender subject to the notification requirements);
- that the offender is not: remanded or committed to custody by order of a court; serving a sentence of imprisonment or a term of service detention; detained in hospital; or outside the UK;
- that the address of each set of premises to which the warrant relates is either the home address which was last notified in accordance with Part 2 of the Sexual Offences Act 2003, or there are reasonable grounds to believe that the registered sex offender resides there or may regularly be found there;
- that it is necessary for the constable to enter and search the premises for the purpose of assessing the risk posed by the offender;
- that on at least two occasions, a constable has sought entry to the premises in order to search them for that purpose and has been unable to obtain entry for that purpose.

The warrant may also authorise entry to and search of premises on more than one occasion if, on the application, the magistrate is satisfied that it is necessary to authorise multiple entries for the purpose of risk assessment. When a warrant authorises multiple entries, the number of entries authorised may be unlimited or limited to a maximum.

If more than one address is to be searched, then the constable will need to attempt (and fail) to enter each address for which the warrant is sought.

In circumstances where a constable has been allowed into the premises to search for the purposes of risk assessment, but not allowed into parts of the premises (e.g. a particular room), this will count as being 'unable to obtain entry' for the purposes of risk assessment.

As a warrant does not grant a power of seizure, where evidence of a crime is found during the course of a search under such a warrant, constables can use their general power of seizure under s. 19 of PACE.

Crime, para. 1.12.2.13

13 | Child Protection

STUDY PREPARATION

It is important that officers recognise the significance of some victims particularly children and their vulnerabilities. Operational officers deal with situations involving these persons on a daily basis; it is important to recognise your powers. Make sure you know the differences between the two offences under the Child Abduction Act 1984 (person connected and not connected to a child). The emotive issue of child cruelty is also covered here as well as legislation aimed directly at child protection, e.g. the Children Act 2004.

QUESTIONS

Question 13.1

STRAUSS is a Swiss national living in the UK. He had an affair with MERCHANT and she had a daughter as a result of that affair. Although they were not married at the time the child was born, they did marry, but then divorced. When the girl reached 16, STRAUSS took her to Austria intending that they would live there together. MERCHANT did not know and complains to the police that the child has been abducted and that STRAUSS was not the child's father; she has medical proof that STRAUSS is not the child's father, although he does not know this.

Has STRAUSS committed an offence of child abduction contrary to s. 1 of the Child Abduction Act 1984?

A No, as the child concerned is not covered by this legislation due to her age.

B No, as he reasonably believed he was the father of the child and no further consent is necessary.

C Yes, even though he had reasonable grounds for believing he was the father he did not have the mother's consent to take the child.

D Yes, as he took the child out of the country without the appropriate consent, that of the child's mother and father.

Question 13.2

MURTY, aged 16, was a single parent, her baby was 18 months old. One winter, the baby developed a severe case of influenza, which resulted in hypothermia. Eventually the baby died. The baby had been ill for some time, and MURTY had not taken her to the doctor. MURTY was arrested for the offence of child cruelty when she reported the death to the police.

What, if anything, would the prosecution have to prove in order to convict MURTY of this offence?

A That her actions in denying medical care were wilful.

B That she was reckless in denying medical care to the child.

C That she intended to deny medical care to the child.

D Nothing, MURTY is 16 years old and therefore below the age of those to which this offence applies, i.e. over 16 years of age.

Question 13.3

CRAWSHAY invited a 15-year-old girl, whom he reasonably believed to have attained the age of 16, back to his house. He had consensual sex with her that night. The following day he was made aware that in fact the girl was only 15 and that she had been reported missing by her foster parents. When he returned home he told her what he knew and she said she was happy to stay with him. The police called some time later and CRAWSHAY denied ever seeing the girl.

Considering only s. 2 of the Child Abduction Act 1984, which of the following is correct?

A He has committed this offence as he removed the child from lawful control when he first took her home.

B He has committed the offence when he allows the girl to remain out of lawful control by denying she is there.

C He has not committed the offence as the girl consented to remain with him.

D He has not committed this offence as when he first took her he reasonably believed she had attained the age of 16.

Question 13.4

In relation to the offence of child cruelty contrary to the Children and Young Persons Act 1933, a person will be presumed to have neglected the child where it is proved that the child was an infant under a certain age and that they died as a result of suffocation while in bed with someone of over a certain age who was under the influence of drink when they went to bed.

What are those relevant ages?

A An infant under 2 years of age and a person 16 years or older.

B An infant under 3 years of age and a person 16 years or older.

C An infant under 2 years of age and a person 18 years or older.

D An infant under 3 years of age and a person 18 years or older.

Question 13.5

ANITA, aged 15, agreed to babysit her neighbours' 2-year-old child, while her neighbours went out for the evening. During the evening, ANITA's boyfriend rang her and asked if he could see her. ANITA checked that the child was asleep, then slipped out of the house to meet her boyfriend. She had been gone from the house for about half an hour, when neighbours found the child wandering down the street in his pyjamas. The child was not injured during the incident.

In relation to the Children and Young Persons Act 1933, which of the following is correct?

A ANITA has committed an offence of child cruelty through her neglect.

B ANITA has committed an offence of child cruelty as her actions are wilful.

C ANITA does not commit an offence of child cruelty in these circumstances.

D ANITA does not commit an offence of child cruelty as the child was not injured.

Question 13.6

YILMAZ had an affair with a woman six years ago and she had a child. YILMAZ believed he was the father of the child, but in fact he wasn't the biological father, nor was he married to the woman. He has contacted the mother recently asking to take the child on holiday to Turkey but she has refused. YILMAZ then meets the child after school and takes him home with a view to taking him on holiday; however after several hours of the child crying he can't stand it and takes the child home to the mother.

Has YILMAZ committed an offence contrary to s. 2 of the Child Abduction Act 1984?

A Yes, as his intention was to remove the child from the United Kingdom.

B Yes, as he has removed the child from the mother who had lawful control.

C No, as he didn't actually remove the child from the United Kingdom.

D No, as he reasonably believed he was the father of the child when he took it.

Question 13.7

Child cruelty is covered by s. 1 of the Children and Young Persons Act 1933 which outlines what would amount to the criminal offence of child cruelty.

Which of the following is correct?

A The offence can only be committed by a positive act and not by omission.

B The acts must have occurred in a manner that caused unnecessary suffering or injury to health.

C The acts must have occurred in a manner that caused unnecessary suffering or injury to health with intention to do so.

D The acts must have occurred in a manner likely to cause unnecessary suffering or injury to health, there is no need to show that any such suffering or injury actually came about.

Question 13.8

LILLEY has three children who are profoundly deaf; he himself suffers from Usher's Syndrome, which means that he has tunnel vision and night blindness. He is registered blind, and has been without a valid driving licence since it was withdrawn on medical grounds by the DVLA. Despite this, LILLEY regularly drove his children to school, but has been warned by social services that this must stop, and he had agreed it would. Two days later, social services had information that LILLEY had driven the children several hundred miles to be assessed by another school for deaf children. On learning what had happened, the family's social worker instructed the council's legal department to apply for an emergency protection order (EPO) pursuant to s. 44 of the Children Act 1989, which was granted. The police were informed and they intercepted the vehicle on the motorway being driven home with the children as passengers. The officers invoked their powers under s. 46 of the Children Act 1989 and took the children into police protection.

In relation to police action, which of the following is correct?

A The s. 46 power to remove a child cannot be exercised where an EPO is in force in respect of the child.

B The police should invoke the powers under s. 46 as the statutory scheme accords primacy to that procedure.

C Where a police officer knows that an EPO is in force, they should not exercise the power of removing a child under s. 46, unless there are immediate and compelling reasons to do so.

D Where a police officer knows that an EPO is in force, they should not exercise the power of removing a child under s. 46, unless there are compelling reasons to do so.

Question 13.9

Section 46 of the Children Act 1989 deals with the protection of children in certain situations.

In relation to the section, which of the following statements is correct?

A A constable or social worker may remove a child to suitable accommodation.

B A constable in uniform may remove a child to suitable accommodation.

C A constable may only remove a child to a police station or hospital.

D A constable may remove a child to suitable accommodation.

Question 13.10

MICHAEL is 11 years old and is living with his 24-year-old cousin, although she has no parental responsibility for him. MICHAEL becomes subject to police protection in line with s. 46 of the Children Act 1989.

Which of the following is correct in relation to whether the designated officer can allow the cousin to have contact with MICHAEL whilst in police protection?

A The cousin can have no contact with MICHAEL as she has no parental responsibility for him.

B The cousin would be entitled to contact with MICHAEL as he is currently living with her even though she has no parental responsibility.

C The cousin *should* be allowed contact provided the designated officer believes it to be reasonable and in the child's best interest.

D The sister *must* be allowed contact unless the designated officer believes it would not be reasonable and in the child's best interest.

Question 13.11

An 11-year-old child has been made subject of an emergency protection order under s. 44 of the Children Act 1989 taken out by social services and has been placed into temporary foster care. The child's father contacts her on her mobile phone and tells her that if she comes back to the family home she will be safe and taken away on a special holiday to see her grandmother who lives in France.

Has the father committed an offence of acting in contravention of a protection order?

A Yes, as the father has induced, assisted or incited the child to run away from foster care.

B Yes, as the father has induced, assisted or incited the child to run away from foster care and intends taking the child abroad.

C No, as the child wasn't directly in 'care' within the local authority area as foster care is not 'care' for the purposes of the legislation.

D No, as the offence would only be complete if the child actually leaves, or is taken away from the foster care by the father.

Question 13.12

PRINCE is the divorced father of three children aged 16, 14 and 12. He takes them on a skiing holiday to France for a week with the consent of his wife, and at the end of that time he calls her to say he will not be returning the children to her, he is going to settle in France with them.

Considering the offence under s. 1 of the Child Abduction Act 1984 (abduction by person connected with a child) only, which of the following statements is correct?

A PRINCE commits the offence in relation to all three children and has no defence.

B PRINCE commits the offence in relation to the two younger children and has no defence.

C PRINCE commits the offence, but would have a defence as he is out of the United Kingdom for a period of less than one month.

D PRINCE does not commit this offence at all in these circumstances.

Question 13.13

MAYNARD has been arrested for having in his book shop publications that are considered to be so violent that an offence of having a harmful publications contrary to s. 2 of the Children and Young Persons (Harmful Publications) Act 1955 is committed.

Which, if any, of the following would be a defence for MAYNARD in relation to the commission of this offence?

A That he had not examined the contents of the work and had no reasonable cause to suspect that it was one to which the Act applies.

B That he had examined the contents of the work and had no reasonable cause to suspect that it was one to which the Act applies.

C That the contents themselves were not acts of violence or cruelty.

D There is no defence in law to this offence.

ANSWERS

Answer 13.1

Answer **A** — Section 1 of the Child Abduction Act 1984 states:

(1) Subject to subsections (5) and (8) below, a person connected with a child under the age of 16 commits an offence if he takes or sends the child out of the United Kingdom without the appropriate consent.

'Connected with a Child'

Section 1 of the Child Abduction Act 1984 states:

(2) A person is connected with the child for the purposes of this section if—
   (a) he is a parent of the child; or
   (b) in the case of a child whose parents were not married to each other at the time of his birth, there are reasonable grounds for believing that he is the father of the child; or
   (c) he is a guardian of the child; or
   (ca) he is a special guardian of the child; or
   (d) he is a person in whose favour a residence order is in force with respect to the child; or
   (e) he has custody of the child.

As the girl is 16 years of age this offence is not relevant; answers B, C and D are therefore incorrect.

Crime, para. 1.13.2.1

Answer 13.2

Answer **A** — Section 1 of the Children and Young Persons Act 1933 states:

(1) If any person who has attained the age of 16 years and has responsibility for any child or young person under that age, wilfully assaults, ill-treats, neglects, abandons, or exposes him, or causes or procures him to be assaulted, ill-treated, neglected, abandoned, or exposed, in a manner likely to cause him unnecessary suffering or injury to health (including injury to or loss of sight, or hearing, or limb or organ of the body, and any mental derangement), that person shall be guilty of a misdemeanour.

If a parent or other person legally liable to maintain the child or young person, or a guardian, has failed to provide adequate food, clothing, medical aid or lodging for the child or young person, they will be deemed to have neglected the child or young person for these purposes (see s. 1(2)).

As MURTY has reached the age of 16 she can commit this offence; answer D is therefore incorrect. The prosecution must prove that this was wilful (not reckless or intentional, which is why answers B and C are incorrect).

Crime, para. 1.13.3

Answer 13.3

Answer **B** — The offence under s. 2 of the 1984 Act can be committed in two ways:

- Remove the child from lawful control.
- Keep the child from lawful control.

There is also a statutory defence under s. 2(3) which states it is not an offence if at the time it was committed the defendant believed the child had attained the age of 16. In relation to when CRAWSHAY removed the child, effectively the first limb of the offence, he would not have committed it due to his belief; answer A is therefore incorrect.

However, later that defence is removed when he finds out the child's real age, and as such even though he did not commit the first limb he did commit the second limb when he kept the child; answer D is therefore incorrect.

Unlike the offence of kidnapping, consent of the victim in s. 2 is irrelevant; answer C is therefore incorrect.

Crime, paras 1.13.2.3, 1.13.2.4

Answer 13.4

Answer **B** — Section 1(2) of the Children and Young Persons Act 1933 states:

(b) where it is proved that the death of an infant under three years of age was caused by suffocation (not being suffocation caused by disease or the presence of any foreign body in the throat or air passages of the infant) while the infant was in bed with some other person who has attained the age of sixteen years, that other person shall, if he was, when he went to bed, under the influence of drink, be deemed to have neglected the infant in a manner likely to cause injury to its health.

This is answer B; answers A, C and D are therefore incorrect.

Crime, para. 1.13.3

Answer 13.5

Answer **C** — To be guilty of an offence under s. 1 of the Children and Young Persons Act 1933, an accused must have been over the age of 16 at the time of the offence, and must have 'had responsibility' for the child or young person in question. Although s. 1 creates just one offence, it may take a number of different forms. It may take the form of positive abuse (assault, ill-treatment, abandonment or exposure) or of mere neglect, or it may take the form of causing or procuring abuse or neglect. The abuse or neglect in question must be committed 'in a manner likely to cause unnecessary suffering or injury to health', but the offence is essentially a conduct crime rather than a result crime. It need not therefore be shown that any such injury was caused (answer D is therefore incorrect). ANITA's actions may well have amounted to an offence under the Act, but she is outside the scope of the legislation by virtue of her age; answers A and B are therefore incorrect.

Crime, para. 1.13.3

Answer 13.6

Answer **D** — There are two offences of child abduction under the Child Abduction Act 1984; s. 1, person connected with a child and s. 2 person not connected with a child. So is YILMAZ connected to the child? The answer to this lies in s. 1(2) which states:

A person is connected with the child for the purposes of this section if—
(a) he is a parent of the child; or
(b) in the case of a child whose parents were not married to each other at the time of his birth, there are reasonable grounds for believing that he is the father of the child; or
(c) he is a guardian of the child; or
(ca) he is a special guardian of the child; or
(d) he is a person in whose favour a residence order is in force with respect to the child; or
(e) he has custody of the child.

So YILMAZ could never commit an offence contrary to s. 2 as he is not a person not connected with a child, and indeed this is reflected in s. 2(3) of the 1984 Act; answer B is therefore incorrect.

Removing the child from the UK is the remit of s. 1 and has no application to s. 2; answers A and C are therefore incorrect.

Crime, paras 1.13.2.1, 1.13.2.2

Answer 13.7

Answer **D** — It is an offence of child cruelty when a person, in relation to a child:

> wilfully assaults, ill-treats, neglects, abandons, or exposes him, or causes or procures him to be assaulted, ill-treated, neglected, abandoned, or exposed, in a manner likely to cause him unnecessary suffering or injury to health ...

(Children and Young Persons Act 1933, s. 1)

This section creates only one single offence, albeit one that can be committed in many different ways, by both positive acts and omission (see *R* v *Hayles* [1969] 1 QB 364); answer A is therefore incorrect. Although any aspect of neglect must be shown to have occurred in a manner likely to cause unnecessary suffering or injury to health, there is no need to show that any such suffering or injury actually came about; answers B and C are therefore incorrect.

Crime, para. 1.13.3

Answer 13.8

Answer **D** — This scenario mirrors the case of *Langley* v *Liverpool City Council and Chief Constable of Merseyside* [2006] 1 WLR 375. In that case the police invoked their powers under s. 46 of the Children Act 1989 despite an EPO being in existence that the social services were going to raise when the children returned home.

The Court of Appeal considered the proper approach in these circumstances to be as follows:

- There is no express provision in the Act prohibiting the police from invoking s. 46 where an EPO is in place and it is not desirable to imply a restriction which prohibits a constable from removing a child under s. 46 where he or she has reasonable cause to believe that the child would otherwise be likely to suffer significant harm; answer A is therefore incorrect.
- The s. 46 power to remove a child can therefore be exercised even where an EPO is in force in respect of the child.
- Where a police officer knows that an EPO is in force, he or she should not exercise the power of removing a child under s. 46, unless there are compelling reasons to do so; answer C is therefore incorrect as there is no mention of 'immediately'.
- The statutory scheme accords primacy to the EPO procedure under s. 44 because removal under that section is sanctioned by the court and involves a more elaborate, sophisticated and complete process of removal than under s. 46; answer B is therefore incorrect.

- Consequently, the removal of children should usually be effected pursuant to an EPO, and s. 46 should only be invoked where it is not reasonably practicable to execute an EPO.
- In deciding whether it is practicable to execute an EPO, the police should always have regard to the paramount need to protect children from significant harm.
- Failure to follow the statutory procedure may amount to the police officer's removal of the child under s. 46 being declared unlawful; answer C is therefore incorrect.

Crime, para. 1.13.4

Answer 13.9

Answer **D** — Section 46 states that where a constable has reasonable cause to believe that a child would otherwise be likely to suffer significant harm, he or she may remove that child to suitable accommodation and keep him or her there. Answer A is incorrect, as the section allows only a constable to remove the child (known as police protection). There is no requirement for the officer to be in uniform (answer B is therefore incorrect). The section does not specify that the child should only be taken to a police station or hospital (although these may be suitable places); the child may be taken to any suitable accommodation (which is why answer C is incorrect).

Crime, para. 1.13.4

Answer 13.10

Answer **C** — Section 46(10) of the Children Act 1989 states:

Where a child has been taken into police protection, the designated officer shall allow—
(a) the child's parents;
(b) any person who is not a parent of the child but who has parental responsibility for him;
(c) any person with whom the child was living immediately before he was taken into police protection;
(d) any person in whose favour a contact order is in force with respect to the child;
(e) any person who is allowed to have contact with the child by virtue of an order under section 34; and
(f) any person acting on behalf of any of those persons,
to have such contact (if any) with the child as, in the opinion of the designated officer, is both reasonable and in the child's best interests.

So clearly it is the decision of the designated officer what, if any, contact should be had with the child whilst in police protection (answer B is therefore incorrect) considering:

- what is reasonable;
- what is in the child's best interest.

There is no 'must' about the cousin's contact and therefore answer D is incorrect. Even though the cousin has no parental responsibility contact could be allowed if the designated officer thinks it is appropriate; answer A is therefore incorrect.

Crime, para. 1.13.4.1

Answer 13.11

Answer **A** — Acting in contravention of a protection order or power exercised under s. 46 of the Children Act 1989 (police protection power) is an offence contrary to s. 49 of the 1989 Act.

Section 49 of the Children Act 1989 states:

(1) A person shall be guilty of an offence if, knowingly and without lawful authority or reasonable excuse, he—
    (a) takes a child to whom this section applies away from the responsible person;
    (b) keeps such a child away from the responsible person; or
    (c) induces, assists or incites such a child to run away or stay away from the responsible person.

So the offence is complete when a person induces, assists or incites a child to run away, and does not necessarily involve actually taking the child away, although that action is also an offence under this section; answer D is therefore incorrect. In this section 'the responsible person' means any person who for the time being has care of him by virtue of the care order, the emergency protection order, or s. 46, as the case may be. This would include the foster carer; answer C is therefore incorrect.

The legislation does not mention an intention to take the child abroad, referring only to taking the child, or inducing the child to leave the place they were put if they were in care, subject to an EPO or police protection powers (s. 49(2)); answer B is therefore incorrect.

Crime, para. 1.13.4.2

Answer 13.12

Answer **D** — Section 1 of the Child Abduction Act 1984 states:

> (1) Subject to subsections (5) and (8) below, a person connected with a child under the age of 16 commits an offence if he takes or sends the child out of the United Kingdom without the appropriate consent.

So the offence itself only relates to children under 16; for that reason alone answer A is incorrect.

The offence can only be committed by a person 'connected with' the child, and this is defined in s. 1(2) of the Child Abduction Act 1984, which would include the children's father.

Such a person must either take, or be responsible for sending, the child out of the United Kingdom himself. This offence is not committed by holding the child within the jurisdiction, nor where the child is lawfully taken out the country and return is then refused; answers A, B and C are therefore incorrect.

Had the father taken the children to France without the consent of the mother then the offence may have been committed. This would have led to the various defences kicking in, one of which is that he is out of the United Kingdom for a period of less than one month. However, as the offence was not committed no defence is necessary.

Crime, para. 1.13.2.1

Answer 13.13

Answer **A** — Section 2 of the Children and Young Persons (Harmful Publications) Act 1955 states:

> (1) A person who prints, publishes, sells or lets on hire a work to which this Act applies, or has any such work in his possession for the purpose of selling it or letting it on hire, shall be guilty of an offence...

A prosecution for this offence can only be brought with the consent of the Attorney General (or Solicitor General). The sort of 'works' to which the Act applies are set out in s. 1 and include books, magazines or other like works of a kind likely to fall into the hands of children or young persons which consist wholly or mainly of stories told in pictures which portray:

- the commission of crimes, or
- acts of violence or cruelty, or
- incidents of a repulsive or horrible nature,

in such a way that the work as a whole would tend to corrupt a child or young person.

There is a defence to this charge (answer D is therefore incorrect). Section 2 of the Children and Young Persons (Harmful Publications) Act 1955, s. 2 states:

(1) ...in any proceedings taken under this subsection against a person in respect of selling or letting on hire a work or of having it in his possession for the purpose of selling it or letting it on hire, it shall be a defence for him to prove that he had not examined the contents of the work and had no reasonable cause to suspect that it was one to which this Act applies.

So he has to show that he had not examined the contents (answer B is therefore incorrect) and it is irrelevant what his view of the contents are; answer C is therefore incorrect.

Crime, para. 1.13.5

Theft and Related Offences

STUDY PREPARATION

To use the police vernacular, many subjects in this chapter are your 'bread and butter' offences. In the *Police Q & A Road Policing* book, we stress the importance of knowing basic definitions, in order to recognise the more complex offences. The same applies to many dishonesty offences. You simply cannot get away with not knowing the components that make up the definition of theft. Learning this will assist you with robbery, handling, burglary and aggravated burglary. Similarly, the concept of dishonesty is important to understanding—and proving—a number of offences.

Following on from this, you must be able to recognise the difference between the burglary offences under s. 9(1)(a) and s. 9(1)(b) of the Theft Act 1968, and when a person commits the aggravated offence, by having with them certain articles.

Learning the definitions of robbery and handling will also be crucial, as well as the offences under s. 12 of the Act (taking and aggravated vehicle-taking). There are other offences contained in the chapter that you may not come across regularly, such as abstracting electricity and blackmail.

QUESTIONS

Question 14.1

VENTHAM goes into a shop intending to steal a dress and she has brought a label with a barcode on it with her, much cheaper than the actual price of the dress she wants. She picks up the dress and replaces the label and starts to walk towards the till; however she believes she is being followed by a store detective so she puts the dress down and walks off. Ten minutes later she returns and picks the dress up again this time going through the till and buying the dress at a much cheaper price.

In relation to theft which of the following is correct?

A VENTHAM commits theft when she picks up the dress initially.

B VENTHAM commits theft when she changes the price tag.

C VENTHAM commits theft when she picks up the dress for the second time.

D VENTHAM does not commit theft, she commits a Fraud Act offence when she pays for the dress at a cheaper price.

Question 14.2

SWART is in a nightclub during licensing hours and goes to the toilet where he falls asleep as he is very drunk. When he wakes he takes a picture off the wall that he really likes intending to keep it. He then goes back into the main part of the club although it is now closed. He cannot get out so he uses a chair to smash a window and jumps out, unfortunately straight into the arms of a passing police officer.

At what point, if any, does SWART commit aggravated burglary?

A When he takes the picture.

B When he re-enters the nightclub.

C When he breaks the window.

D He does not commit burglary at any point.

Question 14.3

McDOUGAL is shopping in a department store and absent mindedly puts a dress into her own bag. She pays for other items and leaves the store without paying for the dress in her own bag. She gets on a bus and goes home. At home she discovers the dress and wonders if it suits her. She tries it on and likes it so she decides to keep it.

When does McDOUGAL appropriate the dress as defined by s. 3 of the Theft Act 1968?

A When she puts the item in her bag.

B When she leaves the store without paying.

C When she tries the dress on.

D When she decides to keep the dress.

Question 14.4

BEYNON believes that his neighbour's dog keeps excreting in his garden so he breaks into his house one night with the intention of committing GBH on his neighbour, however no one is in so BEYNON breaks several items in the house.

In relation to the offence of burglary (under s. 9 of the Theft Act 1968), which of the following is correct?

A BEYNON commits both s. 9(1)(a) and s. 9(1)(b) offences when he enters the house.

B BEYNON only commits an offence contrary to s. 9(1)(a) when he enters the house.

C BEYNON commits an offence contrary to s. 9(1)(b) when he damages the property.

D BEYNON does not commit a burglary offence as he had no intention to commit damage when he entered and did not actually commit GBH.

Question 14.5

OLSEN is a homeless person and is walking along a canal bank late at night. He breaks into a canal barge to see if there is any food in there he can steal, however he is tired and sleeps the night. The following day he spends all day on the barge and sleeps there that night. He decides then to move on and steals some tins of food on his way out. The canal barge itself was in fact uninhabited at this time as it had been re-possessed by the bank and was awaiting sale.

In considering only if the canal barge would be a 'building' for the purposes of burglary, which of the following is correct?

A Yes, a canal barge is always a 'building' as it is a structure of a permanent nature.

B Yes, the canal barge is always a 'building' as it is capable of being inhabited.

C No, the canal barge will not be a 'building' as it was uninhabited at the time it was entered.

D No, the canal barge will not be a 'building' as it was unoccupied at the time it was entered.

Question 14.6

CUTHBERT organises a gang to carry out a burglary at a large country house. He plans it meticulously and has various roles for all his accomplices. One of those, BRITZ, is asked to carry a large knife in case they are disturbed; all the gang know that BRITZ will be carrying a knife and all agree that they will use it if they have to. The gang enter the house and steal several items; BRITZ stayed outside the house on guard with his knife.

Who, if anyone, has committed aggravated burglary contrary to s. 10 of the Theft Act 1968?

A All the gang commits aggravated burglary as they are all aware of the knife.

B All the gang commits aggravated burglary as they are all aware of the knife and all agree to its use if necessary.

C Only BRITZ as he was the one actually carrying the knife.

D No one at all commits aggravated burglary.

Question 14.7

GRIFFITHS asked his colleague MORGAN if he could borrow her motor van to take his family on holiday for the weekend to West Wales. MORGAN agreed; however, GRIFFITHS had misled MORGAN, and actually takes the motor van to a pop festival with some friends. He returns it in good condition at the end of the weekend.

Has GRIFFITHS committed an offence (under s. 12 of the Theft Act 1968) of taking a vehicle without the owner's consent?

A Yes, he obtained MORGAN's permission by deception.

B Yes, but only if the journey was further than the agreed destination.

C No, his deception did not negate the consent he obtained.

D Yes, unless he could show he believed MORGAN would have consented.

Question 14.8

ELLIS and McWHIRTER were in a supermarket car park when they saw a car with the keys in the ignition. They decided to take the vehicle and ELLIS got in the driver's seat; McWHIRTER sat in the front passenger seat. While he was reversing out of the parking place, ELLIS struck KANG, a shopper who was walking past. Both ELLIS and McWHIRTER got out of the car and ran off, leaving KANG behind with a bruised hip.

Has an offence been committed (under s. 12A of the Theft Act 1968) of aggravated vehicle-taking?

A No, the vehicle was not driven on a road.

B Yes, but only by ELLIS, the driver.

C Only if it can be shown that the vehicle was driven dangerously.

D Yes, by both ELLIS and McWHIRTER.

Question 14.9

SEYMOUR was working for a company that was going through financial difficulties, and as a result, he was laid off. One Friday evening, SEYMOUR entered the company office through an insecure window. In order to cause financial hardship to the owners, he linked all the computers up to the Internet, intending that they should all stay on for the weekend.

Has SEYMOUR committed the offence of abstracting electricity by his actions?

A Yes, the offence is complete in these circumstances.

B Yes, but a charge of burglary would be more appropriate.

C No, because he has not abstracted or diverted electricity.

D No, using a telephone would not amount to using electricity.

Question 14.10

RENNIE and ELLIOT met one evening to discuss breaking into an electrical warehouse. It was agreed that RENNIE would break in and hand the goods to ELLIOT outside in his van. They were joined by SEDGMORE, who agreed to keep the goods in his house for a few weeks, and MALROW, who owned a second-hand store and would sell the goods. They agreed that the burglary would take place the following night.

Who, if anyone, has committed the offence of handling stolen goods in these circumstances?

A ELLIOT, SEDGMORE and MALROW only.

B All four have committed the offence.

C Only SEDGMORE and MALROW have committed the offence.

D None of these people has committed the offence.

Question 14.11

STUARTSON has been arrested for handling stolen goods and the officers dealing with the case are deciding what they would need to prove in order to secure a conviction in relation to 'stolen goods'.

In relation to this which of the following is correct?

A They only have to show that the goods were actually stolen.

B They would have to show that the goods were stolen by way of conviction of the 'thief'.

C They would have to show that the goods were actually stolen, and by whom they were stolen.

D They would have to show that the goods were actually stolen, and name the actual loser.

Question 14.12

LATIMER and BOWEN went for a meal in their favourite restaurant, one where they ate regularly. During the meal they consumed two bottles of wine each. For a laugh, at the end of the meal they both went to the toilet and climbed out of the window. They intended returning the next day to pay for the meal; however, the restaurant owner did not know this and called the police.

Have LATIMER and BOWEN committed an offence (under s. 3 of the Theft Act 1978) of making off without payment?

A Yes, but they would have a defence if they could show that they thought the owner would have consented in the circumstances.

B No, because they have not deceived the owner into thinking they would pay for the meals.

C No, they have not committed the offence in these circumstances as they intended returning to pay.

D Yes, they have committed the offence, regardless of their intention to pay, and would have no defence in the circumstances.

Question 14.13

GWYNN was at his friend PETERS' flat and he had with him a stolen credit card, which he had recently used to obtain goods by deception. GWYNN gave the card to EDDINGTON, so that EDDINGTON could use it the next day. GWYNN had no intention of using the card again.

Which of the following statements is true, in relation to s. 25 of the Theft Act 1968, regarding 'going equipped'?

A An offence has been committed by EDDINGTON only, as GWYNN did not intend using the card again.

B An offence has been committed by GWYNN and EDDINGTON in these circumstances.

C No offence has been committed by either EDDINGTON or GWYNN in these circumstances.

D An offence has been committed by GWYNN; EDDINGTON commits no offence in these circumstances.

Question 14.14

EVANS telephones the parents of a 14-year-old boy stating that he knew the boy walked home from school alone and that one day he might go missing. To avoid that, EVANS asks the parents if they think their son is worth £10,000.

Has EVANS committed the offence of blackmail in these circumstances?

A Yes, provided the parents fear their son may be kidnapped.

B Yes, as EVANS has made unwarranted demands with menaces.

C No, as no actual demand has been made.

D No, as the child is currently free to come and go as he pleases.

Question 14.15

DRAPER is walking along the street when his friend pulls up next to him in a car. DRAPER gets in the car and notices that the ignition barrel is missing and asks if the vehicle has been stolen. His friend tells him it hasn't and that the ignition barrel is only broken; DRAPER does not believe him and suspects that the vehicle has been stolen. Despite this belief, DRAPER allows himself to be carried in the vehicle. However, a few miles into their journey they are stopped by police as the car was in fact taken without the owner's consent.

Has DRAPER committed the offence under s. 12(1) of the Theft Act 1968, of allowing himself to be carried?

A Yes, the fact he suspects the car to be stolen and his presence in it is enough; movement of the car was irrelevant.

B Yes, as he suspects the car to be stolen and allows himself to be carried in it.

C No, mere suspicion is not enough, he must know the car is stolen and allow himself to be carried in it.

D No, mere suspicion is not enough, he must know the car is stolen; movement of the car is irrelevant.

Question 14.16

MUNRO commits a robbery and steals a mobile phone. He gives it to COMMONS, who works for a mobile telephone company, who alters the unique device identifier and sells the phone on to an unsuspecting buyer.

Considering the Mobile Telephones (Re-Programming) Act 2002, which of the following is true?

A This is an offence from the moment the phone is altered; there is no defence.

B This is an offence from the moment the phone is sold; there is no defence.

C This is an offence from the moment the phone is altered; there is a statutory defence however.

D This is an offence from the moment the phone is sold; there is a statutory defence however.

Question 14.17

McIVOR visits his doctor in absolute agony due to a back injury. He demands an injection of a new wonder pain-killing drug, but as it is very expensive his doctor refuses and prescribes a strong pain-killer instead. Infuriated, McIVOR pulls a knife from his pocket and threatens to kill the doctor unless he gets the new drug; in fear for his life, the doctor gives him the injection. McIVOR apologises for his behaviour and leaves.

With respect to blackmail, which of the following is true?

A The offence is complete when the doctor gives McIVOR the injection.

B The offence is complete when McIVOR threatens the doctor.

C This is not blackmail as McIVOR has had no 'gain'.

D This is not blackmail as the doctor has had no loss, the drug belonging to the NHS.

Question 14.18

NICHOLAS drove his van at the request of his friend to collect some copper wire, and he was surprised when he was directed to stop beside a large hedge. NICHOLAS was even more surprised when his friend started to load up his van with the heavy-duty copper wire that was hidden below this bush, but not suspecting wrongdoing he assisted. On arrival at a local scrap yard he was even more surprised to be arrested by police officers investigating the theft of copper wire from an electrical power substation next to the hedge. The police, however, have no evidence that NICHOLAS stole the wire, although he has numerous previous convictions for handling stolen goods. When questioned about the wire he said he had no knowledge that the goods were stolen, and that he 'asked no questions and was told no lies'.

In relation to a possible charge of handling stolen goods against NICHOLAS which of the following is correct?

A He should be charged with both receiving or arranging to receive stolen goods and assisting or acting for the benefit of another.

B He should be charged with either receiving or arranging to receive stolen goods and assisting or acting for the benefit of another, but not both.

C He must be charged with receiving or arranging to receive stolen goods as it was obvious the goods were stolen.

D He should not be charged with any handling offence as he had no knowledge that the goods were stolen.

Question 14.19

DOUGLAS worked in a petrol station owned by RANKIN. At the end of her shift one day she was told that her son had been in a car accident and was in hospital. DOUGLAS did not have a car and when she finished work, she took £10 from the till to pay for a taxi to take her to the hospital as she had no cash on her. In fact she had plenty of money in her bank account, but she didn't want to waste time by going to a cash point. DOUGLAS intended paying the money back the next day, thinking that RANKIN would not mind. RANKIN found that the till was short of money the next day and confronted DOUGLAS. RANKIN did mind that the money had been taken and contacted the police to report a theft.

Would DOUGLAS be able to claim a defence to the offence of theft in these circumstances?

A No, because RANKIN did not consent to the money being taken, and therefore it was theft.

B No, as she could have got her own money had she taken reasonable steps to get it.

C Yes, if she believed that RANKIN would have consented if he had known she was taking the money and the circumstances in which it was taken.

D Yes, if she believed that RANKIN would have consented if he had known she was taking the money.

Question 14.20

CRAWFORD obtains several thousand pounds in cash by stealing it from his elderly neighbour. CRAWFORD deposits the cash in his own account but transfers it electronically to the bank account held by his friend ELMS, who is initially unaware of the transfer. A few days later ELMS discovers the money in his account, and when he asks where it came from, CRAWFORD tells him the truth. ELMS agrees to keep it to assist CRAWFORD.

At what point, if any, does ELMS commit an offence of dishonestly retaining a wrongful credit contrary to s. 24A of the Theft Act 1968?

A He commits an offence under s. 24A as soon as the money is transferred into his account.

B He commits an offence under s. 24A as soon as he becomes aware that the money was stolen.

C He commits an offence under s. 24A as soon as he becomes aware that the money was stolen and fails to have it cancelled.

D He does not commit an offence contrary to s. 24A but will commit an offence of handling stolen goods as he assists in the retention of the funds.

Question 14.21

MATHERSON was a landlord who refused to return his tenant, GUTHRIE's deposit when the tenancy was terminated by MATHERSON. GUTHRIE believed he had been asked to leave without justification and that the deposit was being unfairly withheld. GUTHRIE and a friend went to MATHERSON's house and burst in when the door opened; the friend held MATHERSON tightly whilst GUTHRIE searched the house. GUTHRIE was hoping to take cash he thought that he was entitled to, however not finding any he took items of value. GUTHRIE claims that he intended to keep the items until MATHERSON returned his deposit and if this failed he would sell the items and then use the money for a deposit on another flat, returning the money left over to the landlord. He would have taken that course of action as he knew he was entitled to cash but thought he had no right to take the items as he did.

Is GUTHRIE guilty of robbery?
A Yes, he has used force to obtain items that do not belong to him.
B Yes, he has used force to obtain items that he had no rights to.
C No, he honestly believed he had a legal right to deprive MATHERSON of the items.
D No, GUTHRIE did not apply the force himself in order to obtain the items.

Question 14.22

JEAVONS has bought title on a property from a business. JEAVONS suspected when he bought the title that the land, and therefore the title, could have been obtained by fraud, however he still buys the title.

Would this title be criminal property as defined in s. 340 of the Proceeds of Crime Act 2002?
A Yes, provided that the 'title' was obtained by criminal conduct.
B Yes, even though it is only suspected that the 'title' was obtained by criminal conduct.
C No, property relates to more than just money, however it must be real or personal property.
D No, the 'title' would not be property, however the actual land bought may be if it was obtained by criminal conduct.

Question 14.23

GUTHERIDGE is a car dealer and his wife is an accountant. GUTHERIDGE obtains a luxury car for a very low price and sells it at a high price. When it comes to dealing with the taxes on that car his wife suspects that GUTHERIDGE may have benefited from criminal conduct as she suspects that the car was stolen. However she carries on and puts the sale through her husband's company books, and does not mention her concerns to him. In fact the car was obtained and sold lawfully by GUTHERIDGE.

Consider the offence of entering into or becoming concerned in a money launder-ing arrangement, contrary to s. 328(1) of the Proceeds of Crime Act 2002.

A This could well be that offence even though the property was not 'criminal property'.

B This could well be that offence but only if GUTHERIDGE's wife claimed less tax than was expected to be paid.

C This could not be that offence as it was based merely on suspicion and not knowledge.

D This could not be that offence as the property was not obtained for benefit by criminal conduct.

ANSWERS

Answer 14.1

Answer **A** — There are five key elements to the offence of theft. These are:

- dishonesty;
- appropriation;
- property;
- belonging to another;
- intention of permanently depriving.

So VENTHAM commits theft when she picks up the dress with the intention of permanently depriving the owner of it. She may well go on to commit a fraud offence but she meets all the elements of theft when she picks up the dress; answer D is therefore incorrect.

In *R* v *Gomez* [1993] AC 442 the House of Lords considered 'appropriation'; there may be an appropriation of the same property on more than one occasion. However, once property has been stolen (as opposed to merely appropriated), that same property cannot be stolen again by the same thief (*R* v *Atakpu* [1994] QB 69). So although the property was appropriated when the tag was changed and when it was picked up again, essentially theft cannot be committed that second or third time and answers B and C are therefore incorrect.

Crime, para. 1.14.2.3

Answer 14.2

Answer **D** — Burglary is dealt with by s. 9(1) of the Theft Act 1968 and the principles contained therein should be followed to determine when the offence is, or is not, committed.

Section 9(1)(a) burglary is committed where someone enters any building or part of a building as a trespasser and with intent to commit:

- stealing;
- inflicting grievous bodily harm;
- causing unlawful damage.

Section 9(1)(b) burglary is committed where someone having entered any building or part of a building as a trespasser:

- steals;
- inflicts, attempts to inflict grievous bodily harm.

So we need to consider the entries and intentions of the accused.

- Enters nightclub—not a trespasser, intention to drink = no burglary offence.
- Enters toilet—pub still open so not a trespasser, intention to ...! = no burglary offence.
- Whilst in cubicle—steals, s. 9(1)(b) is not committed as he didn't enter as a trespasser = no burglary offence.
- Back into nightclub—enters as a trespasser, nightclub is closed, intention to leave = no burglary offence.
- In nightclub—caused damage and was there as a trespasser, not one of the s. 9(1)(b) offences = no burglary offence.

So, no offence of burglary is committed, answers A, B and C are therefore incorrect.

Crime, paras 1.14.3 (all sections), 1.14.4 (all sections)

Answer 14.3

Answer **C** — Section 3 of the Theft Act 1968 states:

(1) Any assumption by a person of the rights of an owner amounts to an appropriation, and this includes, where he has come by the property (innocently or not) without stealing it, any later assumption of a right to it by keeping or dealing with it as owner.

If a person, having come by property—innocently or not—without stealing it, later assumes any rights to it by keeping it or treating it as his/her own, then he/she 'appropriates' that property (s. 3(1)).

The point of appropriation is therefore when she treats it as her own by trying it on; answers A, B and D are therefore incorrect.

Crime, para. 1.14.2.3

Answer 14.4

Answer **B** — Section 9 of the Theft Act 1968 states:

(1) A person is guilty of burglary if—
   (a) he enters any building or part of a building as a trespasser and with intent to commit any such offence as is mentioned in subsection (2) below; or

(b) having entered any building or part of a building as a trespasser he steals or attempts to steal anything in the building or that part of it or inflicts or attempts to inflict on any person therein any grievous bodily harm.

(2) The offences referred to in subsection (1)(a) above are offences of stealing anything in the building or part of a building in question, of inflicting on any person therein any grievous bodily harm and of doing unlawful damage to the building or anything therein.

So a s. 9(1)(b) offence can only be committed after entry; answer A is therefore incorrect. He commits a s. 9(1)(a) offence when he enters intending GBH, but s. 9(1)(b) does not include criminal damage so he does not commit that; answers C and D are therefore incorrect.

Crime, paras 1.14.3.1, 1.14.3.5

Answer 14.5

Answer **C** — Section 9 of the Theft Act 1968 states:

(4) References in subsections (1) and (2) above to a building,...and the reference in subsection (3), above, to a building which is a dwelling, shall apply also to an inhabited vehicle or vessel, and shall apply to any such vehicle or vessel at times when the person having a habitation in it is not there as well as at times when he is.

The effect of s. 9(4) is to include inhabited vehicles and vessels (such as houseboats or motor homes) within the term. A canal boat that is not inhabited is not a building as whilst it may be capable of habitation, it is not being lived in; answers A and B are therefore incorrect.

What is important with a canal barge then is whether it is inhabited or not; if it is inhabited then it would be a building as per s. 9(4) even though at the time entry was made it was unoccupied; answer D is therefore incorrect.

Crime, para. 1.14.3.2

Answer 14.6

Answer **D** — Section 10 of the Theft Act 1968 states:

(1) A person is guilty of aggravated burglary if he commits any burglary and at the time has with him any firearm or imitation firearm, any weapon of offence, or any explosive;...

An aggravated burglary is committed when a person commits an offence of burglary (either a s. 9(1)(a) or a s. 9(1)(b) offence) and at the time he has with him his WIFE.

W — Weapon of offence
I — Imitation firearm
F — Firearm
E — Explosive

So there are essentially two factors; a burglary committed and at the time it is committed it is done with a WIFE.

So who of the gang has committed burglary? Those who entered the building with the intention of stealing. So that is all the gang except BRITZ who remained outside the building. So BRITZ never commits burglary so he cannot commit aggravated burglary and as he was the one with a WIFE none of the gang, who committed burglary, committed aggravated burglary; answers A, B and C are therefore incorrect.

Crime, para. 1.14.4

Answer 14.7

Answer **C** — An offence under s. 12 is committed by a person who takes a vehicle without the owner's consent or other lawful authority, for his own or another's use.

The issue of consent was dealt with in the case of *R* v *Peart* [1970] 2 QB 672. The defendant was convicted of the offence, after he falsely represented to the owner of a car that he needed it to drive from Bedlington to Alnwick to sign a contract. The owner let him have the vehicle, provided he returned it that day. As he had intended all along, Peart drove the car instead to Burnley in the evening.

The Court of Appeal subsequently quashed Peart's conviction, by following the decision in *Whittaker* v *Campbell* [1984] QB 318, where it was held that *there is no general principle of law that fraud vitiates consent.*

Consequently, even if consent is obtained by fraud, it is still consent (making answer A incorrect). The case of *Peart* shows that even though the journey taken was different from the one agreed, an offence is still not committed (making answer B incorrect).

Lastly, the defence provided under s. 12(6) would apply *where an offence has been committed.* Since an offence has not been committed in these circumstances, the defence would not apply (which is why answer D is incorrect).

Crime, paras 1.14.5, 1.14.5.1

Answer 14.8

Answer **D** — First, a person must commit an offence under s. 12(1) of the Theft Act 1968 either by taking the vehicle, *or* by being carried in it. Then, under s. 12A, it must be proved that at any time after the vehicle was taken (whether by him or another) and before it was recovered:

- it was driven dangerously on a road or public place; *or*
- owing to the driving of the vehicle, an accident occurred whereby injury was caused to any person; *or*
- owing to the driving of the vehicle, an accident occurred whereby damage was caused to any property other than the vehicle; *or*
- damage was caused to the vehicle.

The Act does not specify that the accident involving an injury to a person should occur on a road (making answer A incorrect).

All that the prosecution has to prove is that *one* of these circumstances occurred before the car was recovered (*Dawes* v *DPP* (1995) 1 Cr App R 65) (answer C is incorrect for this reason).

Answer B is incorrect because the offence may be committed by either the driver or the passenger, provided one of the circumstances apply.

Crime, paras 1.14.5, 1.14.6

Answer 14.9

Answer **A** — Under s. 13 of the Theft Act 1968, a person who dishonestly uses, without due authority, or dishonestly causes to be *wasted or diverted*, any electricity, shall be guilty of an offence.

As electricity is not 'property', a specific offence was created to deal with its dishonest use or waste. For this reason electricity cannot be 'stolen', and therefore its dishonest use or wastage cannot form an element of burglary (making answer B incorrect).

Diverting a domestic electrical supply so as to bypass the meter, or using another's telephone without authority (*Low* v *Blease* [1975] Crim LR 513) would be examples of this offence, as would unauthorised surfing on the Internet by an employee at work, provided in each case that dishonesty was present (making answers C and D incorrect).

Crime, para. 1.14.11

Answer 14.10

Answer **D** — Quite simply, there can be no offence under s. 22 of the Theft Act 1968, unless goods have been stolen (answers A and B are therefore incorrect). Even though two of the participants have arranged to receive stolen goods, they will not commit the offence until the burglary takes place (answer C is therefore also incorrect).

If the plan ever does come to fruition, RENNIE, as the person stealing the goods, would not commit the offence. It is debatable whether ELLIOT would do so, if he assisted with the burglary, as he might be guilty of that offence.

Crime, para. 1.14.16

Answer 14.11

Answer **A** — For goods to be handled they have to be stolen, if goods are not stolen there is no handling. Whether they are so stolen is a question of fact for a jury or magistrate(s). There is no need to prove that the thief, blackmailer, etc. has been convicted of the primary offence before prosecuting the alleged handler, neither is it always necessary to identify who that person was; answers B, C and D are therefore incorrect.

However, care needs to be taken if a defendant is to be accused of handling goods stolen from a specific person or place. If that is the case then ownership of the goods will become an integral part of the prosecution case and it will be necessary to provide evidence proving that aspect of the offence (*Iqbal* v *DPP* [2004] EWHC 2567 (Admin)).

Crime, paras 1.14.16, 1.14.16.1

Answer 14.12

Answer **C** — This is a typical question where police officers would think practically and decide, 'I would arrest those, where it was necessary to do so'. Avoid this approach and answer questions purely as points of law.

A person commits an offence under s. 3 of the Theft Act 1978 if, knowing that payment on the spot for goods supplied or services received is required, he or she dishonestly makes off without paying *with intent to avoid payment.*

In the scenario, even though the couple have made off without paying, there is no offence if they intend to defer payment to a later date (even though morally their actions may be regarded as wrong!). (Answer D is therefore incorrect.)

There is no requirement that the person practised some deception to prove the offence; simply making off with the required intent is enough (which is why answer B is incorrect).

The defence in answer A has been made up and does not exist.

Crime, para. 1.14.13

Answer 14.13

Answer **C** — A person commits an offence under s. 25 of the Theft Act 1968 when, not at his place of abode, he has with him any article for use in the course of or in connection with any burglary or theft.

The offence is designed as a preventative measure and therefore cannot be committed by a deed done in the past. The offence will be committed by a person who has an article with him or her for use by *someone else* (*R v Ellames* [1974] 1 WLR 1391).

Applying the Act to this scenario, GWYNN was not at his place of abode and had with him a credit card, which he intended EDDINGTON to use in the future in a cheat—this is neither theft nor burglary.

The question asks you specifically about s. 25 of the Theft Act 1968, not the Fraud Act 2006 (this would have been an offence in that statute). No offence under s. 25; answers A, B and D are therefore incorrect.

Crime, para. 1.14.8

Answer 14.14

Answer **B** — Section 21 of the Theft Act 1968 states:

(1) A person is guilty of blackmail if, with a view to gain for himself or another or with intent to cause loss to another, he makes any unwarranted demand with menaces; and for this purpose a demand with menaces is unwarranted unless the person making it does so in the belief—
    (a) that he has reasonable grounds for making the demand; and
    (b) that the use of the menaces is a proper means of reinforcing the demand.
(2) The nature of the act or omission demanded is immaterial, and it is also immaterial whether the menaces relate to action to be taken by the person making the demand.

This definition is deliberately drafted in such a way as to penalise the making of the demand, rather than the obtaining of property or the intimidation of the victim. In other words, it is a 'conduct crime'; answer A is therefore incorrect.

'Demands' are not defined in the Act. A demand need not be expressed openly. So where someone phones parents and asks them whether they regard the child as being worth £10,000, would clearly be regarded as having 'demanded' that sum irrespective of the fact the child is free to come and go; answers C and D are therefore incorrect.

Crime, para. 1.14.10

Answer 14.15

Answer **C** — The person who commits this offence must know that the conveyance has been taken without the consent of the owner or other lawful authority. If that person only 'suspects' that the conveyance has been taken, the offence is not committed; answers A and B are therefore incorrect. Further, the conveyance must actually move when the person drives it or allows themselves to be carried in or on it; answer D is therefore incorrect.

Crime, para. 1.14.5.6

Answer 14.16

Answer **C** — This offence was created to try to prevent the increasing criminal activity involving mobile handsets. The offence is committed where the unique identifier is either changed or interfered with, and is not reliant on a future sale of the phone; answers B and D are therefore incorrect. There is, however, a statutory defence, exclusive to manufacturers or those with written consent of the manufacturers; answer A is therefore incorrect.

Crime, para. 1.14.15

Answer 14.17

Answer **B** — The points to prove for an offence of blackmail are:

- with a view to gain;
- for self or another; *or*
- with intent to cause loss to another;
- made an unwarranted demand with menaces.

Using a knife to threaten to kill someone is most certainly an unwarranted demand ('unwarranted demand' is defined as an unreasonable or unfair demand) and menacing!

'Menaces' is loosely delineated as a threat (including a veiled one) of any action detrimental or unpleasant to the person addressed. And the offence is complete at the time the demand is made, not when its desired consequences are brought about; answer A is therefore incorrect.

As the demand must be made with a view to the person's gain, has McIVOR actually 'gained'? The gain must be in money or other property and can be temporary or permanent. In a case not mentioned in the manual, it was held that the drug was property and the injection involved 'gain' to the accused as he achieved pain relief. The fact that it was injected into him rather than being handed over did not mean that McIVOR did not gain that property; answer C is therefore incorrect. There does not have to be a loss, provided the demand is made with a view to gain; answer D is therefore incorrect.

Crime, para. 1.14.10.1

Answer 14.18

Answer **A** — Although generally speaking a charge should specify exactly what it is the person is actually accused of, and that where alternatives exist, to charge both would be bad for duplicity, handling stolen goods is an exception to this.

In *R v Nicklin* [1977] 1 WLR 403 the accused was charged with handling stolen property by dishonestly receiving it, knowing or believing it to be stolen, contrary to s. 22(1) of the Theft Act 1968. The defendant pleaded not guilty to that charge but accepted that he had assisted in the removal of the stolen property (the circumstances mirror the scenario of this question). He was found guilty of handling stolen goods and dishonestly assisting in the removal or disposing of them for the benefit of another knowing or believing the same to have been stolen. He appealed (understandably) that he had been convicted of an offence with which he was not even charged!

His appeal was allowed and the conviction quashed. The Court of Appeal stated *per curiam* that a conviction of a particular type of handling can be upheld where the indictment simply alleges the offence of handling and the generalised form has led to no injustice or confusion; but the better practice is to particularise the form of handling for which the defendant is blamed. If there is any uncertainty about which form of handling two counts will generally cover every form; one count for the first limb of s. 22(1) of the Theft Act 1968, dishonestly receiving, and a second count for the second limb, dishonestly undertaking or assisting in the retention, removal, disposal or realisation or arranging to do those things.

It is not bad for duplicity to charge both strands of the offence; answer B is therefore incorrect. In this scenario to charge only one strand would be wrong, following *Nicklin* a conviction would not be forthcoming; answer C is therefore incorrect.

You must show that the defendant knew or believed the goods to be stolen. Mere suspicion, however strong, will not be enough (*R v Griffiths* (1974) 60 Cr App R 14). Deliberate 'blindness' to the true identity of the goods would suffice but the distinction is a fine one in practice. It can be very difficult to prove knowledge or belief on the part of, say, a second-hand dealer who 'asks no questions'. Because there are practical difficulties in proving the required *mens rea*, s. 27(3) of the 1968 Act makes special provision to allow evidence of the defendant's previous convictions, or previous recent involvement with stolen goods, to be admitted; in these circumstances there would be more than enough evidence to charge the defendant, not to charge would be erroneous and therefore answer D is incorrect.

Crime, para. 1.14.16.4

Answer 14.19

Answer **C** — Under s. 2(1)(b) of the Theft Act 1968, a person's appropriation of property belonging to another is not to be regarded as dishonest if he/she appropriates the property in the belief that he or she would have the other's consent if the other knew of the appropriation *and* the circumstances of it. Therefore, the person appropriating the property must believe both elements, i.e. that the other person would have consented had he/she known of the appropriation and the circumstances of it. Answer D is therefore incorrect.

It is the belief of the person appropriating the property that is important, regardless of the belief of the owner. Therefore, even though RANKIN would state that he did not consent to the money being taken, if DOUGLAS can convince the court of these two elements, she may have a defence. Answer A is therefore incorrect. This includes occasions where the defendant had access to other funds, which could have been obtained by taking reasonable steps as this directly relates to the circumstances under which the defendant took the money, i.e. urgency in attending at the hospital; answer B is therefore incorrect.

Crime, para. 1.14.2.1

Answer 14.20

Answer **C** — One consequence of the decision of the House of Lords in *R v Preddy* [1996] AC 815 is that, where a person dishonestly obtains a money transfer from another the sum thereby credited to the first person's account can no longer be cat-egorised as stolen goods. This indeed was the view of the Law Commission when reviewing the impact of *Preddy*. Furthermore, even where a person, A, pays stolen bank notes directly into his account, the proceeds of a subsequent transfer from that account to an account held by another person B cannot be classed as stolen goods, because any credit balance thereby created in B's account is an entirely different chose ('thing in action') from the credit balance which previously represented the stolen money in A's account. B's credit balance admittedly represents the proceeds of A's original crime, but it has never done so in the hands of the original thief, and any argument that it does so in the hands of a handler of the stolen property (i.e. B) is circular, because that presupposes the very point it seeks to establish, namely that the funds in B's account are stolen goods! As they are not 'stolen goods' and therefore cannot be 'handled', answer D is therefore incorrect.

Section 24A of the Theft Act 1968 addresses this problem in two ways.

First, s. 24A(2A) broadens the scope of s. 24A to cases in which the accused dishon-estly retains a credit which he knows or correctly believes derives from an offence of:

> (2A) A credit to an account is wrongful to the extent that it derives from—
> (a) theft;
> (b) blackmail;
> (c) fraud (contrary to section 1 of the Fraud Act 2006); or
> (d) stolen goods.

If, for example, A pays stolen money into his account and transfers the funds from that account to an account owned by B, a wrongful credit has been made to B's account, and B may commit a s. 24A offence if he dishonestly retains it, knowing or believing it to be derived from one or other of those offences. In this scenario this is exactly what happened, and the s. 24A offence is complete only when the defendant dishonestly retained it; answers A and B are therefore incorrect.

Secondly s. 24A(8) provides that any money dishonestly withdrawn from an account to which a wrongful credit has been made can be classed once again as stolen goods.

It is curious that the proceeds of A's original theft can be classed as stolen goods when paid into A's own bank account, yet cease to be stolen goods when effectively 'transferred' to B's account, and yet revert to being stolen goods when dishonestly withdrawn as cash by B; but that is the law.

Any volunteers for a transfer to fraud investigation?

Crime, para. 1.14.14

Answer 14.21

Answer **B** — Section 8 of the Theft Act 1968 provides:

> (1) A person is guilty of robbery if he steals, and immediately before or at the time of doing so, and in order to do so, he uses force on any person or puts or seeks to put any person in fear of being then and there subjected to force...

So there has to be a theft, with all the requirements (dishonesty, etc.) that go with s. 1 of the Theft Act 1968. In *R* v *Forrester* [1992] Crim LR 793 the landlord refused to return the defendant's deposit when the tenancy was terminated by the landlord. The defendant believed he had been asked to leave without justification and that the deposit was being unfairly withheld. The defendant and a friend went to the landlord's house and burst in when the door was opened. The friend held the landlord whilst the defendant seized some items. The defendant's defence was that he intended to keep the items until the landlord returned his deposit and if this failed he would sell the items and use the money for a deposit on another flat and would return the money left over to the landlord. The conviction for robbery was upheld by the Court of Appeal. It was held that he knew he had no right to the items themselves and so could not claim that he was not dishonest under s. 2(1)(a) of the Theft Act 1968. This may have been different had he actually taken cash, and not items, but he was not entitled to take the items; answer C is therefore incorrect. Note the difference between answers A and B; even if the items did not belong to him, the accused could take them provided the elements of s. 2(1)(a) of the Theft Act 1968 were met, i.e. he had a right in law to take them. Answer A is therefore incorrect.

It is also immaterial who actually uses the force and to whom. Provided there is force used on a person to 'steal' the offence of robbery is complete and answer D is therefore incorrect.

Crime, para. 1.14.9

Answer 14.22

Answer **B** — Section 340 of the Proceeds of Crime Act 2002 states:

> (3) Property is criminal property if—
> > (a) it constitutes a person's benefit from criminal conduct or it represents such a benefit (in whole or part and whether directly or indirectly), and
> > (b) the alleged offender knows or suspects that it constitutes or represents such a benefit.

It is enough therefore that the suspect suspects that the property may have come to him through criminal conduct; answer A is therefore incorrect.

The property itself which may comprise the benefit from criminal conduct is widely defined to include money, all forms of property or real estate, things in action and other intangible or incorporeal property; answers C and D are therefore incorrect.

Crime, para. 1.14.17.3

Answer 14.23

Answer **D** — Section 328 of the Proceeds of Crime Act 2002 states:

(1) A person commits an offence if he enters into or becomes concerned in an arrangement which he knows or suspects facilitates (by whatever means) the acquisition, retention, use or control of criminal property by or on behalf of another person.

Thus the prosecution has to prove that:

- the defendant enters into or becomes concerned in an arrangement;
- which he knows or suspects (answer C is therefore incorrect) facilitates (by whatever means) the acquisition, retention, use or control;
- of criminal property;
- by or on behalf of another person.

Although her actions can be at least dubious, she cannot commit this offence as the property concerned would have to be criminal property, as defined in s. 340 of the 2002 Act which it is not; answer A is therefore incorrect.

Answer B may well be an offence, but not under this Act, it is therefore incorrect.

Crime, para. 1.14.17.5

15 | Fraud

QUESTIONS

Question 15.1

JOKEVSKI was stopped and lawfully searched by a police officer who discovered several credit cards on him, all of which were not in his name. The officer believed that the cards were going to be used for fraud offences, and JOKEVSKI claims that he was on the way home from committing those offences. However despite several enquiries no victims have been identified and therefore no charges could be brought.

In relation to these circumstances could JOKEVSKI be charged with possession or control of articles for use in frauds contrary to s. 6 of the Fraud Act 2006?

A Yes, he has articles in his possession for use in the course of or in connection with any fraud.

B Yes, he has articles in his possession for use in the course of or in connection with any fraud and has actually used them.

C No, as the articles were used in offences that have previously taken place.

D No, as no actual victims have been identified.

Question 15.2

BRANDRICK claims that he is a Nigerian prince and that he is due to inherit a fortune. He sends out emails asking for people to send him £10 to enable him to pay his legal fees and that he will then share his fortune with those who donate cash. He intends keeping any money that is sent to him; however, no one believes him and no money is sent.

Has BRANDRICK committed the offence of fraud by false representation contrary to s. 2 of the Fraud Act 2006?

A Yes, as he made a representation he knows is misleading.

B Yes, as he made a representation he knows is, or might be, untrue or misleading.

C No, as the representation was not made to a specific individual or a machine.

D No, as no one actually believed the fraud and sent money.

Question 15.3

RAMAGE is a member of a gym to which she took PASSARO. At the gym there was a new person working in reception. RAMAGE showed her membership card to the receptionist, saying, 'She's a member, too, but she forgot her card'. PASSARO was not a member, but said nothing and was allowed entry, without paying the usual fee for guests. Both RAMAGE and PASSARO had agreed to do this before attending at the gym in order to secure free entry for PASSARO.

Who, if anyone, has committed an offence (under s. 2 of the Fraud Act 2006) of fraud by misrepresentation?

A Both have committed the offence in these circumstances.

B RAMAGE only, as PASSARO made no representation that she was a member.

C PASSARO only as RAMAGE herself made no 'gain', whereas PASSARO gained entry to the gym for free.

D Neither, as no actual 'gain' was made by either of them as they received no money or property.

Question 15.4

FOWLER has a rare genetic disorder that he knows would preclude him from gaining life insurance. He is filling out a form for life insurance. The form asks specific questions about various medical conditions, but does not mention his specifically. So he correctly states he does not suffer from any of the conditions mentioned on the form and he signs the form.

Considering the Fraud Act 2006 which of the following is correct?

A FOWLER has falsely represented that he is in good health and has committed an offence contrary to s. 2.

B FOWLER has failed to disclose information and has committed an offence contrary to s. 3.

C FOWLER has falsely represented that he is in good health, and has also failed to disclose information; he has committed two offences, s. 2 and s. 3.

D FOWLER has not committed any offences as he has not falsely represented or failed to disclose as he has only signed to say that he does not suffer from any of the conditions mentioned.

Question 15.5

YOSHIMI was a sales representative and was given a company mobile phone. According to company rules, employees had to pay for private telephone calls. At the end of each month, YOSHIMI received a copy of the mobile phone bill and was required to highlight any private calls made and pay for them by cheque or cash. YOSHIMI knew that the accounting department was always busy and the bills were never examined closely. As a result, YOSHIMI regularly made international calls to family in America, but never declared these as private calls and never paid for them.

Could YOSHIMI be found guilty of the offence of false accounting, under s. 17 of the Theft Act 1968?

A No, an offence under this section cannot be committed by an omission alone; there must be an act done by the accused.

B Yes, provided it can be shown that YOSHIMI intended to permanently deprive the company of the money owed.

C Yes, an offence under this section may be committed by an omission alone.

D No, an offence under this section cannot be committed unless it is shown that documents were falsified, defaced or destroyed.

Question 15.6

CHANNING is highly skilled in the forgery field, and produced a sophisticated set of plates from which he made a forged £20 note. Using a high specification laser copier, he photocopied a large quantity of these notes. Before releasing the notes, he spent some in local shops to test their quality.

Which elements of 'false instrument' would CHANNING be guilty of in these circumstances?

A Making and using a false instrument.

B Copying and making a false instrument.

C Using a false instrument only.

D He is not guilty of any false instrument offence.

Question 15.7

ALBRIGHT, who is 15 years old, wishes to watch his local football team play at home in the FA Cup against West Ham United. However the tickets are too expensive for him and he decides he will climb a fence to watch the game. He does so and enjoys the game, however what he did not know was that for this special game anyone under 16 years of age was given free entry, on proof of age.

Which of the following is correct in relation to an offence under s. 11 of the Fraud Act 2006, obtaining services dishonestly?

A ALBRIGHT has committed an offence of obtaining services dishonestly as his intention was not to pay; the fact the game was free is irrelevant.

B ALBRIGHT has committed an offence of obtaining services dishonestly as he did not enter the ground properly, producing proof of age.

C ALBRIGHT has not obtained services dishonestly, the offence is not inchoate: it requires the actual obtaining of a service, and watching football is not such a service.

D ALBRIGHT has not obtained services dishonestly, whatever his intentions, for his age the service was provided for free.

Question 15.8

ENGLISH is in possession of a pen as he walks down the High Street. He goes into the bank and obtains an application form for a credit card, which he fills out fraudulently. He obtains the card a few days later, and has it in his possession as he goes to a shop to buy goods he has no intention of paying for. He presents the card to the person on the cash till in the shop. From the moment he left his home with that pen in his pocket his sole intention was to obtain a credit card and then goods fraudulently.

In relation to an offence contrary to s. 6 of the Fraud Act 2006, possession of articles for use in fraud, which of the following is correct?

A The offence is complete when ENGLISH is in possession of the pen.

B The offence is complete when ENGLISH is in possession of the credit card application form.

C The offence is complete when ENGLISH is in possession of the credit card.

D The offence is complete when ENGLISH is in possession of the credit card, with intention to use it fraudulently.

Question 15.9

Officers from the fraud squad are investigating BARLEY, who works as a bank employee, following a complaint from her employer. BARLEY is suspected of having dishonestly obtained a transfer of £10,000, by a deception, from the bank account of a customer into her own account. The officers have been unable to identify the account from which the money was taken. The investigation has revealed that only £5,000 was credited to BARLEY's own account and that this sum of money was transferred out immediately, to an unknown account. The investigating officers have been unable to trace the remaining £5,000, which they believe was transferred to another account also.

In these circumstances has BARLEY committed an offence of fraud by abuse of position contrary to s. 4 of the Fraud Act 2006?

A Yes, but only if the investigating officers can prove that BARLEY unlawfully retained some or all of the money.

B Yes, there need be no consequences to the unlawful act and the offence is complete where no money was retained.

C No, because the amount credited to BARLEY's account is less than the amount debited from the customer's account.

D No, unless they can identify the account from which the £10,000 was taken.

Question 15.10

CIPLINSKI works for a leading commodities, financial futures and options broker. As such she is privy to sensitive information, although in work she cannot access any customer funds. Over the last month she has been transferring details of the broker's customer accounts from her work computer to her own laptop, with the intention of using the information to fraudulently transfer funds from their accounts to hers. She resigns from the brokers, and only when not employed by them does she try to transfer the money. Unfortunately for her she is found out and arrested by the police prior to any transfer of funds to her own account.

In relation to s. 4 of the Fraud Act 2006, fraud by abuse of position, at what point, if any, is the offence committed?

A When CIPLINSKI begins to transfer details to her own laptop.

B When CIPLINSKI accesses the information on her laptop with the intention of obtaining funds fraudulently.

C The offence cannot be committed as at the point when the transfer is arranged, CIPLINSKI is no longer in a position in which she was expected to safeguard, or not to act against, the financial interests of another person.

D The offence cannot be committed as CIPLINSKI was never in a position in which she was expected to safeguard, or not to act against, the financial interests of another person as she never had access to their funds in work.

Question 15.11

Section 2 of the Fraud Act 2006 creates an offence of fraud by false representation, and outlines when a representation is false.

In relation to s. 2 of the Fraud Act 2006, when would a representation be 'false'?

A A representation is false if it is completely untrue and the person making it knows this to be the case.

B A representation is false if it is completely untrue and the person making it knows this is or knows this might be the case.

C A representation is false if it is untrue or misleading and the person making it knows this to be the case.

D A representation is false if it is untrue or misleading and the person making it knows this is or knows this might be the case.

Question 15.12

GIVENS is a plumber who visits a house to give a quote on the job. He returns home and writes a letter to the householder asking for a £500 deposit to be sent to him. At the time he sent the letter GIVENS has no intentions of carrying out the work and only wishes to take the householder's money. The householder receives the letter, but does not send any money.

In relation to s. 2 of the Fraud Act 2006, fraud by false representation, which of the following is correct?

A The offence has been committed, and it was committed when the letter was posted.

B The offence has been committed, and it was committed when the letter was received by the householder.

C An offence has not been committed as the householder did not send any money.

D An offence has not been committed, but an attempt to commit the offence has been.

ANSWERS

Answer 15.1

Answer **C** — Section 6 of the Fraud Act 2006 states:

(1) A person is guilty of an offence if he has in his possession or under his control any article for use in the course of or in connection with any fraud.

The offence under s. 6 can be committed anywhere at all, including the home of the defendant. The offence is not only committed when the defendant has articles in his possession but also when he has them in his control—a term that indicates that the defendant may be some distance away from the articles and yet still commits the offence. The offence under s. 6 applies to all fraud offences under the 2006 Act. However, much like the offence of 'going equipped', the offence is only committed in respect of future offences and not offences that have already taken place; answers A and B are therefore incorrect. There is no need to identify victims for this offence; answer D is therefore incorrect.

Crime, para. 1.15.7

Answer 15.2

Answer **B** — Section 2 of the Fraud Act 2006 states:

(1) A person is in breach of this section if he—
    (a) dishonestly makes a false representation, and
    (b) intends, by making the representation—
        (i) to make a gain for himself or another, or
        (ii) to cause loss to another or to expose another to the risk of loss.
(2) A representation is false if—
    (a) it is untrue or misleading, and
    (b) the person making it knows that it is, or might be, untrue or misleading [answer A is therefore incorrect].
(3) 'Representation' means any representation as to fact or law, including a representation as to the state of mind of—
    (a) the person making the representation, or
    (b) any other person.
(4) A representation may be express or implied.

(5) For the purposes of this section a representation may be regarded as made if it (or anything implying it) is submitted in any form to any system or device designed to receive, convey or respond to communications (with or without human intervention).

Section 2(1)(b) refers to 'gain' and 'loss' and that the person making the representation must do so with the intention of making a gain or causing a loss or risk of loss to another. The gain or loss does not actually have to take place; answer D is therefore incorrect.

The offence would also be committed by someone who engages in 'phishing'. This is the practice of sending out emails in bulk, purporting to represent a well-known brand in the hope of sending victims to a bogus website that tricks them into disclosing bank account details. 'Phishing kits' have long been available on the Internet; the offence under s. 2 now covers such activity; answer C is therefore incorrect.

Crime, para. 1.15.3

Answer 15.3

Answer **A** — The elements of the offence under s. 2 of the Fraud Act 2006 are that the defendant:

- made
- a false representation
- dishonestly
- knowing that the representation was or might be untrue or misleading
- with intent to make a gain for himself or another, to cause loss to another or to expose another to risk of loss.

In the scenario RAMAGE makes a false statement about her friend's membership status, with the intention to deceive, knowing the statement to be untrue. PASSARO said nothing. However, a representation may also be implied by conduct, or can be by omission. PASSARO failed to mention the fact she was not a member and her actions in walking past the receptionist as if she were a member (albeit on her friend's word) would be a false representation; answer B is therefore incorrect. The dishonesty would stem from the agreement PASSARO had with RAMAGE to dupe the gym.

It's not just a gain that makes this offence out, it also includes 'loss', that is, losing something that one might ordinarily have obtained, in this case the entry fee; answer D is therefore incorrect. So although RAMAGE made no gain, as she would have had free entry in any case, she is compliant in an act that causes a loss to the gym; answer C is therefore incorrect.

Crime, para. 1.15.3

Answer 15.4

Answer **B** — Fraud by false representation as outlined in the Fraud Act 2006 relates to a representation which is false if it is untrue or misleading and the person making it knows this is or knows this might be the case. Therefore, an untrue statement made in the honest belief that it is in fact true would not suffice. This is what FOWLER does when he correctly signs to say that none of the illnesses mentioned applies to him. He cannot commit an offence contrary to s. 2; answers A and C are therefore incorrect.

Section 3 creates an offence of dishonestly failing to disclose information where there is a legal duty to do so. The term 'legal duty' has not been defined but will include duties under oral contracts as well as written contracts and where a person intentionally failed to disclose information relating to a heart condition when making an application for life insurance; answer D is therefore incorrect.

Crime, para. 1.15.4

Answer 15.5

Answer **C** — Section 17 of the Theft Act 1968 creates *two* offences: destroying, defacing, falsifying, etc. accounts and documents (s. 17(1)(a)); and using false or misleading accounts or documents in furnishing information (s. 17(1)(b)). An offence under s. 17 can be committed by omission as well as by an act. Failing to make an entry in an accounts book, altering a till receipt or supplying an auditor with records that are incomplete may, if accompanied by the other ingredients, amount to an offence. In *R v Shama* [1990] 1 WLR 661 the Court of Appeal upheld the conviction of a telephone operator who had failed even to start filling out standard forms provided by his employer for the recording of international calls. He was held to have falsified the forms by leaving them unmarked; answers A and D are therefore incorrect.

Unlike the offence of theft there is no requirement to prove an intention permanently to deprive—but there is a need to show dishonesty on behalf of the accused. Answer B is therefore incorrect.

Crime, para. 1.15.11.1

Answer 15.6

Answer **D** — Quite simply, offences classed as forgery include virtually every kind of document *except* bank notes. Therefore, as he has been involved in 'forging' bank notes, CHANNING cannot commit the offences of making and using a false instrument (answer A is therefore incorrect), copying and making a false instrument (answer B is therefore incorrect) and using a false instrument (answer C is therefore incorrect). Offences relating to currency are dealt with by the Forgery and Counterfeiting Act 1981.

Crime, para. 1.15.11.4

Answer 15.7

Answer **D** — Section 11 of the Fraud Act 2006 makes it an offence for any person, by any dishonest act, to obtain services for which payment is required, with intent to avoid payment. The person must know that the services are made available on the basis that they are chargeable, or that they might be. It is not possible to commit the offence by omission alone and it can be committed only where the dishonest act was done with the intent not to pay for the services as expected. This offence replaces the offence of obtaining services by deception in s. 1 of the Theft Act 1978, though the new offence contains no deception element.

The offence is not inchoate: it requires the actual obtaining of the service. For example, data or software may be made available on the Internet to a certain category of person who has paid for access rights to that service. A person dishonestly using false credit card details or other false personal information to obtain the service would be committing an offence under this clause. However, the section would also cover a situation where a person climbs over a wall and watches a football match without paying the entrance fee—such a person is not deceiving the provider of the service directly, but is obtaining a service, which is provided on the basis that people will pay for it; answer C is therefore incorrect.

However, where services obtained are free, s. 11 cannot ever be charged, no matter the circumstances and intention of the defendant. In this scenario the services are free for those under 16, therefore anyone within that age range could not commit the offence. Proof of age is a restriction placed by the football administrators, not the law. For instance if ALBRIGHT had attempted formal entry and had been turned away because he had no proof of age with him, and had then climbed the fence he would still not be guilty of an offence under s. 11 of the 2006 Act; answers A and B are therefore incorrect.

Crime, para. 1.15.10

Answer 15.8

Answer **A** — Section 6 of the Fraud Act 2006 states:

(1) A person is guilty of an offence if he has in his possession or under his control any article for use in the course of or in connection with any fraud ...

Section 6 makes it an offence for a person to possess or have under his control any article for use in the course of or in connection with any fraud. This wording draws on that of the existing law in s. 25 of the Theft Act 1968 and s. 24 of the Theft Act (Northern Ireland) 1969. (These provisions make it an offence for a person to 'go equipped' to commit a burglary, theft or cheat, although they apply only when the offender is not at his place of abode.) The intention is to attract the case law on s. 25, which has established that proof is required that the defendant had the article for the purpose or with the intention that it be used in the course of or in connection with the offence, and that a general intention to commit fraud will suffice.

It is any article that could be used in any of the fraud offences of the 2006 Act, and begins when the accused has the pen, together with the necessary intent; answers B, C and D are therefore incorrect.

Crime, para. 1.15.7

Answer 15.9

Answer **B** — The elements of the offence under s. 4 of the Fraud Act 2006 are that the defendant:

- occupies a position in which he was expected to safeguard, or not to act against, the financial interests of another person
- abused that position
- dishonestly
- intending by that abuse to make a gain/cause a loss
- the abuse may consist of an omission rather than an act.

Like the other two offences (contained in ss. 2 and 3 of the 2006 Act), s. 4 is entirely offender focused. It is complete once the defendant carries out the act that is the abuse of his position. It is immaterial whether or not he is successful in his enterprise and whether or not any gain or loss is actually made.

BARLEY clearly occupies a position of trust and abused that position by dishonestly transferring money to her own account, albeit fleetingly. For this offence there is no need to prove where the fraudulently obtained funds came from, nor that any of those funds were actually available to the defendant. The offence revolves around the dishonest intentions of the defendant; answers A, C and D are therefore incorrect.

Crime, para. 1.15.5

Answer 15.10

Answer **A** — The elements of the offence under s. 4 of the Fraud Act 2006 are that the defendant:

- occupies a position in which he was expected to safeguard, or not to act against, the financial interests of another person
- abused that position
- dishonestly
- intending by that abuse to make a gain/cause a loss
- the abuse may consist of an omission rather than an act.

This offence is committed when a person 'occupying a position' abuses it by transferring information that they intend to use in making a gain or causing a loss. Although when CIPLINSKI actually attempts to access another person's funds she is no longer 'occupying a position' the offence was complete when she transferred the information from the work computer to her home one; answers B and C are therefore incorrect.

Even though at work she cannot access funds, she is still, as an employee of the brokers, responsible for not acting against the financial interests of the broker; answer D is therefore incorrect.

Crime, para. 1.15.5

Answer 15.11

Answer **D** — Section 2(2) of the Fraud Act 2006 states:

(2) A representation is false if—
    (a) it is untrue or misleading, and
    (b) the person making it knows that it is, or might be, untrue or misleading.

A representation is false if it is untrue or misleading and the person making it knows this is or knows this might be the case. Therefore, an untrue statement made in the honest belief that it is in fact true would not suffice. The words 'or might be' must involve a subjective belief on the part of the person making the representation.

So the representation does not have to be completely untrue, misleading is enough; answers A and B for that reason are untrue. The person making the statement need only believe that the statement may be untrue or misleading; for that reason answer C is therefore incorrect (as is answer A again).

Crime, para. 1.15.3

Answer 15.12

Answer **A** — Section 2(1) of the Fraud Act 2006 states:

(1) A person is in breach of this section if he—
    (a) dishonestly makes a false representation, and
    (b) intends, by making the representation—
        (i) to make a gain for himself or another, or
        (ii) to cause loss to another or to expose another to the risk of loss.
(2) A representation is false if—
    (a) it is untrue or misleading, and
    (b) the person making it knows that it is, or might be, untrue or misleading.
(3) 'Representation' means any representation as to fact or law, including a representation as to the state of mind of—
    (a) the person making the representation, or
    (b) any other person.
(4) A representation may be express or implied ...

There has certainly been a false representation, give me £500 for doing nothing!

Deception offences under the Theft Acts 1968 and 1978 required the 'target' of the deception to be deceived by the words or conduct of the defendant; if this element were not present there would only be an attempted deception. The Fraud Act 2006 removes this requirement so that where a defendant makes a false representation knowing that it is false or might be, the offence of fraud is complete; answers C and D are therefore incorrect.

The offence is complete the moment the false representation is made. The representation need never be heard nor communicated to the recipient and if carried out by post, would be complete when the letter is posted (*Treacy* v *DPP* [1971] AC 537); answer B is therefore incorrect.

Crime, para. 1.15.3

16 | Criminal Damage

STUDY PREPARATION

The definition of criminal damage needs attention in the first instance, and you will have to know the various components, such as lawful excuse, protection, recklessness, damage, property and belonging to another. In addition to these statutory issues there are many decided cases on each of these points.

It is important to learn the basic definition, before turning to the aggravated offences. Each one of these is similar to the other, with the defendant'intent being of key significance. It is also worth paying attention to contamination of goods. Although the offences associated with the definition are reasonably long and complicated, this is an area that may receive considerable further attention in the current climate of terrorist threats.

QUESTIONS

Question 16.1

NEWLING runs a computer company specialising in software. Whilst waiting one day for a meeting with a potential client he drops the memory stick with a vital program on it on the floor. A rival sees the opportunity and stamps on the memory stick, breaking it completely. NEWLING is unable to give his presentation and does not get a contract.

In relation only to the program, has it been criminally damaged?

A Yes, as it is the intellectual property of NEWLING.

B Yes, as it is capable of being displayed it is real property.

C No, as it is not tangible property.

D Not unless it is the only copy of the program.

Question 16.2

BOYD and FARR take apples off the tree on their neighbour's property and throw them to each other; several fall to the ground and are bruised.

Have the apples been criminally damaged?

A Yes, as they have been damaged and may be unusable.

B Yes, provided that the apples had a propriety purpose.

C No, the apples are not damaged only bruised.

D No, as apples growing on a tree are not 'property' under the Criminal Damage Act 1971.

Question 16.3

HOARE is angry that he was turned down for a job with a local bus company and plots revenge. He gets an automatic pistol and attends at the garage. He then fires the bullet at an empty bus. He misses and the bullet breaks a nearby window and a shard of glass imbeds itself in an employee's neck causing life-threatening injuries.

Ignoring other offences, has HOARE committed aggravated damage contrary to s. 1(2) of the Criminal Damage Act 1971?

A Yes, as damage was caused that endangered life.

B Yes, as HOARE was reckless in firing a gun that life could have been endangered.

C No, as the damage caused was not intended to be caused by HOARE.

D No, as HOARE was not reckless as to the danger to life that was caused.

Question 16.4

When proving an offence under s. 1(2) of the Criminal Damage Act 1971 (aggravated criminal damage), *mens rea* must be shown.

In which of the following circumstances is the offence made out?

A The person intended to cause criminal damage and intended to endanger a person's life.

B The person intended or was reckless as to whether damage would be caused, and intended or was reckless as to whether life would be endangered.

C The person intended or was reckless as to whether a person's life would be endangered.

D The person intended to cause criminal damage only, and was reckless as to whether a person's life would be endangered.

Question 16.5

Section 54 of the Anti-social Behaviour Act 2003 makes it an offence to sell aerosol paint to certain people.

To which of the following people would it be illegal to sell aerosol paint?

A Someone who is 16 years of age or under.
B Someone who is or appears to be 16 years of age or under.
C Someone who is under 16 years of age.
D Someone who is or appears to be under 16 years of age.

Question 16.6

Criminal damage under s. 2 of the Criminal Damage Act 1971 is an offence of intent.

When considering an offence under s. 2 (threats to destroy or damage property) what must the prosecution prove?

A That the accused intended that the victim would fear that the damage would be carried out immediately.
B That the accused intended to cause damage and intended to induce fear that damage would be carried out.
C That the accused intended that the victim would fear that the damage would be carried out.
D That the victim did in fact fear that the accused would carry out the threat to cause damage.

Question 16.7

FRANCIS and PRAFFITOUS are members of an animal rights group. PRAFFITOUS applied for a job in a zoo, and they planned that if he was successful, he would damage customers' cars by placing sharp tacks under the tyres. FRANCIS bought ten packets of tacks at a DIY store the day before PRAFFITOUS' interview, intending to give them to him if he got the job.

Has either person committed an offence under s. 3 of the Criminal Damage Act 1971 (having articles with intent to damage property)?

A Only FRANCIS; he has control of the articles, intending that PRAFFITOUS should use them to cause damage.
B Neither person, as FRANCIS does not intend to use the articles himself to cause criminal damage.
C Both people, because of their joint intent that PRAFFITOUS should use the articles to cause damage.

D Neither person, as the intent to commit damage is conditional on PRAFFITOUS being successful in his interview.

Question 16.8

DENNIS works in a butcher's shop. As a joke, on 1 April he came in early and sprinkled icing sugar on some meat on display. He then left a note for his boss, claiming to be from an animal rights group, saying they had sprinkled rat poison on the food. Unfortunately, before he was able to stop him, his boss threw the meat away.

Has DENNIS committed an offence under s. 38 of the Public Order Act 1986 (contamination of goods)?

A Yes, because he has caused economic loss to his employer.

B No, because he has not caused public alarm or anxiety.

C No, because he has not actually contaminated any goods.

D No, because he only intended his employer to treat it as a joke.

Question 16.9

Section 2 of the Criminal Damage Act 1971 makes it an offence, in certain circumstances, to threaten to damage or destroy your own property.

Which of the following is true in relation to this offence?

A It is an offence to threaten to damage your own property regardless of the circumstances.

B It is an offence to threaten to damage your own property, but only where there is danger to your own or any other person's life.

C It is an offence to threaten to damage your own property, but only where there is danger to any other person's life.

D It is an offence to threaten to damage your own property under *any* circumstances.

Question 16.10

FAWKES was arrested for an offence of being in charge of a motor vehicle whilst over the prescribed limit and following a reading that showed he was well over the prescribed limit he was placed in a cell and detained. FAWKES was angry that in his view he had not been properly given his rights, and so he put the blanket he had been given down the toilet and flushed it until the cell floor was flooded. As a result of his actions the cell had to be closed until it had been cleaned, and the blanket had to be sent to be cleaned and dried.

In relation to a possible charge of criminal damage in relation to FAWKES's actions, which of the following is correct?

A It would only be criminal damage to the blanket had the toilet contained urine or faeces when it was put down there.

B It would only be criminal damage to the cell as that had to be taken out of service and was out of commission.

C It would be criminal damage in relation to both as the blanket could not be used until it had been dried out and the flooded cell remained out of action until the water was cleared.

D It would not be criminal damage in either case as both would dry, and when dry they would return to their original state.

Question 16.11

A bailiff is trying to repossess a car from outside a house. The person who owned the car, JOHNSON, comes out and puts a hole in all four tyres using a screwdriver.

Has JOHNSON committed the offence of criminal damage?

A Yes, as he has lost all rights to the car as it is being taken by a bailiff.

B Yes, even though the car belongs to him the bailiff has an interest in the car.

C No, as the car has not yet been reduced into the possession of the bailiff.

D No, as the car has not yet been reduced into the possession of the person to whom the re-possession is being made.

Question 16.12

DOWNTON sets fire to the factory where he works and causes damage to it. He is arrested for causing criminal damage and states that he was acting on behalf of the owner of the factory who wanted to claim against the insurance company.

Has DOWNTON committed criminal damage contrary to s. 1 of the Criminal Damage Act 1971?

A Yes, as he has caused damage to property belonging to another.

B Yes, as he has committed the damage in aggravating circumstances; to commit a fraud offence.

C No, he was acting with the permission of the owner therefore he did not damage property belonging to another.

D No, he has not committed the offence as he does not have the required *mens rea*.

Question 16.13

COULTER is an animal lover and hates people who eat meat. She sends a letter to her local supermarket stating she intends to sprinkle rat poison over all their meat. Her intention is to cause harm to persons who eat meat. She then makes several stickers that say 'Don't eat dead animals' which she intends putting on the meat at the supermarket. However she is stopped by a police officer prior to arrival at the supermarket, who discovers the stickers and the rat poison. In fact the supermarket has taken no action at all as a result of the letter she sent to them.

In relation to contamination of goods which of the following is correct?

A An offence is committed in relation to the letter only.

B An offence is committed in relation to the letter and the stickers.

C An offence is not committed as both the letter and the stickers related to future actions.

D An offence is not committed as the supermarket took no action.

ANSWERS

Answer 16.1

Answer **C** — Section 10 of the Criminal Damage Act 1971 describes 'property' as:

(1) In this Act 'property' means property of a tangible nature, whether real or personal, including money and—
   (a) including wild creatures which have been tamed or are ordinarily kept in captivity and any other wild creatures or their carcasses if, but only if, they have been reduced into possession ... or are in the course of being reduced into possession; but
   (b) not including mushrooms growing wild on any land or flowers, fruit or foliage of a plant growing wild on any land.

Quite simply tangible means 'touchable' and you cannot touch a computer program or any other intellectual property; answers A and B are therefore incorrect. Even if the program was the only copy it would not be criminal damage, although other offences may apply; answer D is therefore incorrect.

Crime, para. 1.16.2.3

Answer 16.2

Answer **A** — Section 1 of the Criminal Damage Act 1971 states:

(1) A person who without lawful excuse destroys or damages any property belonging to another intending to destroy or damage any such property or being reckless as to whether any such property would be destroyed or damaged shall be guilty of an offence.

Although a key feature of the 1971 Act, the terms 'destroy' or 'damage' are not defined. The courts have taken a wide view when interpreting these terms. 'Destroying' property would suggest that it has been rendered useless but there is no need to prove that 'damage' to property is in any way permanent or irreparable; answer C is therefore incorrect.

Property is defined in the 1971 Act by s. 10 which states:

(1) In this Act 'property' means property of a tangible nature, whether real or personal, including money and—
   (a) including wild creatures which have been tamed or are ordinarily kept in captivity and any other wild creatures or their carcasses if, but only if, they have been reduced into possession ... or are in the course of being reduced into possession; but
   (b) not including mushrooms growing wild on any land or flowers, fruit or foliage of a plant growing wild on any land.

So, apples on a tree would be included as they were on someone's property and their ultimate use is immaterial; answers B and D are therefore incorrect.

Crime, paras 1.16.2.1, 1.16.2.2

Answer 16.3

Answer **D** — Section 1(2) of the Criminal Damage Act 1971 states:

A person who without lawful excuse destroys or damages any property, whether belonging to himself or another—
(a) intending to destroy or damage any property or being reckless as to whether any property would be destroyed or damaged; and
(b) intending by the destruction or damage to endanger the life of another or being reckless as to whether the life of another would be thereby endangered;
shall be guilty of an offence.

So there are two elements to the offence:

- intentional or reckless damage;
- and intentional or reckless endangerment to life caused by that damage.

In the scenario HOARE intended to damage the bus, but as it was empty he could neither have intended nor been reckless as to whether life would be endangered by the damage he intended; answer B is therefore incorrect.

The damage that was actually caused by HOARE did endanger life. However, without the necessary intent or recklessness this will not be enough; answer A is therefore incorrect. Further to this the damage caused was not intended by HOARE, although it could have been reckless had he been aware that it was a risk. However, the endangerment to life was neither intended nor could have been foreseen by HOARE; answer C is therefore incorrect. There is clearly danger to life caused by firing a live bullet! However, for the offence in question it is the damage that is caused that must endanger life and not the bullet (*R* v *Steer* [1988] AC 111).

Crime, para. 1.16.3

Answer 16.4

Answer **B** — A person is guilty of an offence under s. 1(2) of the Criminal Damage Act 1971, if they damage/destroy property intending *or* reckless as to whether damage is caused to their own property, or another's, *and* they intend *or* are reckless as to whether a person's life is endangered.

Either the elements of intent *or* recklessness must be proved in relation to both the damage and the endangerment to life for this offence to be made out. All four answers are fairly similar, but only answer B contains all the elements required to prove the offence. Consequently, answers A, C and D are incorrect.

Please note the change in the concept of recklessness brought about by the decision of the House of Lords in *R* v *G & R* [2003] 3 WLR 1060.

Crime, para. 1.16.3

Answer 16.5

Answer **C** — A person commits the offence by selling the aerosol to a person under 16 years of age. There is a defence courtesy of s. 54(4) of the Anti-social Behaviour Act 2003, for the person who reasonably believes the person was not under the age of 16 and took all reasonable steps to determine the purchaser's age. The section makes no mention of the apparent age of the purchaser; answers A, B and D are incorrect.

Crime, para. 1.16.7

Answer 16.6

Answer **C** — This is an offence of intention; that is, the key element is the *defendant's intention* that the person receiving the threat fears it would be carried out.

The s. 2 offence under the Criminal Damage Act 1971, which originates from the need to tackle protection racketeers, is very straightforward: there is no need to show that the other person actually feared or even believed that the threat would be carried out (making answer D incorrect).

Also, there is no need to show that the defendant intended to carry out the threat; nor does it matter whether the threat was even capable of being carried out (which is why answer B is incorrect).

Answers A and C are similar; however, C is correct because there is no requirement to show that the accused intended to cause fear of *immediate* damage.

Crime, para. 1.16.5

Answer 16.7

Answer **A** — Section 3 of the Criminal Damage Act 1971 states:

A person who has anything in his custody or under his control, intending without lawful excuse to use it or cause or permit another to use it—

(a) to destroy or damage any property belonging to some other person; or

(b) to destroy or damage his own or the user's property in a way which he knows is likely to endanger the life of some other person;

shall be guilty of an offence.

Answer B is incorrect as a person may have control of articles which he or she intends to permit another to use. Answer C is incorrect as PRAFFITOUS did not have the articles in his custody or control at any time.

Answer D is incorrect because a conditional intention to use an article if given circumstances arise will amount to an offence (*R* v *Buckingham* (1976) 63 Cr App R 159).

Crime, para. 1.16.6

Answer 16.8

Answer **D** — Under s. 38 of the Public Order Act 1986, it is necessary to prove that a person contaminated or interfered with goods, or made it appear that goods have been contaminated or interfered with, or threatened or claimed to have done so.

However, the person must have done so *with the intention* of causing public alarm or anxiety, or of causing injury to members of the public consuming or using the goods, or of causing economic loss to any person by reason of the goods being shunned by members of the public, or of causing economic loss to any person by reason of steps taken to avoid such alarm or anxiety, injury or loss.

Therefore, even though DENNIS in the circumstances may have contaminated goods, and even caused economic loss, he did not do so with the required intention and cannot be guilty of this offence. (Answer A is therefore incorrect.)

Had DENNIS been proved to have had the required intent, answers B and C would still be incorrect, because there is no need to prove a person actually caused public alarm/anxiety, and the offence may be committed without actually contaminating goods.

Crime, para. 1.16.8

Answer 16.9

Answer **C** — Section 2(b) of the Criminal Damage Act 1971 states it is an offence for a person to threaten:

(b) to destroy or damage his own property in a way which he knows is likely to endanger the life of that other or a third person;

So you can threaten to damage your own property, but it is only an offence where another's life is in danger. Consequently answers A, B and D are incorrect.

Crime, para. 1.16.5

Answer 16.10

Answer **C** — Although a key feature of the Criminal Damage Act 1971, strangely enough the terms 'destroy' or 'damage' are not defined. The courts have often been left to muse over what is and what is not 'damaged', and have taken an eclectic view when interpreting these terms. 'Destroying' property would suggest that it has been rendered useless, but there is no need to prove that 'damage' to property is in any way permanent or irreparable.

The *Concise Oxford Dictionary* explains damage as 'harm or injury impairing the value or usefulness of something...'. In *Morphitis* v *Salmon* [1990] Crim LR 48, the transcript of Auld J's judgment reads:

> The authorities show that the term 'damage' for the purpose of this provision, should be widely interpreted so as to conclude not only permanent or temporary physical harm, but also permanent or temporary impairment of value or usefulness.

This view was endorsed in *R* v *Fiak* [2005] EWCA Crim 2381; in that case the defendant had been arrested and placed in a police cell which he flooded by stuffing a blanket down the cell lavatory and repeatedly flushing. The defendant argued that there was no evidence that the blanket or the cell had been 'damaged'; the water had been clean and both the blanket and the cell could be used again when dry. This argument of course assumes the absence of any possible contamination or infection from the lavatory itself, and the confident expectation that there would be none (how many police cell toilets would this apply to?). The Court of Appeal disagreed and held that, while the effect of the defendant's actions in relation to the blanket and the cell was remediable, the reality was that the blanket could not be used until it had been dried and the flooded cell was out of action until the water had been cleared. Therefore both had sustained damage for the purposes of the Act; answers A, B and D are therefore incorrect.

Crime, para. 1.16.2.1

Answer 16.11

Answer **B** — Section 1 of the Criminal Damage Act 1971 states:

(1) A person who without lawful excuse destroys or damages any property belonging to another intending to destroy or damage any such property or being reckless as to whether any such property would be destroyed or damaged shall be guilty of an offence.

The only factor here is 'belonging to another'—this is defined in s. 10 of the 1971 Act as:

(2) Property shall be treated for the purposes of this Act as belonging to any person—
  (d) having the custody or control of it;
  (e) having in it any proprietary right or interest (not being an equitable interest arising only from an agreement to transfer or grant an interest); or
  (f) having a charge on it.

This extended meaning of 'belonging to another' is similar to that used in the Theft Act 1968. One result is that if a person damages his/her own property, he/she may still commit the offence of simple criminal damage if that property also 'belongs to' someone else; answers C and D are therefore incorrect. However, JOHNSON as the owner would still also have a propriety interest in the car as technically it still belongs to him; answer A is therefore incorrect.

Crime, para. 1.16.2.3

Answer 16.12

Answer **C** — Simple damage is committed where:

A person who without lawful excuse destroys or damages any property belonging to another intending to destroy or damage any such property or being reckless as to whether any such property would be destroyed or damaged shall be guilty of an offence

(Section 1 of the Criminal Damage Act 1971).

Clearly DOWNTON does have the necessary intent as he intended to damage it; answer D is therefore incorrect.

It is not an offence to damage your own property unless there are aggravating circumstances. Even if the intention in doing so is to carry out some further offence—such as a fraudulent insurance claim—this fact still does not make it an offence under s. 1(1) of the Criminal Damage Act 1971 (*R* v *Denton* [1981] 1 WLR 1446) and as DOWNTON believed he was acting on behalf of the owner he should be in no worse position; answers A and B are therefore incorrect.

Crime, para. 1.16.2.6

Answer 16.13

Answer **A** — Section 38 of the Public Order Act 1986 creates two offences. The first involves the contamination of, interference with or placing of goods with the intentions set out at s. 38(1)(a)–(d):

(a) of causing public alarm or anxiety, or
(b) of causing injury to members of the public consuming or using the goods, or
(c) of causing economic loss to any person by reason of the goods being shunned by members of the public, or
(d) of causing economic loss to any person by reason of steps taken to avoid any such alarm or anxiety, injury or loss.

This is a crime of 'specific' intent and the particular intention of the defendant must be proved.

Section 38(2) involves the making of threats to do, *or* the claiming *to have done* any of the acts in s. 38(1), with any of the intentions set out at s. 38(1)(a), (c) or (d). It is difficult to see how a threat or claim made with the intention of causing injury to the public (s. 38(1)(b)) would not also amount to an intention to cause them alarm or anxiety. In this case clearly her intention is to alarm people so much they stop eating meat.

The offence is complete when the threat is issued with the necessary intent, and being a crime of specific intent it does not require any action from the person threatened. It is immaterial that no action has yet been taken, or that the shop ignored the letter; answers C and D are therefore incorrect.

Under s. 38(3) of the 1986 Act:

It is an offence for a person to be in possession of any of the following articles with a view to the commission of an offence under subsection (1)—
(a) materials to be used for contaminating or interfering with goods or making it appear that goods have been contaminated or interfered with, or
(b) goods which have been contaminated or interfered with, or which appear to have been contaminated or interfered with.

Being in possession of the poison would fit the criteria laid out here, however do the stickers make it appear that goods have been contaminated? The answer is no, so the stickers themselves do not constitute an offence under this section. Had the stickers said 'contaminated meat—danger!' then this would have been enough; answer B is therefore incorrect.

Crime, para. 1.16.8

17 Offences Against the Administration of Justice and Public Interest

STUDY PREPARATION

This chapter tests your knowledge of those offences which exist to deter people from interfering with the proper course of justice. Included in this chapter are questions relating to perjury, false statements, contempt of court and corruption. The common law offence of perverting the course of justice is included, as are the statutory offences of intimidating witnesses and jurors. Particular crimes relating to those who assist offenders by protecting or hiding them are tested, as are those relating to wasting police time—an area that may also come into greater use as pressures on police resources intensify.

QUESTIONS

Question 17.1

REYNOLDS is an expert witness employed by a defence team in relation to a charge of causing death by dangerous driving. He is asked by the prosecution, whilst giving evidence, whether in his expert opinion the damage caused to the bottom of the car could have been caused by the vehicle being driven too quickly along the rough unmade road. He states that in his opinion it could not have been caused by driving too quickly; although he does actually believe it could have been caused by excess speed he did not want to affect the defence as he was called as a defence witness.

In these circumstances has REYNOLDS committed perjury?

A Yes, he has made a statement he knows to be false or believes not to be true.

B Yes, he has made a statement he knows to be false or believes not to be true and did so with the intent of misleading the court.

C No, as he was asked for an opinion and as an expert witness he is entitled to give an opinion.

D No, as the damage to the car would not be a material fact as the cause of the damage could only be a matter of opinion.

Question 17.2

CLANCY has been charged with committing a robbery which he denies; he asks his sister to provide an alibi for him stating he was with her at the time of the offence. His sister is very suspicious about whether CLANCY did commit the robbery or not but does not believe he actually did it. She provides an alibi for him; however she is not believed and the prosecution goes ahead.

Has CLANCY's sister committed an offence of assisting an offender contrary to s. 4 of the Criminal Law Act 1967?

A Yes, as she has committed an act with intent to impede his prosecution.

B Yes, as she has committed an act with intent to impede his prosecution and she has suspicion that he did actually commit the offence.

C No, as she did not know or believe him to be guilty of the offence; mere suspicion is not enough.

D No, as an offence has to have been committed and CLANCY denies committing the offence.

Question 17.3

ESCOTT is giving evidence for the defence in court as a sworn witness on behalf of his friend who has been accused of assaulting his wife. ESCOTT states that he knew for a fact that his friend's wife was having an affair and that he told his friend about that. In fact this statement is not correct and ESCOTT suspects that it might be false as his friend asked him to make the statement.

In these circumstances has ESCOTT committed perjury?

A Yes, he has made a statement he knows to be false or does not believe to be true.

B Yes, he has made a statement he knows to be false or does not believe to be true and it is material to the case.

C No, it is not a material fact, in relation to the actual assault which is a physical act.

D No, it is not a material fact as it relates to the wife and not the defendant.

Question 17.4

SCHUMANN contacts police to state he is a witness to a murder. He did see the suspect in the area but he makes up several facts that cause the police to make enquiries that were not necessary. However whilst engaged on one of these unnecessary enquiries they actually obtain definitive evidence against the suspect.

Which of the following statements is true in relation to wasting police time?

A SCHUMANN is guilty of wasting police time as he caused several hours of wasted time.

B SCHUMANN is guilty of wasting police time as he caused wasteful employment of the police.

C SCHUMANN is not guilty of wasting police time as he did provide some useful information, i.e. seeing the suspect in the area.

D SCHUMANN is not guilty of wasting police time; as a result of information he gave actual evidence was obtained.

Question 17.5

MILLIGAN has been sold laminate flooring, which is defective, and has issued a county court claim against ACME Co. Ltd, who supplied the goods. FRANKS is an expert laminate floor fitter and intends to give evidence on MILLIGAN's behalf at court. In order to prevent this, ACME's managing director has written a letter to FRANKS warning him that he will lose business if he gives evidence against the company.

Does this letter amount to intimidation of a witness?

A Yes, provided there was intention to intimidate FRANKS.

B Yes, provided the company were reckless as to whether FRANKS would be intimidated.

C No, as the threat was not made in person.

D No, intimidating witnesses applies only to criminal court cases, not county court cases.

Question 17.6

SUMMERS is an accredited Police Community Support Officer (PCSO) and is dealing with ARTHURS for a fixed penalty offence. He requires ARTHURS to provide his name and address. ARTHURS refuses and SUMMERS exercises his power of detention as provided by sch. 4 to the Police Reform Act 2002. ARTHURS is less than impressed at this, and pushes the PCSO over and makes good his escape.

Consider the offence at common law of escaping. Which of the following is correct?

A ARTHURS has committed this offence; the offence is complete.

B ARTHURS has committed this offence provided he remains at liberty for at least 24 hours.

C ARTHURS has not committed this offence, as it relates to escaping from prisons, etc.

D ARTHURS has not committed this offence, as it relates to lawful custody, i.e. by a police officer.

Question 17.7

RUDDOCK picks up a hammer and uses it to assault O'CONNEL. He then runs out of the shop where the assault took place and bumps into a neighbour who knows who RUDDOCK is. Thinking he will be able to identify him he tells the neighbour to 'keep your nose out if your missus wants to keep her good looks'. The neighbour is confused as he has no idea what has happened, but he is worried never the less.

In relation to witness intimidation, which of the following is correct?

A This is witness intimidation as it is intended that the investigation be obstructed.

B This is witness intimidation as an offence has taken place and the neighbour may well be a witness.

C This is not witness intimidation as an investigation has not commenced.

D This is not witness intimidation as the neighbour is unaware what the threat is about.

Question 17.8

Constable EVANS has written a statement regarding the arrest of an offender that he witnessed. The officer has stated that he saw the accused in possession of the drugs found on him by his sergeant. In fact the constable did not actually see the accused with the drugs on him, the sergeant told him that he had taken the drugs from him and he believed that to be true. The accused had pleaded guilty and both officers' statements have been read out in court. Neither officer was present when this happened.

In relation to this which of the following is correct?

A The constable has committed perjury as he has made a statement which he knows to be false or does not believe to be true.

B The constable has made a false statement in criminal proceedings as he has made a statement which he knows to be false or does not believe to be true.

C The officer has not committed perjury as he made a statement he thought was true; the fact it wasn't is irrelevant.

D The officer has not made a false statement in criminal proceedings as he made a statement he thought was true; the fact it wasn't is irrelevant.

Question 17.9

CLEASE was a witness in a trial at Crown Court. Two days before the trial he was approached by the defendant, ALDUESCUE who pleaded with him to lie in court. When CLEASE refused, ALDUESCUE became aggressive and threatened CLEASE. CLEASE stated that he found the actions of ALDUESCUE to have been intimidating, but that he himself did not feel intimidated, and he went on to give truthful evidence in court.

Has an offence of intimidating a witness been committed contrary to s. 51 of the Criminal Justice and Public Order Act 1994?

A No, as CLEASE went on to give evidence in court.

B No, as CLEASE was not actually intimidated.

C Yes, but only because ALDUESCUE asked CLEASE to lie.

D Yes, as ALDUESCUE has committed an act which intimidates.

Question 17.10

HARKANNIN attended a police station and made an allegation of rape against a taxi driver, whom she stated had driven her home the previous evening. HARKANNIN said that she did not know the identity of the person who raped her and could not describe the taxi or the driver as she had been extremely intoxicated at the time. The police spent the next two days investigating the incident, but HARKANNIN later told them that she had made up the story because she had been late going home that night and she had a jealous boyfriend.

Would HARKANNIN's actions amount to an offence against the administration of justice and public interest in these circumstances?

A No, because a course of justice had not commenced before HARKANNIN made the allegation.

B No, because HARKANNIN did not identify any individual who may have been arrested or inconvenienced by her statement.

C Yes, HARKANNIN's conduct could amount to perverting the course of justice, as there were possible consequences of detention, arrest, charge or prosecution.

D Yes, this could amount to an offence of wasting police time as over 24 hours' police time had been used, but it could never be perverting the course of justice.

Question 17.11

LEDERER has been convicted of theft at Crown Court and given a custodial sentence. A private security company is responsible for transporting detainees to the local prison. Whilst en route to the prison BRANDRICK rams the prison van with his Transit van and then overpowers the guards; subsequently he assists LEDERER to escape by unlocking his cell on the prison van.

In relation to the offence of assisting escape contrary to s. 39 of the Prison Act 1952, which of the following is true in respect of BRANDRICK's actions?

A He commits the offence when he rams the prison van with the intention of assisting the escape.

B He commits the offence only where he physically assisted the escape by unlocking the cell.

C He does not commit the offence as it relates only to escape from police or prison transport, not from a private security company.

D He does not commit this offence as it does not relate to prisoners in transit to or from prison.

Question 17.12

AKELLO has committed an armed robbery and is looking to avoid detection by the police. AKELLO asks his friend to help him avoid arrest, telling him that he is wanted for theft. His friend agrees to hide him for a few days, and does so.

Has an offence of assisting an offender been committed by the friend in these circumstances?

A Yes, provided the friend's action actually delayed the arrest of AKELLO.

B Yes, as his friend's actions were intended to hinder the arrest of AKELLO.

C No, as the friend did not know or believe that AKELLO was wanted for the more serious offence.

D No, as the friend has not lied to the police, or taken any positive steps to impede his arrest.

Question 17.13

DALISH had his motorbike stolen and reported it to the police. A short time later he received information that a local youth was riding round on the bike. DALISH went to see the youth. When he attended at the house he saw the motorbike in the front garden, undamaged. The father of the youth who stole the bike offers to give DALISH some free parts for the bike if he doesn't report it to the police and DALISH accepts the money and only tells the police that he has found his motorbike and it was undamaged.

Has DALISH committed an offence of concealing a relevant offence contrary to s. 5 of the Criminal Law Act 1967?

A Yes, as he has agreed to accept money for his silence.

B Yes, as he has agreed to accept money for his silence which goes beyond reasonable compensation.

C No, as the agreement he reached was not with the person who stole the motorbike.

D No, as free parts for the bike would be seen as reasonable consideration.

ANSWERS

Answer 17.1

Answer **A** — Section 1(1) of the Perjury Act 1911 states:

> If any person lawfully sworn as a witness or as an interpreter in a judicial proceeding wilfully makes a statement material in that proceeding, which he knows to be false or does not believe to be true, he shall be guilty of perjury...

To prove perjury you must also show that the defendant *knew* the statement to be false or *did not believe it to be true*. There is no intent with this offence and it is committed in the conditions described; answer B is therefore incorrect.

Evidence of an opinion provided by a witness who does not genuinely hold such an opinion may also be perjury. This is true even where it is 'expert opinion'. It would be perjury if that opinion was one he knew to be false or did not believe to be true; answer C is therefore incorrect.

A 'statement material in that proceeding' means that the content of the evidence tendered in that case must have some importance to it and not just be of passing relevance. Would damage caused by excessive speed be material in a driving offence? Answer D is therefore incorrect.

Crime, para. 1.17.2

Answer 17.2

Answer **C** — Section 4 of the Criminal Law Act 1967 states:

(1) Where a person has committed a relevant offence, any other person who, knowing or believing him to be guilty of the offence or of some other relevant offence, does without lawful authority or reasonable excuse any act with intent to impede his apprehension or prosecution shall be guilty of an offence.

(1A) In this section and section 5 below, 'relevant offence' means—

    (a) an offence for which the sentence is fixed by law,

    (b) an offence for which a person of 18 years or over (not previously convicted) may be sentenced to imprisonment for a term of five years (or might be so sentenced but for the restrictions imposed by section 33 of the Magistrates' Courts Act 1980).

It must be shown that the defendant knew or believed the person to be guilty of that, *or some other* relevant offence. Mere *suspicion*, however strong, that the 'assisted' person had committed a relevant offence will not be enough; answers A and B are therefore incorrect.

Merely denying an offence has been committed is not enough to say it hasn't; once charged the offence would be said to have been committed. If this were not the case then this offence would be ineffective as everyone would deny the offence! Answer D is therefore incorrect.

Crime, para. 1.17.7

Answer 17.3

Answer **B** — Section 1 of the Perjury Act 1911 states:

(1) If any person lawfully sworn as a witness or as an interpreter in a judicial proceeding wilfully makes a statement material in that proceeding, which he knows to be false or does not believe to be true, he shall be guilty of perjury...

(2) The expression 'judicial proceeding' includes a proceeding before any court, tribunal, or person having by law power to hear, receive, and examine evidence on oath.

(3) Where a statement made for the purposes of a judicial proceeding is not made before the tribunal itself, but is made on oath before a person authorised by law to administer an oath to the person who makes the statement, and to record or authenticate the statement, it shall, for the purposes of this section, be treated as having been made in a judicial proceeding.

A 'statement material in that proceeding' means that the content of the evidence tendered in that case must have some importance to it and not just be of passing relevance. Whether something is material to a case is a question of law for a judge to decide. Although the affair has no relevance to the actual physical assault it is of importance as it would be a relevant fact; answers C and D are therefore incorrect.

So the fact alluded to must be false or believed to be untrue and material to the case; answer A is therefore incorrect.

Crime, para. 1.17.2

Answer 17.4

Answer **B** — Section 5 of the Criminal Law Act 1967 states:

(2) Where a person causes any wasteful employment of the police by knowingly making to any person a false report tending to show that an offence has been committed, or to give rise to apprehension for the safety of any persons or property, or tending to show that he has information material to any police inquiry, he shall be liable...

It is widely thought that there is a minimum number of hours which must be wasted before a prosecution can be brought for this offence. There is no reliable authority on this point; answer A is therefore incorrect.

The fact that he gave some evidence, or by luck the police actually obtained evidence, is immaterial to the fact he wasted police time by giving a false report; answers C and D are therefore incorrect.

Crime, para. 1.17.10

Answer 17.5

Answer **A** — Section 39 of the Criminal Justice and Police Act 2001 extended the offences of intimidation of witness offences outlined in s. 51 of the Criminal Justice and Public Order Act 1994 to proceedings in civil cases. The 1994 Act applies to the investigation or trial of those in criminal proceedings. Answer D is therefore incorrect. The new offence is very similar to the 1994 Act offence and is an offence of specific intent, so recklessness will not suffice (answer B is therefore incorrect). The offence includes doing any act, provided it was with the intention of intimidating a witness and provided the defendant knew the person might be a witness. This would include writing letters, making phone calls, etc., and is not limited to personal threats (answer C is also incorrect).

Crime, para. 1.17.5.2

Answer 17.6

Answer **A** — This offence applies to persons in lawful custody, anywhere. It is not restricted to custody units, prison, etc. Answer C is therefore incorrect. Whether a person is 'in custody' or not is a question of fact and the word 'custody' is to be given its ordinary meaning (*E v DPP* [2002] Crim LR 737). This could be shown by providing evidence that the person's liberty was restricted (as it is in the question), and that it was lawful (sch. 4 to the 2002 Act provides this). This custody is not restricted to sworn police officers and would include police community support officers (PCSOs), Investigating Officers or Escort Officers (who are given powers by the 2002 Act); answer D is therefore incorrect. The offence of escaping is completed immediately that liberty is obtained and is not subject to time restrictions on such liberty; therefore, answer B is incorrect.

Crime, para. 1.17.9

Answer 17.7

Answer **C** — Section 51 of the Criminal Justice and Public Order Act 1994 states:

(1) A person commits an offence if—
  (a) he does an act which intimidates, and is intended to intimidate, another person ('the victim'),
  (b) he does the act knowing or believing that the victim is assisting in the investigation of an offence or is a witness or potential witness or a juror or potential juror in proceedings for an offence, and
  (c) he does it intending thereby to cause the investigation or the course of justice to be obstructed, perverted or interfered with.
(2) A person commits an offence if—
  (a) he does an act which harms, and is intended to harm, another person or, intending to cause another person to fear harm, he threatens to do an act which would harm that other person,
  (b) he does or threatens to do the act knowing or believing that the person harmed or threatened to be harmed ('the victim'), or some other person, has assisted in an investigation into an offence or has given evidence or particular evidence in proceedings for an offence, or has acted as a juror or concurred in a particular verdict in proceedings for an offence, and
  (c) he does or threatens to do it because of that knowledge or belief.

What is important then is the knowledge and belief that the person threatened is assisting in the investigation of an offence or is a witness or potential witness or a juror or potential juror in proceedings for an offence, and that the belief must have some substance to it. In this particular scenario a threat has been made, however it would not fit within the criteria for this offence; answers A and B are therefore incorrect.

It is immaterial what the victim feels. The offence could be made out even if the victim was not actually in fear; answer D is therefore incorrect.

Crime, para. 1.17.5.1

Answer 17.8

Answer **D** — Perjury is committed by persons giving evidence that is false or they do not believe it to be true when sworn as witnesses at court; making a false statement relates to a written statement being tendered in evidence (the bit at the top of an MG11). In this scenario perjury could never be committed as neither officer was a sworn witness; answers A and C are therefore incorrect.

Like perjury making a false statement in criminal proceedings contrary to s. 89 of the Criminal Justice Act 1967 is concerned with someone who wilfully makes a statement material in those proceedings which he knows to be false or does not believe to be true. In the scenario the officer makes a statement he believes to be true, and that is the important factor, his belief. The fact he is incorrect is immaterial. Had he not believed the sergeant and still made the statement, however, he would have been liable; answer B is therefore incorrect.

Crime, para. 1.17.3

Answer 17.9

Answer **D** — Section 51 of the Criminal Justice and Public Order Act 1994 states:

(1) A person commits an offence if—
   (a) he does an act which intimidates, and is intended to intimidate, another person ('the victim')...

In a decision that seems to contradict the specific wording in the previous extract, the Court of Appeal held, *inter alia*, that intimidation does not have to be successful, in that the victim does not actually have to be deterred from giving evidence or put in fear. Answers A and B are therefore incorrect. Whilst it will be material evidence if the victim was neither deterred from giving evidence nor put in fear, a person may intimidate another person without the victim being intimidated (*R* v *Patrascu* [2004] EWCA Crim 2417). Note that this section extends well beyond simply asking a person to lie, and can include other ways of obstructing justice through witness intimidation. Answer C is therefore incorrect.

Crime, para. 1.17.5.1

Answer 17.10

Answer **C** — It is an offence at common law to do an act tending and intended to pervert the course of public justice. 'The course of public justice' includes the process of criminal investigation (see *R* v *Rowell* [1978] 1 WLR 132)—it is not necessary that an investigation has commenced *before* the person makes a false complaint, such as the one previously. Answer A is therefore incorrect.

The conduct referred to in the scenario *may* amount to an offence of wasting police time (contrary to s. 5 of the Criminal Law Act 1967), although contrary to popular belief there is no minimum number of hours which must be wasted before a prosecution can be brought for this offence. However, it has also been held to amount to perverting the course of justice (see *R* v *Goodwin* (1989) 11 Cr App R (S) 194, where a false allegation of rape was made to the police). Answer D is therefore incorrect.

Where a person makes a false allegation to the police justifying a criminal investigation with the possible consequences of detention, arrest, charge or prosecution, and that person intends that the allegation be taken seriously, the offence of perverting the course of justice is *prima facie* made out. This will be the case *whether or not the allegation is capable of identifying specific individuals* (see *R* v *Cotter* [2002] 2 Cr App R 29, a case involving the boyfriend of a well-known black Olympic athlete who falsely claimed to have been attacked as part of a racist campaign). Answer B is therefore incorrect.

Crime, para. 1.17.4

Answer 17.11

Answer **D** — Section 39 of the Prison Act 1952 states:

(1) A person who—
    (a) assists a prisoner in escaping or attempting to escape from a prison, or
    (b) intending to facilitate the escape of a prisoner—
        (i) brings, throws or otherwise conveys anything into a prison,
        (ii) causes another person to bring, throw or otherwise convey anything into a prison, or
        (iii) gives anything to a prisoner or leaves anything in any place (whether inside or outside a prison), is guilty of an offence.

The wording of the section seems to indicate that it only relates to 'escaping' from a prison, and this was verified by the Court of Appeal in *R* v *Moss and Harte* (1986) 82 Cr App R 117 where it was held that the offence under s. 39 of the 1952 Act does not apply to a prisoner who escapes while in transit to or from prison; answers A, B and C are therefore incorrect.

Crime, para. 1.17.9

Answer 17.12

Answer **B** — For there to be an offence under s. 4 of the Criminal Law Act 1967 (assisting offenders) there must first have been a relevant offence committed by someone. That relevant offence must, in the case of this offence, have been committed by the 'assisted' person, in this case armed robbery.

The defendant can commit the offence before the person he or she has assisted is convicted of committing the relevant offence.

It must be shown that the defendant knew or believed the person to be guilty of that, or some other relevant offence. Therefore, if the defendant believed that the 'assisted' person had committed a robbery when in fact he or she had committed a theft, that mistaken part of the defendant's belief will not prevent a conviction for this offence; answer C is therefore incorrect.

The relevant offences are:

(a) an offence for which the sentence is fixed by law,
(b) an offence for which a person of 18 years or over (not previously convicted) may be sentenced to imprisonment for a term of five years (or might be so sentenced but for the restrictions imposed by s. 33 of the Magistrates' Courts Act 1980).

This offence must involve some positive act by the defendant; simply doing or saying nothing will not suffice. In this case the positive act of hiding the accused would be enough, irrespective of whether that actually delayed their arrest; answers A and D are therefore incorrect.

Crime, para. 1.17.7

Answer 17.13

Answer **B** — Section 5 of the Criminal Law Act 1967 states:

(1) Where a person has committed a relevant offence, any other person who, knowing or believing that the offence or some other relevant offence has been committed, and that he has information which might be of material assistance in securing the prosecution or conviction of an offender for it, accepts or agrees to accept for not disclosing that information any consideration other than the making good of loss or injury caused by the offence, or the making of reasonable compensation for that loss or injury, shall be liable...

The main focus of this offence is:

• the acceptance of, or agreement to accept 'consideration' (i.e. anything of value);
• beyond reasonable compensation for loss/injury caused by the relevant offence;
• in exchange for not disclosing material information.

In this scenario all three points are present so the offence is complete.

The legislation does not state that the agreement has to be with the person who committed the offence, only that one was committed; answer C is therefore incorrect. Had any part on the motorbike been broken or damaged, then the replacement part may well have been reasonable compensation, however as this is not the case answer D is therefore incorrect.

There has to be more than just an agreement of silence for the 'consideration', it must go beyond any consideration other than the making good of loss or injury caused by the offence, or the making of reasonable compensation for that loss or injury; answer A is therefore incorrect.

Crime, para. 1.17.8

18 | Offences Arising from Immigration, Asylum and People Exploitation

STUDY PREPARATION

This chapter deals with one of the most contentious policing issues of modern times, that of illegal entry to the United Kingdom. The events of 11 September 2001 prompted swift and considerable changes to immigration offences throughout the world. Immigration, asylum and exploitation of people has become an increasingly significant area of criminal activity in Wales and England, and central government has been swift to react with legislative changes to deal with the escalating problem. The unlawful exploitation of vulnerable people has, as it should be, been a priority; legislation dealing with that is tested here.

QUESTIONS

Question 18.1

HASSANI is originally from Pakistan, but is now a British citizen. His brother (who is not a British citizen) wishes to come to Britain on a permanent basis, but has falsely filled out an entry application stating he is coming on holiday. HASSANI has signed this form to say that his brother will stay with him on holiday for two weeks. HASSANI knows this to be false.

Who, if either, commits an offence under s. 24A of the Immigration Act 1971?

A The offence only applies to British citizens, so only HASSANI commits it.

B Both HASSANI and his brother, as the offender's nationality is of no relevance.

C The offence is aimed specifically at non-British citizens, so the offence is committed only by the brother.

D Neither, this offence applies only to applications for citizenship.

Question 18.2

ROBERTS is the leader of a group that is aimed at assisting asylum seekers to enter the UK. It is funded through contributions from charity. The group assists a male from Afghanistan to enter the UK, in the belief that he would claim asylum. However upon arrival he does not make a claim under the Refugee Convention or the European Convention on Human Rights.

Considering the offence of helping an asylum seeker to enter the United Kingdom contrary to s. 25A of the Immigration Act 1971, which of the following is correct?

A The offence is complete, as the person did not in fact claim asylum when they entered the UK.

B The offence is complete even though the person did not in fact claim asylum when they entered the UK.

C The offence is not complete as there was no gain for the group, financial or otherwise.

D The offence is not complete, as the person did not in fact claim asylum when they entered the UK.

Question 18.3

Under s. 2 of the Asylum and Immigration (Treatment of Claimants etc.) Act 2004, a person will commit an offence if, when at a leave or asylum interview, he or she does not have with him or her a passport or other document establishing his or her nationality or citizenship. Section 2(3) of the Act provides a time period, during which a person may produce the passport or document, to avoid prosecution for the offence.

In relation to this period, when must the passport or document be produced?

A Within three days to the Secretary of State.

B Within three days to an immigration officer or to the Secretary of State.

C Within seven days to the Secretary of State.

D Within seven days to an immigration officer or to the Secretary of State.

Question 18.4

ELBEGDORJ owns a warehouse which processes fresh fish and shellfish. The product is caught locally and then sold on to small businesses in a local coastal town. ELBEG-DORJ has formed a relationship with SOWDEN, who supplies workers to the ware-house during the summer months, when business increases due to tourism. ELBEGDORJ is aware that SOWDEN does not have a licence to procure the workers' services, but being grateful for the extra help, asks no questions. ELBEGDORJ pays the workers a minimum wage, but does not pay SOWDEN for supplying them.

Would ELBEGDORJ be guilty of an offence under the Gangmasters (Licensing) Act 2004?

A No, because the workers are not gathering produce.

B No, only SOWDEN commits an offence, by supplying the workers.

C No, because the workers are paid for their services.

D Yes, ELBEGDORJ commits an offence by entering into an arrangement with SOWDEN.

Question 18.5

The Gangmasters (Licensing) Act 2004 regulates certain aspects of unlawful exploita-tion of vulnerable groups of people within England and Wales, in relation to work that they are expected to do.

Which of the following would be a 'worker' within the meaning of the Act?

A Any worker working in manual labour, i.e. building sites.

B Any worker employed in the shellfish industry.

C Any worker employed as a sex slave/prostitute.

D Any worker in any industry at all.

Question 18.6

It is an offence under s. 4 of the Asylum and Immigration (Treatment of Claimants etc.) Act 2004 to traffic people for exploitation.

The definition of exploitation can be found in s. 4(4) of the Act. Which of the following is *specifically* listed in the definition?

A Exploiting a person for the purposes of organ transplants.

B Exploiting a person for the purpose of prostitution.

C Exploiting a person for the purpose of enforced marriage.

D Exploiting a person for the purpose of child pornography.

Question 18.7

UREN is a transport manager for a haulage company, which operates in the UK and Europe. UREN is aware that several of his drivers transport illegal immigrants into the UK. However, because his role includes allocating workloads, he is often asked by drivers to swap routes at the last minute. UREN suspects that the drivers request these changes to allow them to pick up people, but he turns a blind eye and generally accedes to their requests. UREN is not involved in any of the arrangements, but he believes that most of the people transported may be exploited by being used as cheap labour.

Would UREN be guilty of an offence under s. 4 of the Asylum and Immigration (Treatment of Claimants etc.) Act 2004 (trafficking people for exploitation)?

A Yes, but only if it can be shown that he holds more than a mere belief that the people will be exploited.

B No, because he does not arrange to transport the people.

C Yes, he would be guilty of the offence in these circumstances alone.

D No, because he is not directly involved in the exploitation of people.

Question 18.8

ALBERTS and SMYTHE were both British citizens and were taking an extended holiday in Spain, staying on SMYTHE's yacht. ALBERTS met and fell in love with ALLONSO, a Spanish citizen, and they decided they could not be apart when ALBERTS was due to return to Britain. ALLONSO was deported from the UK some two years previously but has not told either ALBERTS or SMYTHE and she persuades ALBERTS to take her back to the UK on the yacht and thereby avoid immigration. ALBERTS believes that as ALLONSO is an EU Member State national there would be no problem in ALLONSO arriving in this manner, and SMYTHE agrees to the use of his yacht for this purpose. ALBERTS unfortunately does not have good sea legs and has to fly back to the UK. SMYTHE and ALLONSO arrive at Brixham in Devon on the yacht and are met there by ALBERTS after they had disembarked from the yacht.

Which of the following statements is correct, in respect of the offence of assisting entry to the United Kingdom in breach of a deportation order contrary to s. 25B of the Immigration Act 1971?

A Only SMYTHE commits the offence, as the person who actually brought ALLONSO into the country.

B Only ALBERTS commits the offence, as it was his scheme to bring ALLONSO to the UK by this method.

C Both ALBERTS and SMYTHE commit the offence as they colluded together to assist ALLONSO's arrival.

D Neither ALBERTS nor SMYTHE commit the offence in these circumstances.

Question 18.9

A small boat has arrived at a quiet harbour and on board are persons illegally entering the UK. There are offences contrary to s. 25 of the Immigration Act 1971 being committed.

Can the police seize the boat?

A Yes, provided the captain only is arrested for the s. 25 offence.

B Yes, provided the owner only is arrested for the s. 25 offence.

C Yes, provided either the captain or the owner is arrested for the s. 25 offence.

D Yes, provided either the captain or the owner is suspected of committing the s. 25 offence.

Question 18.10

OSTANI is an asylum seeker and has been issued with a registration card by the Secretary of State. OSTANI alters his name on the card. He does nothing with the card himself but allows his friend to use it to obtain benefits.

Has OSTANI committed an offence of misuse of a registration card contrary to s. 26A of the Immigration Act 1971?

A Yes, it is an offence to alter any detail contained on a registration card.

B Yes, although the holder can amend some details it is an offence to alter any personal details on a registration card.

C No, there was no intention to deceive by OSTANI and this is required for the offence to be committed.

D No, as using the card in these circumstances would be a fraud offence rather than an offence of altering the registration card.

Question 18.11

Consider the offence of use of deception to enter or remain in the UK, contrary to s. 24A of the Immigration Act 1971, and what is required to prove the offence.

In relation to s. 24A of the Immigration Act 1971 which of the following is correct?

A The entire course of conduct of the defendant must amount to a deception for the offence to be complete.

B The deception can be by the defendant, or any person on behalf of the defendant.

C The deception can be by the defendant, or any person on behalf of the defendant, provided the deception related to the defendant.

D Although the entire course of conduct need not amount to a deception, it will be necessary to show that the defendant carried out some act of deception.

ANSWERS

Answer 18.1

Answer **C** — Section 24A of the Immigration Act 1971 is aimed at the actions of non-British citizens only, so as a British citizen, HASSANI can never commit this offence (answers A and B are therefore incorrect). It applies to any application to obtain or seek to obtain leave to enter the UK in any circumstances, including holidays, and therefore answer D is incorrect. HASSANI's brother commits the offence as he uses means which include deception to achieve his leave to enter.

Crime, para. 1.18.2.3

Answer 18.2

Answer **C** — Section 25A of the Immigration Act 1971 states:

(1) A person commits an offence if—
   (a) he knowingly and for gain facilitates the arrival in, or the entry into, the United Kingdom of an individual, and
   (b) he knows or has reasonable cause to believe that the individual is an asylum-seeker.

Section 25A of the Immigration Act 1971 reproduces the offence which was previously set out in s. 25(1)(b) of the Immigration Act 1971.

The offence must be done for 'gain', financial or otherwise, where there is no gain there is no offence; answers A and B are therefore incorrect.

The accused must know of or 'have reasonable cause to believe' that the individual he/she is assisting is an 'asylum-seeker'. 'Asylum-seeker' is defined in s. 25A(2) as someone who 'intends' to claim that to remove him from the United Kingdom would be a breach of the United Kingdom's obligations under (a) the Refugee Convention or (b) the European Convention on Human Rights. This presumably means that a person could be guilty of this offence even though the immigrant did not make a claim under the Refugee Convention or the European Convention on Human Rights. It seems therefore that, provided it can be established that the immigrant intended to make such a claim, this would suffice for the purposes of the offence; answer D is therefore incorrect.

Crime, para. 1.18.3.1

Answer 18.3

Answer **B** — The passport or document must be provided to an immigration officer or to the Secretary of State within a period of three days, beginning with the date of that interview. Answers A, C and D are therefore incorrect.

Crime, para. 1.18.5

Answer 18.4

Answer **D** — An unlicensed gangmaster is a person who illegally supplies people to conduct the work listed in s. 3 of the Gangmasters (Licensing) Act 2004. The work listed in this section is essentially agricultural work, gathering shellfish *and includes* processing or packaging any produce derived from agricultural work, shellfish, fish or products derived from shellfish or fish. Answer A is therefore incorrect.

Section 6 of the Act makes provision for licences to be issued by the Gangmasters Licensing Authority (GLA) to suitable persons. It is an offence to act as a gangmaster without a licence (see s. 12(1)). It is a further summary offence to enter into an arrangement with a gangmaster where, in supplying the workers or services, the gangmaster contravenes s. 6 (s. 13(1)). Answer B is therefore incorrect. Lastly, it is irrelevant that the workers were paid for their services—the offence is complete when ELBEGDORJ enters into an arrangement with SOWDEN. Answer C is therefore incorrect.

Crime, para. 1.18.3.4

Answer 18.5

Answer **B** — In summary a gangmaster is a person who supplies a worker to do work to which the 2004 Act applies for another person (s. 3 of the Gangmasters (Licensing) Act 2004). The work listed in this section is essentially agricultural work, gathering shellfish and includes processing or packaging any produce derived from agricultural work, shellfish, fish or products derived from shellfish or fish. Answers A, C and D are therefore incorrect.

Crime, para. 1.18.3.4

Answer 18.6

Answer **A** — The definition of exploitation under s. 4(4) is fairly wide and includes where a person is:

- a victim of behaviour that contravenes Art. 4 of the European Convention on Human Rights (slavery and forced labour);
- encouraged, required or expected to do anything as a result of which they (or another person) would commit an offence under the Human Organ Transplants Act 1989;
- subjected to force, threats or deception designed to induce them to provide services, provide another person with benefits or enable another person to acquire benefits of any kind;
- requested or induced to undertake *any activity* having been chosen on the grounds they are mentally or physically ill or disabled, young or have a family relationship with a person and a person without the illness, disability, youth or family relationship would be likely to refuse the request or resist the inducement.

Of the choices in this question, only exploiting a person for the purposes of organ transplants appears specifically in the list. Therefore answers B, C and D are incorrect. However, any of the other scenarios may fall within the offence, depending on the circumstances.

Crime, para. 1.18.3.3

Answer 18.7

Answer **C** — An offence is committed under s. 4(1) of the Asylum and Immigration (Treatment of Claimants etc.) Act 2004, when a person arranges *or* facilitates the arrival in the UK of an individual (the 'passenger'). The dictionary definition of 'facilitate' includes to 'smooth the progress of', 'make easy', or 'make possible'. Even though UREN is not directly involved in the arrangements, he could certainly be accused of facilitating the arrival of the passengers. Answer B is therefore incorrect.

Section 4(1) continues that the person will be guilty of the offence, if he or she:

    (a) intends to exploit the passenger in the UK or elsewhere, or
    (b) believes another person is likely to exploit the passenger in the UK or elsewhere.

Therefore, even though UREN is not directly involved in the exploitation of the passengers, he commits the offence because of his belief that they will be exploited (and therefore answer D is incorrect). Answer A is incorrect because the prosecution would have to show a *belief* by the accused and no more. The definition of 'exploitation' under s. 4(4) includes where a person is a victim of Art. 4 of the Human Rights Convention—slavery and forced labour.

It should be noted that there are further offences contained in s. 4, namely, arranging or facilitating the travel within the UK of a passenger, with the same intent

(s. 4(2)), and arranging or facilitating the *departure* from the UK of that person with the same intent (s. 4(3)).

Crime, para. 1.18.3.3

Answer 18.8

Answer **D** — An offence of assisting entry to the United Kingdom in breach of a deportation order contrary to s. 25B of the Immigration Act 1971 is committed *inter alia* where the defendant does an act which assists the individual to arrive in, enter or remain in the United Kingdom, and that person is subject to a deportation order.

The defendant must have known or had reasonable cause for believing that their act facilitated assisting the entry in breach of that deportation order, therefore they must have known/had reasonable cause to believe that there was such an order in existence. As in the scenario neither man knew of the deportation order so they commit no offence; answers A, B and C are therefore incorrect.

It should be noted that ALLONSO, however, may be guilty of an offence under s. 24(1)(a) of the 1971 Act, of being a person who is not a British citizen who knowingly enters the UK in breach of a deportation order or without leave.

Crime, para. 1.18.3.1

Answer 18.9

Answer **C** — Where a person has been arrested for an offence under s. 25, 25A or 25B, a police officer may detain any vehicle or certain smaller ships and aircraft where they have reasonable grounds for believing that:

- the vehicle, ship or aircraft has been used or was intended to be used in carrying out the arrangements in respect of the offence; and
- the person arrested is the owner, driver or, in the case of a ship or aircraft, the captain.

So where the owner or the captain is arrested, and not just suspected for one of the offences, the boat can be seized; answers A, B and D are therefore incorrect.

Crime, para. 1.18.3.2

Answer 18.10

Answer **A** — Section 26A of the Immigration Act 1971 states:

(3) A person commits an offence if he—
   (a) makes a false registration card,
   (b) alters a registration card with intent to deceive or to enable another to deceive...
       [answer B is therefore incorrect].

A registration card here is a document which:

- carries information about a person (whether or not wholly or partly electronically); and
- is issued by the Secretary of State to the person wholly or partly in connection with a claim for asylum (whether or not made by that person) (s. 26A(1)).

It is enough that the card is altered and another enabled to make a deception; answer C is therefore incorrect. Although a fraud offence may be committed this offence is also committed; answer D is therefore incorrect.

Crime, para. 1.18.4

Answer 18.11

Answer **D** — This offence (contrary to the Immigration Act 1971, s. 24A) is relatively new and is broadly aimed at the more calculated actions by non-British citizens to get (or try to get) leave to enter or stay in the United Kingdom, or to evade deportation.

'Deception' here would appear to have its ordinary meaning and is not defined within the 1971 Act. It is worth noting that the relevant criminal conduct (*actus reus*) by the defendant here can be any means which includes deception by him/her.

Therefore, although the entire course of conduct by the defendant need not amount to a deception (answer A is therefore incorrect), it will be necessary to show that the defendant himself/herself carried out some act of deception (e.g. giving false details, providing misleading information, etc.).

It will not be enough for this offence to show that someone else practised a deception in order to bring about the consequences at s. 24A(1)(a) and (1)(b) for another person; answers B and C are therefore incorrect.

Crime, para. 1.18.2.3

Question Checklist

The following checklist is designed to help you keep track of your progress when answering the multiple-choice questions. If you fill this in after one attempt at each question, you will be able to check how many you have got right and which questions you need to revisit a second time. Also available online, to download visit www.blackstonespolicemanuals.com.

	First attempt Correct (✓)	Second attempt Correct (✓)
1 State of Mind		
1.1		
1.2		
1.3		
1.4		
1.5		
1.6		
1.7		
1.8		
1.9		
2 Criminal Conduct		
2.1		
2.2		
2.3		
2.4		
2.5		
2.6		
2.7		
2.8		
2.9		
2.10		
2.11		

	First attempt Correct (✓)	Second attempt Correct (✓)
2.12		
2.13		
3 Incomplete Offences and Police Investigations		
3.1		
3.2		
3.3		
3.4		
3.5		
3.6		
3.7		
3.8		
3.9		
3.10		
3.11		
3.12		
3.13		
4 General Defences		
4.1		
4.2		
4.3		
4.4		
4.5		

	First attempt Correct (✓)	Second attempt Correct (✓)
4.6		
4.7		
4.8		
4.9		
4.10		
4.11		
4.12		
4.13		
4.14		
4.15		

5 Homicide

	First attempt Correct (✓)	Second attempt Correct (✓)
5.1		
5.2		
5.3		
5.4		
5.5		
5.6		
5.7		
5.8		
5.9		
5.10		
5.11		
5.12		

6 Misuse of Drugs

	First attempt Correct (✓)	Second attempt Correct (✓)
6.1		
6.2		
6.3		
6.4		
6.5		
6.6		
6.7		
6.8		
6.9		
6.10		
6.11		
6.12		
6.13		

	First attempt Correct (✓)	Second attempt Correct (✓)
6.14		
6.15		
6.16		
6.17		
6.18		
6.19		

7 Firearms and Gun Crime

	First attempt Correct (✓)	Second attempt Correct (✓)
7.1		
7.2		
7.3		
7.4		
7.5		
7.6		
7.7		
7.8		
7.9		
7.10		
7.11		
7.12		
7.13		
7.14		
7.15		
7.16		
7.17		

8 Racially and Religiously Aggravated Offences

	First attempt Correct (✓)	Second attempt Correct (✓)
8.1		
8.2		
8.3		
8.4		
8.5		
8.6		
8.7		

9 Non-Fatal Offences Against the Person

	First attempt Correct (✓)	Second attempt Correct (✓)
9.1		
9.2		
9.3		

	First attempt Correct (✓)	Second attempt Correct (✓)
9.4		
9.5		
9.6		
9.7		
9.8		
9.9		
9.10		
9.11		
9.12		
9.13		
9.14		
9.15		
9.16		

10 Miscellaneous Offences Against the Person

	First attempt Correct (✓)	Second attempt Correct (✓)
10.1		
10.2		
10.3		
10.4		
10.5		
10.6		
10.7		

11 Sexual Offences

	First attempt Correct (✓)	Second attempt Correct (✓)
11.1		
11.2		
11.3		
11.4		
11.5		
11.6		
11.7		
11.8		
11.9		
11.10		
11.11		
11.12		
11.13		
11.14		
11.15		

	First attempt Correct (✓)	Second attempt Correct (✓)
11.16		
11.17		
11.18		
11.19		
11.20		
11.21		
11.22		
11.23		
11.24		
11.25		
11.26		
11.27		

12 Control of Sex Offenders

	First attempt Correct (✓)	Second attempt Correct (✓)
12.1		
12.2		
12.3		
12.4		
12.5		
12.6		
12.7		

13 Child Protection

	First attempt Correct (✓)	Second attempt Correct (✓)
13.1		
13.2		
13.3		
13.4		
13.5		
13.6		
13.7		
13.8		
13.9		
13.10		
13.11		
13.12		
13.13		

14 Theft and Related Offences

	First attempt Correct (✓)	Second attempt Correct (✓)
14.1		

	First attempt Correct (✓)	Second attempt Correct (✓)
14.2		
14.3		
14.4		
14.5		
14.6		
14.7		
14.8		
14.9		
14.10		
14.11		
14.12		
14.13		
14.14		
14.15		
14.16		
14.17		
14.18		
14.19		
14.20		
14.21		
14.22		
14.23		

15 Fraud

	First attempt Correct (✓)	Second attempt Correct (✓)
15.1		
15.2		
15.3		
15.4		
15.5		
15.6		
15.7		
15.8		
15.9		
15.10		
15.11		
15.12		

16 Criminal Damage

	First attempt Correct (✓)	Second attempt Correct (✓)
16.1		
16.2		

	First attempt Correct (✓)	Second attempt Correct (✓)
16.3		
16.4		
16.5		
16.6		
16.7		
16.8		
16.9		
16.10		
16.11		
16.12		
16.13		

17 Offences Against the Administration of Justice and Public Interest

	First attempt Correct (✓)	Second attempt Correct (✓)
17.1		
17.2		
17.3		
17.4		
17.5		
17.6		
17.7		
17.8		
17.9		
17.10		
16.11		
17.12		
17.13		

18 Offences Arising from Immigration, Asylum and People Exploitation

	First attempt Correct (✓)	Second attempt Correct (✓)
18.1		
18.2		
18.3		
18.4		
18.5		
18.6		
18.7		
18.8		
18.9		
18.10		
18.11		

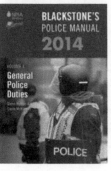

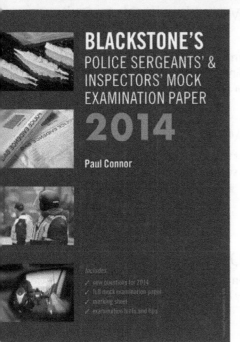

BLACKSTONE'S POLICE PROMOTION EXAMINATION PRODUCTS ONLINE

Blackstone's Police Manuals and Q&As Online Combined

Fast desktop access to the complete text of all four *Blackstone's Police Manuals* plus an extensive online database of 2,000 individually written practice questions to test your knowledge on all areas of the syllabus.

Blackstone's Police Manuals Online

Access to the complete text of the four *Blackstone's Police Manuals* with a quick search facility across all subject areas, legislation, case names, as well as a consolidated A-Z index.

Blackstone's Police Q&As Online

Over 2,000 individually written multiple choice questions, each written in the same format and difficulty as the actual examinations - the perfect way to practice your technique.